More Memories of Growing Up in San Francisco's Chinatown

Edmund S. Wong

Illustrations by
Leland Wong

ISBN: 978-0-578-52218-0

Dedicated to

Perkin Lee

Love ya, Cuz!

CONTENTS

Acknowledgements

I wish to thank all of the individuals who are widely featured in this book. They are, in no particular order: Judy Wing Lee, Irene Dea Collier, Deb Lem, Tommy Lim, Melody Chan Doss-Wambeke, Sherman Wong, Pat Chin, Pat Nishimoto, Cynthia Yee, Mimi Lee, Don Ng, Liz Wong, Raymond Lee, Jack Woo, Harold Lee, Norman Fong, Steven Lee, and Saki Lee. I greatly appreciate your trust and patience as I worked with your most treasured memories. I am also grateful to those among you who shared photographs for me to use in our book. I sincerely hope that this book represents you and those closest to you well. This book is as much for you as it is about you.

Significant parts of this book also result from the assistance of a multitude of individuals who may not actually appear in its pages. Their contributions in the form of support, interest, belief and enthusiasm have been priceless. Thank you all so very much. You are the heart and the soul of Chinatown, San Francisco.

Leland Wong merits special mention. He is not only the illustrator for *More Memories of Growing Up in San Francisco's Chinatown,* but also the founder and administrator of the Facebook page, "We Grew up in San Francisco Chinatown," or as its followers commonly refer to it, WGUISFCT. Many direct contributors to both of my books, *Growing Up in San Francisco's Chinatown* and *More Memories of Growing Up in San Francisco's Chinatown* came to me through their posts in WGUISFCT. Not only did I meet dozens of the page's followers who offered me their memories, stories and photos, but I was also able to find countless ideas and tremendous inspiration for my writing through the site.

Thank you again, Linda Winkler, former colleague at St. Xavier High School in Louisville, Kentucky, for your time and patience in serving as my editor. As with *The Sea Takes No Prisoners*, our first book together, your guidance and wonderfully insightful suggestions have helped me to craft a far better book than I could ever have managed on my own.

Of course, there are my dear wife, Elizabeth and my wonderful daughter, Allison to recognize. What would I have ever done or become without the two of you? Hasn't it just been so much fun being "Chinese?" Love you both.

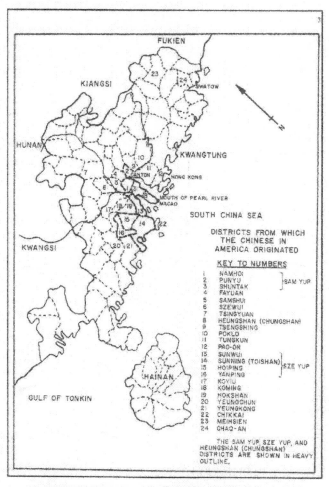

DISTRICTS FROM WHICH
THE CHINESE IN
AMERICA ORIGINATED

KEY TO NUMBERS

1	NAMHOI	
2	PUNYU	SAM YUP
3	SHUNTAK	
4	FAYUAN	
5	SAMSHUI	
6	SZEWUI	
7	TSINSYUAN	
8	HEUNGSHAN (CHUNGSHAN)	
9	TSENGSHING	
10	POKLO	
11	TUNGKUN	
12	PAO-ON	
13	SUNWUI	
14	SUNNING (TOISHAN)	SZE YUP
15	HOIPING	
16	YANPING	
17	KOYIU	
18	KOMING	
19	HOKSHAN	
20	YEUNGCHUN	
21	YEUNGKONG	
22	CHIKKAI	
23	MEIHSIEN	
24	CHAO-AN	

THE SAM YUP, SZE YUP, AND
HEUNGSHAN (CHUNGSHAN)
DISTRICTS ARE SHOWN IN HEAVY
OUTLINE.

Map from Chinn, Thomas W., ed., A History of the Chinese in California, 1969.

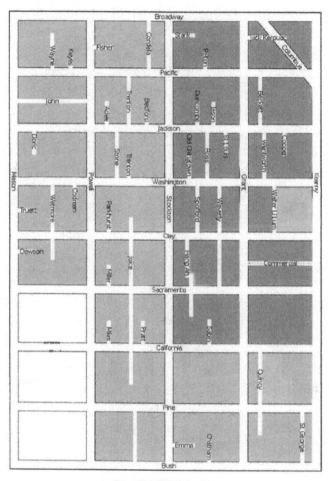

Central Chinatown Street Map
https://commons.wikimedia.org/wiki/
(altered by author)

Orientation of adjacent neighborhoods:

North Beach – North of Broadway
Nob Hill – West of Mason
Financial District – East of Kearny/South of Sacramento
Downtown – South of Bush

1.
First Arrivals and Early Family Life
We Only Want You to Have a Better Life

During the 1950s and 1960s Chinatown was a vibrant home to its baby boomer American-born Chinese children. Most of these Chinatown boomers are first-generation American citizens who, in the United States of today, would likely be classified as "Dreamers." Their parents and grandparents were mostly born in China. Once in the United States, these elders often struggled with language and cultural barriers, and many of them worked long hours in low-skilled and low-paying jobs. Their children and grandchildren, however, typically remember their earliest years as happy ones. They also remember Chinatown fondly and speak of it as a warm, cozy and safe place in which to grow up. With adulthood and the passing of most of those who raised them, the Chinese-Americans who lived in tiny and crowded tenement apartments or in the *Ping Yuen* housing projects and who played in alleys and on sidewalks along the likes of Grant Avenue, Clay Street, Waverly Place, Wentworth and Adele Court are filled with appreciation for the truth so often told to them by those who reared them as youngsters: "We only want you to have a better life than what ours has been."

Allen Leong [1.]
I Would Not Trade Anything for the Type of Childhood We Had

Semi-retired pharmacist and Chinatown native Allen Leong recalls his early years as follows:

I grew up in Chinatown during the fifties and sixties. It was a time when everyone treated each other like family. We went outside to play and we got dirty. We bought chips and candy from the corner store. We ate beans and hotdogs, mac and cheese and peanut butter sandwiches. We played red light-green light, kick the can, Simon says, hide and seek, dodge ball, Red Rover, king of the hill, baseball, softball and football. We could ride our bikes to the store or the park and stay all day. We walked down to Market Street to watch three movies for a dollar. We could go swimming at the YMCA (in Chinatown) or at the North Beach (public) pool. We walked or rode our bikes everywhere and never worried about our safety. If someone had a fight, that was all it was, a fight. Kids weren't afraid of someone pulling a gun back in those days. When it got late, someone, usually one of the neighbors, would stick their head out of a window to yell at their kid that it was dinner time and time to come in for the night. If one kid was called to dinner, we knew it was time for all of us to go on home.

I would not trade anything for the kind of childhood we had. We had all that we needed; we had love, and that is what made us the type of adults we are today. I would give anything for my kids to have this type of childhood. We weren't afraid of anything except our parents who were the ones who gave all of this to us in the first place.

Melody Chan Doss-Wambeke [2.]
How I Got My Name

Melody and her two brothers were all born at the Chinese Hospital on Chinatown's Jackson Street between Powell and Stockton. She was delivered by Dr. Helen Tong Chinn, a 1933 graduate of UC Berkeley's School of Medicine. Dr. Chinn's second-floor office was at 755 Jackson Street. One former child patient remembered that the office was a dingy one in which an unfolded ironing board served in place of an examination table. He also remembers that, in those mid-1950s days, the charge for an office visit was five dollars.

Dr. Chinn was well known throughout Chinatown for having delivered a good number of the community's babies during the Great Depression, World War II, the post-war Baby Boom years, and beyond. She was a staff member of Chinese Hospital and a member of the American Women's Medical Association. Not only did Dr. Chinn deliver Melody and her siblings, but also, as Melody recalls, she gave them their American names as well.

My parents did not speak any English, so it was Dr. Chinn who gave us our American names. I do not know how Melody was chosen, but just think, I could have been named Jane, or Emily, or Jade. My name has three syllables compared to just one for my brother John and two for my other brother, Myron. My mother could never say the last part of my name, 'dy.' Chinese names, or words of any sort, are never very long so she always just called me 'Melo.'

Pronounced aloud, the name would sound like 'may-low' with the approximate tone of "fa" as in "do-re-mi-fa ..." for the "may" part and a long "do" for the "lo" part. Melody continues,

The literal Chinese translation for it would be "beautiful (mei, or may) stature." My parents, however, gave us all our formal Chinese names. My mother was proud that I could always write out my Chinese name in decent calligraphy. To this day, my American name is still unusual. I cannot sing, but I can hum and I have an appreciation for classical and pop music. I studied and played the viola at Galileo High, but even though I was tone deaf, I played well enough by knowing how to read the music.

How My Parents Met and Their First Years in California

My father, Chan Hong Fun, was born in China on November 20,

1904. He was the eldest of three children. During his teen years, he was adopted by another family who did not have a son. He completed a high school education before coming to America in 1922 at age 18. In the 1920s, despite widespread discrimination and suspicious feelings against the Chinese work force, many Chinese came to America to make a better living than they could possibly hope for in China. My father joined his adoptive parents in the San Jose area which in those days was farmland for as far as the eye could see. He worked with them at a flower nursery.

In 1923, my father became very ill, but his limited savings, inability to communicate in English, and strong anti-Chinese sentiments where he was working kept him from looking for medical care. The nearest place that would treat Chinese patients was the Chinese Hospital in San Francisco. I do not know for certain whether the Chinese Hospital had even been established in the 1920s. [3] *I am speculating that my father did not have enough money to pay for transportation to San Francisco from the San Jose area. My father had to bear his illness untreated until he just got better. Unfortunately, whatever he had suffered from never got better. It soon caused him to completely lose his hearing.*

My mother, Suet Yue Fong, was born on September 3, 1929. In 1938, when she was just nine years old, an arrangement was made between families for her to marry the man who would become my father once she reached the age of 17. The original plan was to have her sent to the United States as a child, but Japan had invaded China and a state of war existed between the two Asian countries. World War II and then the civil war between the Communists and the Nationalists followed. My mother's departure was delayed until 1950 when she arrived in America as a mail order bride! She landed in San Francisco without ever having met her husband-to-be. To her dismay, my father was 17 years her senior and he was deaf. In spite of all that, neither of them questioned their duty to their families, and they went ahead and married. I was born in Chinese Hospital in 1951, my brother, Myron, was born in 1952, and my youngest brother, John, was born in 1955.

Melody remembers her mother as a strong-willed immigrant woman

13

who had four siblings: three brothers and one sister. The older brother died in China of unknown circumstances. Once Melody's parents and one of her mother's brothers were settled in San Francisco, they dedicated themselves to bringing her mother's remaining brother, sister and father to the United States. Melody's maternal grandmother had already passed away, so she has no memory of her at all. It took close to twenty years for all three of those who had stayed behind to immigrate. Melody does not know what her uncle and parents did to bring her relatives over. She says that the plans and details were only discussed among the adults. The children were always shooed away from such discussions and told to go do their homework. Of her mother, Melody says,

I wondered if my mother carried any emotional scars from her life China. Even without war, there were often floods that ruined crops and resulted in famine. On top of that there was no law and order. Warlords and bandits were free to come and go as they pleased. They were a terror on ordinary people because they raided their villages for food and anything else they wanted. By the time I was old enough to seriously wonder about these things that I had overheard bits and pieces of as a child I could no longer speak adequate Chinese to ask about them. I somehow knew with great certainty that my mother endured times when food was not readily available. Rice was my mother's lifeline.

I remember growing up eating rice for all our meals. Even the hardened and sometimes burnt crust of the rice that stuck to the bottom of the pan in which it had been boiled was never thrown away. We would scrape the burnt parts into our bowls and eat it along with the unburned rice. Sometimes we would boil the hard and burnt bottom crust until it softened and separated from the pot. We could then eat it like a kind of soup. My mother called it "fahn-del-suey."

It was important to my mother to have all the rice she needed to cook the meals in her kitchen. She could only feel secure knowing that there was at least one full and as yet unused fifty-pound bag of rice sitting in the pantry. After I married, she would regularly ask me if I had enough rice in my kitchen. I would constantly remind her that my husband Ted, being Caucasian, preferred potatoes and I that we kept a small jar of rice that was never empty. She always acted shocked and feared that I would go hungry. She always made sure that I not leave until she could hand me a huge sack filled with rice.

My parents were often separated. My father moved south to work in the Central Valley fields for the long growing season every year. During my parents' time, it was all farmland and there were many fields growing flowers. My father eked out a living as a field hand. He spent many growing seasons in those future Silicon Valley fields. He was an absentee father, but he always sent money home to my mother who always stayed behind with my brothers and me in San Francisco. My mother was a full-time housewife, and she took in piecework sewing at home. Each of my parents worked at any job that would bring rice to the table. By 1970, my mother and father had saved enough money to purchase a two-unit duplex in the Inner Richmond District, a few blocks away from Golden Gate Park and the Conservatory of Flowers.

My Grandfather Was a Chinese Doctor and Herbalist

After Melody's maternal grandfather arrived in San Francisco from China, he lived with the Chan family for a short time. He was an herbalist and a practitioner of Traditional Chinese Medicine, or TCM. There are four diagnostic methods associated with TCM: inspection, auscultation-olfaction, interrogation, and palpation. These methods differ little in essence from the examination technique used by modern practitioners of Western medicine. Inspection involves the visual examination of a patient from which certain general assumptions can be made. Auscultation involves listening to the sounds emanating from the patient while olfaction utilizes the sense of smell to detect tell-tale signs of possible imperfections of health. Interrogation can be roughly compared to the Western practice of obtaining a history and listening to the patient's current complaints. Palpation is the shared technique between Western medicine and TCM of feeling for a pulse as well as pressing or feeling the chest, abdomen, neck, and/or other parts of the body. Melody recalls that,

My parents did not believe in Western medicine and relied on Chinese herbs. I remember strangers who felt ill coming to our home to visit my mother and my grandfather. Since my mother had a very good memory, especially with numbers and faces, she served as my grandfather's assistant. Somehow the news had gotten around that my grandfather was living in our home. Patients, many of whom were family friends, would sit on a chair in the kitchen. My grandfather would then ask basic questions about the visitor's general health. He would then ask the patient to show him his tongue. Following that my grandfather would sit next to the person and take his or her pulse. He was probably feeling for more than just a pulse because he would keep his fingers and hands on a patient's wrist, hands or arm for several minutes at a time. Before too long he would be able to tell the patient about the ailment and write out a prescription in Chinese characters.

My mother would take the prescription and gather and measure all the indicated Chinese ingredients and place them onto a large square sheet of paper. I recall that many of the herbs were stored in large jars that I think my mother kept in a small closet in the upstairs bedroom. After preparing my grandfather's prescription, she would add a small packet of golden raisins to the mix. She then folded everything neatly together and handed it to the patient. The instructions seemed to always be to take the herbal concoction home and boil it in a pan of hot water until it was reduced to a heavy broth. It was certain to be bitter and eating the golden raisins was to make the medicine palatable. After swallowing the medicated broth, the standard instruction was to go to bed and sleep.

Since most visitors often came after dinner, my brothers and I would be told to go do our homework. We were not encouraged to observe or be inquisitive about what was going on with the adults. Our job was to study hard and get good grades.

I remember a time when, as a child, I was given the same treatment I just described. I had some kind of fever. My grandfather looked at my tongue and very carefully and gently felt my wrist and lower arm. He also looked deeply into my eyes but said nothing as he did so. He then wrote a prescription and my mother measured the ingredients and then boiled them in a pot. The broth was dark and heavy and very bitter. I closed my eyes and gulped it down as fast as I could. Then I ate a few pieces of golden raisins. I slept and I recall seeing my grandfather sitting in a corner waiting for me to wake up. The following day, I woke up and felt better, my grandfather took my pulse and I showed him my tongue. He told me I would be all right, and he finally left the room to go to sleep.

My mother was very familiar with Chinese medicinal broths and frequently served them as a part of our Chinese diet. I attempted to learn how to cook from her but she was very fast and very impatient. I was much slower and I attempted to write her "recipes" down on paper but it never went beyond one dish. I never learned to cook the old-fashion way and I had to rely on Chinese recipe books whenever I prepared a Chinese dish for my husband Ted.

I have noticed that today there are at least two or three Chinese herbal shops in my nearby Visitation Valley neighborhood. Today the herbal shops are respected by Western medicine and are legitimized.

My Father

Even while very young, I never thought of my father as disabled for his inability to hear. He always maintained a proud posture and coped well with the Chinese hearing world. My brothers were very aware that, because my father did not hear, his attempts to speak could be disconcerting to those who were unfamiliar to him. It mattered little to us as we had become accustomed to the Chinese-based sounds he made, the gesticulating, and his hand-written Chinese messages. He always called to us by our Chinese names and we were quick to respond.

I have memories of my father coming home from the fields every year in the late fall. He would stay with us through the winter and go back south in the spring. He always brought a gigantic bouquet of chrysanthemums for the family. My mother always reiterated to us that we needed to respect our father despite his long absences. When he was away, he might not always have been directly

17

consulted about family decisions, but he was sure to have been updated by means of letters. At home, he sat at his rightful place, at the head of the table during dinner.

Whenever he was home while I was still attending Chinese school, he would help me with my calligraphy. He used his brushes and ink to show me how to be firm and steady, yet graceful, through each stroke. His was always a strong and steady hand. I was always told that the way you form your characters and the way in which you hold your brush are the surest indicators of your personality and your intellect. Maybe that is the origin of my artistic side.

In 1984, my father turned 80 and finally retired from physical farm work. He came home to live with his family. During his 80th birthday celebration, he brought out his Chinese sword and showed off his Tai Chi /Kung Fu moves. I recall how he smiled at my husband Ted and pointed at him to look at his strong legs and arm muscles. My father flexed his legs and his arms. Ted touched them and told me that my father's muscles were hard as rock! Ted beamed at my father with a big smile and shook his hands.

During his retirement years, my father spent hours puttering around the home that he loved so much. He also often rode the Muni bus to Chinatown where he enjoyed spending his days at the family association. Everyone there, related by surname, was a cousin, so Dad was at ease communicating with everyone through gestures, written notes, and pointing at items in the Chinese newspapers. He liked to shop at Chinatown stores and would ride back home on the bus to surprise the family with treats of Chinese candies, golden raisins, and fruits. We did not own a car and nobody in the family drove until my two brothers entered college. I have ridden the Muni my entire life and I still do not drive.

The Chan family was not big on parties during birthdays. Our family tradition was to celebrate birthdays with fried chicken and chow mein and small cakes. At the ages of 100, 101, and 102, my father celebrated his birthdays with a hearty appetite, chewing a chicken drumstick, and loving his cakes and cookies. When my father's health began to decline, he was admitted to Laguna Honda Hospital.

Despite his deafness, he made friends with the other residents. He was a feisty patient and often resisted taking his medicine or having lab work done, but this never bothered the staff.

My father lived a good and long life and passed on in 2007 at age 102.

Thanking My Parents for The Good Life That I Have

I recall a conversation with my mother when she was in her 70's. My Chinese language proficiency that had faded by the time I was a teen had by now become worrisome at best. I nonetheless pushed ahead, grasping for vocabulary and praying that my tones were still at least reasonable. I told her that I was happy and that my life was a good one. I tried to tell her how much I appreciated her and all the efforts she had made to help me and my two brothers to become college graduates. I also wanted her to know that I finally understood how her application of old village Chinese values had given me such a clear path toward reaching the "American dream." It was a lot to try to convey in what for me had become a foreign language.

My father and my mother who lived until 2013 left me a legacy of a very strong work ethic, honesty, compassion, love of family, sacrifice for the bigger goal, and endurance. They never took a vacation or spent any extra funds on themselves. They have always channeled their resources – up to the very shirts off their backs - for their family. I am now retired and I am proud to have enjoyed the privilege of being both American born and Chinese.

Judy Wing Lee [4.]
Grandpa Was A Wetback

Judy Wing Lee, born in 1947, arrived from Hoiping, China with her parents when she was nine months old. During her family's brief stay at the immigration center located on Sansome Street in San Francisco, her parents, who could only speak Chinese, were told that they should call their little girl "Juliet." They unquestioningly accepted the suggestion, but finding that particular name difficult to pronounce changed it to "Judy."

Sometime in the early 1900s, Judy's paternal grandfather had attempted to enter the United States, but was turned back. He was a victim of the American laws that had been enacted in the late 1800s to specifically exclude Chinese immigration. A second and successful attempt was aided by one of two tongs: The *On Leong* or the *Hip Sing*. Since the two organizations had branched out from their original base in New York City to Cleveland, Judy's grandfather was brought to Ohio.

Chinese tongs have often been depicted as shadowy and secretive societies bent on criminal activities. Tongs are often compared to the Italian Mafia. The tongs nonetheless did much to promote the establishment and flourishing of legitimate Chinese businesses in the United States. Among their many functions, the tongs took it as their duty to assist families in China faced with hardships that were abundant at the time. According to Judy,

I do not know which specific tong helped my grandfather, but some were acting as benevolent societies. The one that helped my grandfather was probably a network formed to help bring villagers from China to earn money to send back to help sustain or improve the living conditions of their families. My grandfather's family had to pay a sum of money to this network so that it would to bring him to Cleveland. They then had to pay more money to have a business set up for him. By making the business become a success, my grandfather would then send money back to the village for his family.

It is likely that the tongs took advantage of the acute labor shortage in Mexico during that country's early twentieth century construction of a national rail system. Eager to find workers from any convenient source the Mexican government did not discriminate against Chinese arrivals. Subsequent migration from Mexico into the United States was not a daunting journey as in those days the US-Mexican border was open. There were no checkpoints, immigration stations, or any other impediment other than nature to open travel. Judy said,

When my grandfather was caught and sent back on his first attempt to enter the United States, he was harshly reprimanded by his brother for his failure. Grandpa felt so deeply disgraced that he tried to commit suicide by drinking poison. My grandma would lament that because of this suicide attempt they could never conceive another child. Because women were not allowed entry to the United States, my grandma never left China. On his second attempt, my grandfather and some others who were travelling together disembarked in Mexico and swam across the Rio Grande – Grandpa was a wetback! Grandpa then went to a railyard where he clung onto a platform on the bottom of a train that took him to Cleveland. Because my grandfather had been caught and deported once before, the tong decided to hide him in a small town. That is how he wound up in Shelby (about 75 miles southwest of Cleveland). *The tong set him up in a laundry business.*

My grandfather washed laundry and lived in an old dilapidated building. Years later, after he too had made his way to Shelby, my father recalled waking up and finding snow that had come through a hole in the roof onto his pillow. My grandfather was known to drink a rice bowl filled with Ng Ka Pi, a Chinese medicinal wine before bed each night. The white townspeople of Shelby were very kind to and protective of my hardworking grandfather. When he was accused of being an illegal alien (again!), a local lawyer stepped up to defend him by calling upon other townspeople to vouch for the fact that my grandfather had been born in San Francisco before the 1906 earthquake.[5.] *Many had grown very fond of him, so they gladly did so. Years afterwards, when we were growing up in Chinatown, some of these good people came out to San Francisco to visit my father and most memorable was a particular mom and daughter who started to cry when they were getting ready to board the train to go back to Ohio.*

In 1976, after I had married, my husband visited Shelby. He met and talked to members of several families who had known and befriended my grandfather. My husband also met the son of the lawyer who had originally concocted the story that ultimately gained citizenship for my grandfather. Forty years later, my husband could still sense the deep kindness that all of the Shelby residents continued to demonstrate for my side of the family. They showed my husband where my grandfather's laundry once stood. At one point in time several of the town's women, Anna Irey and her daughter-in-law Laura, worked for my grandfather, and Anna treated my father like a son. I recall seeing a letter she had sent to him in San Francisco that was signed, "Your Shelby Mother." I was pretty young, but even then, I could feel the love they had for my dad and our family. My father at one point alluded to the idea that Anna and Laura would have been very pleased if my father had married Laura's daughter! This daughter, Janelle, was still alive about ten years ago when my cousin was trying to put our family tree together. Unfortunately, my cousin passed away, so that project remains unfinished. I'm only sorry we didn't stay in contact with Janelle.

My Parents Were Betrothed at Thirteen

Meanwhile, back during the Ohio years, my grandfather had my grandmother buy two sons in order to have the family that he was not able to himself make. My uncle Jack was bought first by my grandmother from another family. Uncle Jack recalled the day my father's biological parents brought him to the house to be sold. My father was about two years old and my uncle was instructed to take my father outside to the garden to play and distract him. When the contract was signed and money exchanged, my father's birth mother asked for the tattered cloth baby carrier back because she had another younger child at home. My father was always haunted by this abandonment and the sadness affected him until the end of his life. He was a troubled soul who would have my uncle recount his recollection of what his birth parents looked like. My mom said sons used to be bought by families who lacked their own to carry on the family name. The saying was something akin to, "if you eat their rice, you become one of them." Sons, whether natural or purchased, were always treated like kings. Girls, on the other hand, were treated brutally as slaves. My grandmother was guilty of beating a little girl on the head so severely that the child died. She was not punished as the act, however cruel, was not particularly uncommon in old China. My mom said that in those days back in China it was better to let your daughters starve to death at home rather than sell them to be abused.

As a legal citizen (through the efforts of the citizens of Shelby), *my grandfather was able to return to China for several visits. Each time he returned to Ohio; he was sure to report that he had a son. He had previously sent a trunk of gifts back to my grandmother which she unpacked once a year. She would have my uncle and father put on the overcoats that my grandfather had packed inside just to take a picture to send to him in Ohio. My uncle recalls there was also coffee in the trunk. My grandmother would sometimes put a small spoonful into a pot of water to boil. She thought of it as something special but, according to my uncle, it was an awful tasting brew.*

My father was 13 when my grandfather sent for him to Shelby. My grandma,[6] *whose other son, my Uncle Jack, had been sent for earlier, was afraid she would be left behind all alone. However, she had earlier arranged for my father to marry my then 13-year old mom-to-be in order to ensure that he would someday return to China. My grandma had seen my mom playing in another village and followed her home where she asked her parents for her to marry my father and they agreed. That family was a very poor one and it was probably glad to get rid of one more mouth to feed.*

Grandmother's Ghost?

Despite having no biological link, my father and Uncle Jack grew up as brothers. They cared and watched out for each other as boys and teenagers. My father went to school in Ohio for a few years where he, as had my grandfather, made many lifelong friends. He was drafted into the army during World War II and served a few years in the Philippines as a staff sergeant in a mobile unit. After the war and following his discharge, my father returned to China with my grandfather. Unfortunately, my grandmother had passed away shortly before they got to China.

When my grandmother lay dying, she instructed my mom to gather and keep the ashes from the burned-out incense that would be used for her funeral. My grandmother instructed my mother to call her name aloud first when she boarded and again when she

23

disembarked from the ship that she would take to America. My mom still wonders how my grandma knew that she would be going to America.

One night after my younger sister had been born, my grandmother visited my mom in a vision to tell her the baby was crying and to ask why she was not tending to her. The vision happened once again after my brother was born. Grandmother stated to my mom that she had heard a son had been born. When my sister and I were little, we found the red packet in which our mother had carried the incense ashes. We felt creeped out about Grandmother's ghostly visits, so we tore the packet open and scattered the ashes. My grandma never visited my mom again.

Decades later, my mom went back to China, had my grandma's bones cremated and brought them to the US to be buried with my grandfather. My mom said she did this because my grandma had always wanted to come to the US and not be left behind and alone without family in China. She felt a strong obligation to fulfill her mother's wishes.

My Mom Recalled A Stench While We Sailed for the USA

My father stayed long enough in China after my grandmother had died for me to be born. When we left China for the United States, my mother was 24 and I was not quite a year old. Even though I was born in China, I was automatically a US citizen because my father, as a World War II veteran, already was one himself. The ship my parents boarded to America was one of the President lines which was actually a converted freighter. The cargo hold was outfitted with hundreds of cots for the passengers. Those passengers who were hardy enough were able to climb the vertical ladder to the ship's deck for fresh air and water. Both my parents were terribly seasick and, along with the other sick passengers, begged the stronger passengers to bring water for them to drink from above. It was late summer, the seas were stormy, and the waves rocked the ship relentlessly. Each time the ship pitched or rolled; unsecured belongings would tumble about the converted cargo-hold's deck. I often tumbled along with everything else and my mom had to keep retrieving me. My mom had no milk and I had to subsist on orange juice which I sucked through a straw. I was probably the only child on the ship. Many children were left behind to be sent for in later years. A lot of passengers took pity on me. They made it a point to protect and take care of me. One such lady, who had to leave her ten-year old son in China, doted on me and became my mom's best friend for life. Everyone remembered my parents because of me.

My mom recalled a stench that she thought was even more foul than that of the sickness from the passengers: the smell of boiling hot dogs. To this day, she still cannot bear that smell. She weighed no more than 80 pounds when she arrived in San Francisco. She vowed that if it meant going by sea she would never return to China.

My father opened a laundry on the corner of Columbus and Greenwich but closed it when a customer scammed him by bringing in a tattered curtain to be cleaned. The customer accused my father of damaging his curtain, sued, and won $50 in judgement. In those days, $50 was equivalent to two months' pay. My father also worked at a number of jobs which included, being a restaurant waiter and at the American Can Company in the East Bay. My parents later opened a gai-chong, or sewing factory, on upper Grant Avenue in North Beach.

Pat Chin [7.]
"Just a Girl," but Finding Her Own Way

Pat Chin, a current and founding member of the *Grant Avenue Follies*, spent her childhood moving from place to place and living with person to person both in and out of San Francisco's Chinatown. The adults in her life held a variety of jobs and rarely had much money. Pat did as well as she could for herself. Looking back at her early life she says,

My earliest recollection of my childhood was that my parents were separated and that, for a while, I lived in a home with other kids. I can only remember that I slept in a room that was filled with cribs for me and other small children. Later, I went to stay with my maternal grandmother just beyond the western edge of Chinatown.

Paw-paw, or grandma, lived on Washington Street between Mason and Taylor. I stayed there along with three other kids who were my cousins. I guess that my mother and my cousins' parents might have paid for our care, but they must not have given paw-paw too much. A lot of our meals were made up of just rice with butter, and I remember being hungry a lot. After a while my father came to have me live with him. First, he was a cook in a rail yard and my bedroom was inside an old train car. After that we moved to Alameda where he ran a restaurant that was in the back of a cocktail lounge.

One day, my mother came to Alameda and brought me back to San Francisco to live with her and her second husband. He had a sewing factory on Stockton Street near Clay Street and the workers made blouses for a clothing line called Fritzi of California. We lived on the mezzanine of the gai-chong just behind and above the main floor where the sewing stations were. The back part was where we slept. The front part of our living area included a huge table that was used during working hours for cutting fabrics. Then stepfather converted to sewing jeans for Levi-Strauss. The Stockton Street factory was too small for that, so he moved
down to Sacramento Street below Kearny to a much larger place. That location came with huge rats in it so we had to keep a few cats around to stave them off. My mother kept an apartment on Grant Avenue where the Empress of China restaurant used to be. That is where we stayed. It was larger than the mezzanine of the first gai chong, and it didn't have rats like the second place. At least I don't remember seeing any.

When my mother was done with husband number two, we moved again and settled at 27 Saint Louis Alley._The alley is on the left-hand side of Jackson Street going up from Grant Avenue to Stockton Street. It is narrow and gloomy and is a dead-end. Our building was a couple of floors tall and had small apartments in it. I can't recall that my mother ever worked. She was constantly on the phone gossiping with her sisters. I had to do all the errands and shopping. I often went to different restaurants to buy food to go. Mother never cooked! I would go to Sun Wah Kue for a waffle which, buttered and dusted with powdered sugar, cost just twenty cents. I sometimes would get a whole pie for fifty cents. They had apple, custard and *orange pies. For dinner, I would go to Tao Lee Yuen where for two dollars, we could get three dishes plus rice. Even without a lot of money, we could at least eat pretty well. I think that one reason Chinatown was such a big tourist draw in those days was the cheap food. It was always tasty and you always got a lot with your order.*

Going to Work and Making Money, but Still Moving Around a Lot

In 1950, I was 15 and I got my first job at one of those art goods stores that catered to tourists on Grant Avenue. The owner kept asking for my Social Security number, but I had never thought about it and I didn't have one. I didn't think about it because I was too young; you had to be at least 16 before you could even apply for a Social Security card. So, after two weeks, he gave me a full month's salary and told me not to come back. I met him many years later and he could not remember me or that he had to let me go because I hadn't gotten a Social Security card. So many employees had come and gone over the many years that he owned the store.

Given the generally frugal nature of Chinese business owners, Pat was probably fortunate to be paid for a full month after only two weeks of work. Shortly after her brief stint on Grant Avenue Pat was hired as a temporary worker selling program ads for one of the many conventions for which San Francisco has always been such a popular venue.
.

Pat finally secured a permanent job at E.F. Hutton, one of the firms that made up "Wall Street West" on Montgomery Street. The brokerage was at the corner of Bush Street just a few blocks from Chinatown. That portion of Montgomery Street would evolve into a part of the City's present-day Financial District. In a time when telephone, telegraph and radio were the primary means of long-distance information transfer Pat worked as a "board marker." She would listen on a headset as another employee read off stock prices from a ticker machine. She would then write the data onto a large board for traders and investors on the floor to see. Her supervisors were so impressed by Pat's work ethic that they were quick to hire some of her family members and friends solely on her recommendation.

While at *Hutton* Pat also worked as an on-call hat check girl at the St. Francis hotel across the street from the City's well-known Union Square. The hotel paid seventy cents per hour and Pat enjoyed watching San Francisco's socialites and debutantes as they regularly passed through the lobby or ball rooms all decked out in their best outfits. She says that she was not called in too often and that her tips were always taken by her immediate supervisors. Despite that, having to get up at 5:30 to go to work at *Hutton* in the dark every morning and leaving high school before graduation Pat enjoyed working. She not only earned her own money, but she encountered positive emotions and support from others such as she never got while living at home. She attributes the lack of family warmth to Chinese custom that was exacerbated by the fact that she was, as she says, "just a girl." Pat stayed at *Hutton* for the better part of three years, but the early hours wore thin and she kept her eyes open for other opportunities. Sometime in 1953 she spotted a newspaper ad posted by the *Chinese Sky Room* stating, "Chinese dancers wanted, no experience necessary, will train!" According to Pat,
I was 17 then, but of course I lied about my age. I knew nothing about dancing or show business, but I was mostly hoping to get a job that paid better than what I was making at Hutton and the St. Francis. The position was for Andy Wong's Chinese Vanities of 1954. The interview was at the choreographer's place on Jackson and Hyde Streets. It wasn't much of an interview and there wasn't anything even close to an audition. I was quickly accepted and started training with Walton Biggerstaff who was the choreographer for the Chinese Sky Room and some other clubs.

It might seem strange that Pat's interview and hiring process were so casual and quick, but the need for Chinese dancers by the clubs was always acute. Despite the traditional disdain for daughters, Chinese girls were forbidden by their families to engage in anything even remotely similar to what they would be needed to do in a night club. The term "dancing" was immediately taken as the equivalent to "prostitution." Shame would pass directly and immediately from the daughter to the rest of the family. Pat did not have close ties to her immediate family, so these issues were less important to her than they were to many other girls. The shortage of applicants forced the clubs to hire anyone who even if not truly Chinese could, with a simple name change, pass for Chinese. One example is that of Tony Wing, the long-time Chinatown performer and private dance instructor who was born Filipino. Ironically, many of his former Chinatown-bred dance students, now in their sixties and seventies are surprised to finally learn that Tony was not really Chinese.

Irene Dea Collier [8.]
"Good Night Irene"

Irene Dea Collier is a retired middle school teacher. Irene's three grown children have combined to give her five grandchildren. She lives in a quiet outer Richmond district neighborhood with her husband of almost fifty years.

Irene's family came from Hoi Ping where she grew up speaking a village dialect of Chinese that is related to Cantonese. While the longstanding American immigration laws that forbade entry by Asian women were no longer in effect by the 1950s, little Irene, her two brothers, and her mother remained in their home village while their father and husband travelled on to San Francisco alone. Uncertain about his prospects in the United States, he felt it prudent to see how things would go before having his family join him in California. Many years later Irene said,

There's always a lot of separation for Chinese immigrant families, and so when we were alone in China, my mother would talk about my father, and as a young child I would hear stories about him, but I really couldn't remember him.

Once settled and able to earn a living, five-year old Irene's father was finally comfortable enough to send for his family. Irene offered her thoughts and memories about her first year in San Francisco,

My mother, brothers, and I left our village in Hoiping, and after a brief stay in Hong Kong, we came to this country. This was in 1953 and when we first moved here, we lived in a residential hotel on

Grant Avenue. It was one room and there were the kids and my mother and my father. I only had my Chinese name until the day my father took me to a local health clinic in the Ping Yuen. The woman in charge said that I needed an American name and suggested a few possibilities to my father. She first asked if he wanted to pick a name from among those of well-known flowers such as Rose, Lily, and Pansy. None appealed to my father, so the woman suggested that he consider her favorite American song, "Good Night, Irene." It was a chart topper in those days and he liked it very much. In retrospect, I am pretty grateful that my father didn't like something like Pansy.

Pigs' Feet, Tails, Tongue and Ears and Chicken Feet

As for her home life while growing up, Irene says that hers was a quiet family. Nobody was much of a talker, and when they did speak, they would do so quietly. Consistent with Chinese tradition, her parents were the absolute authority at home and what they wanted, they got. Silence and obedience were expected all the more of Irene for the simple matter that she was a girl. Irene says that there was never any dinnertime conversation. The norm was to just eat.

My mom was a good cook, but she worked long hours in a sewing factory. Actually, the women who worked in them didn't tend to stay at any particular one for very long periods. There was nothing to do but sit and sew, so the main relief from that monotony was conversation. The women would talk about all kinds of things, but there seemed to always be a lot of gossip. Because of this, jealousy or animosity would arise among the workers and sooner or later someone would just leave to work somewhere else. Of course, it wasn't always bad. The women liked to share recipes. Since meat, which had been so very scarce in China, was relatively abundant in the United States, families began to include more of it into their diets. The women for whom a lot of meat was a rarity typically did not know how to prepare it. Those few who knew would share recipes while sewing and before too long practically every household in Chinatown made the same meat dishes from good but unvarying recipes. You could go to anyone's house for dinner and just eat the same things you usually had at home.

30

The type of meat that was available in China included just the odd parts: pig's feet, tails, tongue, or ears, and chicken feet and wings, for example. There wasn't even too much of these things. After all a pig has only two ears and four feet. Chickens, of course, only have two feet. For my family and the other people in or from our village all of these things became delicacies. This culture of cuisine was carried on here in the United States. It's funny today that these are gourmet items that nowadays are all the rage in certain restaurants. I find it a bit funny that the delicacies of poverty have become such upscale and pricey treats out of Chinatown. When I was a girl, and because I was a girl, I would get just the chicken wings. I didn't mind. I liked them because, when cooked, those wing tips would be crunchy and I enjoyed that. I also got the neck of the chicken a lot. That's become another upscale gourmet delicacy these days: chicken necks!

There used to be a supermarket which carried everyday American grocery items like bread, milk, and eggs, but it also carried many staples needed by a Chinese household. The business was owned by people from our family association. They even called me to work at the checkout counter. I tried to do my job, but I was too slow. Well, I was so slow that the line would back up and the customers would begin to get impatient. It wasn't long before I got sent home. They told my father, "Don't bring her anymore! Just leave her home where she can help her mother!"

After her morning shift at the sewing factory, Irene's mother would take off on her lunch hour to do some quick shopping for the evening meal. She would hurry home with her purchases and prepare each of the evening's dishes. It would be for Irene and her younger brother to come home after school to do the final cooking. They would wash and cook rice, start the soup at the designated time, and place any dishes needing to be steam-cooked onto the stove. She was never to stir fry vegetables, however. The proper preparation of vegetables was something of which Irene's mother was extremely proud. She would not trust that Irene could possibly do it to the satisfaction of her standards. It was also left to Irene and her brother to set the table before dinner and to clear it afterwards and to wash the dishes.

According to Irene, she was a homebody who rarely accompanied her friends or classmates to places popular with Chinatown kids such as Cameron House or the Chinese Playground. Irene instead enjoyed staying home to quietly read or sew. Irene's mother would bring scraps of cloth left over from the sewing factory which mother and daughter would deftly piece together into clothing.

One thing my mother wanted me to help her do when I was in about the third or fourth grade was to help her add up the payments due to her from the sewing factory. She wanted to be sure that she was getting what she deserved because the gai-chong owners were not shy about cheating their workers. We caught them more than once, too. What really agitated us was when we walked downtown to see what the clothing Mom had worked so hard to make sold for. The prices were like twenty and thirty dollars each for things that she got paid a lousy fifty to eighty cents to put together. The injustice of it has stayed with me all these years.

Sherman Wong [9.]
I Grew Up in A Sewing Factory

Sherman Wong was born in San Francisco's Chinese Hospital in December, 1947. His mother, seven months pregnant with Sherman, and older brother, Robert, had arrived in San Francisco aboard one of the President Lines ships barely two months earlier. Many of the President Lines vessels were like the one that brought Judy Wing Lee and her family to San Francisco. They were cargo ships whose holds had been quickly and roughly converted into steerage compartments for immigrants from Asia. These compartments, as spoken about by Judy, lacked amenities and were typically crowded and uncomfortable.

Sherman's father, Wing Shew Wong, had arrived in San Francisco as a paper son sometime during the late-1920s. Sherman's father took advantage of the exemption for merchants that had been written into the otherwise strict immigration policies governing Chinese migrants. With its eyes on the potentially broad and lucrative trade markets in China, the United States was eager to foster as many possible business connections throughout that country.

Wing Shew Wong's original family name was Fong. While the anti-Chinese immigration laws forced him to leave his wife, Yee Yang Soo-Hoo (Wong), and first-born son behind, Sherman's father-to-be gained unfettered entry to San Francisco. He had purchased an established San Francisco-based Chinese businessman's agreement to declare him as one of his natural-born sons. As a merchant's son Wing Shew Wong worked in a family run business named *Ying Fat Lung* located at 909 Grant Avenue in Chinatown. Sherman's uncle, his father's brother, also worked there. While it carried general merchandise, the store also sold foodstuffs that included produce and meats. Among the meats were pork products cooked on the premises. These included *cha-siu* (a form of Chinese barbecued pork) and whole roasted pigs, the meat of which, when cut into serving sized pieces is called *siu-yook*. A number of years later Sherman's father moved to *Quon Wo* on the 800 block of Grant Avenue. This second business was similar to, but smaller than the first one. *Quon Wo* did not have the means for cooking roasted pork products.

Sherman recalls going to the second floor of *Ying Fat Lung* where he watched his uncle attach an entire slaughtered pig to a chain before lowering it into a roasting pit. When done, the pig was raised and cut into manageable sections of *siu-yook* for sale. Both *cha-siu* and *siu-yook* were brought downstairs and hung on hooks behind the store's meat counter. After a customer would indicate how much they needed to buy, the counter man would unhook the meat, vigorously yet precisely cut it into small pieces with a greasy iron-bladed cleaver, weigh it, and wrap it into paper. A piece of *siu-yook* was typically a two-inch square topped by a crunchy layer of deep brown skin. Directly beneath the skin was an under layer of fat which was then followed by a medium brown portion of tender pork. The square of *siu-yook* ended with a bottom made by a thin layer of bone.

After the customer had paid and gone, the counterman would sweep the residue of the pork he had just chopped into a waste bin with the edge of his cleaver. A few brisk swipes more often than not would do the trick. The blade of the cleaver would be given a quick wipe from an increasingly discolored and greasy towel or the edge of the counterman's increasingly stained apron and set aside for the next order.

Once home, the individual *siu-yook* squares would be neatly arranged onto a platter and brought to the dinner table. The platter would be placed alongside other similarly prepared dishes, and with filled rice bowls in hand, the family of diners would employ their chopsticks to deftly retrieve morsels of their preference one at a time.

During World War II Sherman's father enlisted in the US Army. Despite his very limited ability to speak English, the immigrant soldier earned an honorable discharge after the war. The reward of citizenship followed. The privilege of American citizenship allowed Sherman's father to finally bring his wife and older son, by then a teenager, to San Francisco in late 1947. The war years in China had been difficult for Sherman's mother, but he says that she rarely spoke of them. He only knows that she, along with the other inhabitants of her village, spent much of the time trying to avoid hunger or abuse by the occupying Japanese. According to Sherman, whenever his mother had anything to say about those days, she would usually just utter a very brief statement along the lines of,

It was a very difficult time. We had to leave everything behind. Everything was gone and everything changed, so it doesn't do any good to talk about it anymore.

Sherman's reunited family settled briefly, as Pat Chin's family also once had done, into makeshift living quarters within the *gai chong* where his mother had been fortunate enough to immediately find work. The little factory featured a ground floor on which all the sewing machines and work stations were placed and a mezzanine on which racks of finished clothing were stored prior to shipping. Sherman recalls that there was a walled off area of the mezzanine where his family could live. The space was also equipped with a small area for cooking. It was not long, however, until the family

34

relocated to an apartment in Salmon Alley that was on the Chinatown side of Broadway between Mason and Taylor Streets. Sherman guesses that he was about four or five years old at that time. Sherman remembers watching the construction equipment at work during the building of the Broadway Tunnel which opened in 1952. He also recalls accompanying his mother to the sewing factory where she continued to work. He spent the earliest years of his childhood there and states,

"I grew up in a sewing factory!"

Sherman remembers that when he was in the third or fourth grade, he often played with a large cardboard box by his mother's work station. While she attached zippers and buttons onto a variety of garments, young Sherman would pretend that his box was a fort or a castle. This was also the time when Sherman developed a love of reading. There was no book, magazine, or newspaper that he did not enjoy. The tenant upstairs of the sewing factory always had newspapers, several days to a week old, that Sherman would read cover to cover. Sometimes, if she noticed that her son was bored or restless, Sherman's mother would give him a nickel or a dime. He would take the money and run down to the nearby store for a candy bar or a soda.

Family Gatherings and Celebrations

Sherman has said that what he most liked about Chinatown while growing up was that it was a tight knit community. It was a fully self-sufficient neighborhood that was simultaneously Chinese and American. Its grocery stores, like that of Irene Dea Collier's family association, had shelves of Chinese condiments such as *foo-yue* (fermented bean cake) standing adjacent to others holding Corn Flakes and Rice Krispies. A stationary shop would carry fountain pens as well as brushes and ink blocks for calligraphy. There were restaurants where one could get either a cheese sandwich or a bowl of *jook* (rice gruel). There were medical and dental offices, a hospital, building contractors, insurance agents, lawyers, travel agents, places of worship, schools (both American and Chinese), newspapers, radio broadcast studios, movie theaters, and pretty much anything that would sustain a small town anywhere in the country.

Sherman fondly recalls that he always felt comfortable that his friends, neighbors, and even those whom he did not know all seemed to have roots in Chinatown. He liked it that people lived within easy walking distances to where they worked, played, shopped, and gathered socially. He states that people were,

… all together and the alleys and narrow streets of Chinatown added to a pleasing atmosphere of closeness *and togetherness among people.*

Sherman also has good memories of the large family gatherings sponsored by the Chinatown Family Associations and the togetherness he enjoyed at weddings and traditional Red Egg and Ginger parties that were given to celebrate a newborn's first month of life.

Family Associations were originally founded by well-established immigrants. Members would welcome those who bore the same surnames as themselves and help the new arrivals with adjustment to their new country. The family associations, like that of Judy Wing Lee's grandfather, often assisted newcomers to find places to live and work. The associations either owned or rented building space which was commonly used for informal social gatherings. All the cousins could gather to chat or gossip, share news from the old country, discuss politics and social issues, or pass time playing games that included mah-jong. Each association hosted annual banquets where, once again, relatives and friends could gather under one roof to share food and socialize. Since he was just a boy when his parents would take him to the annual Fong Family Association sponsored banquets, Sherman did not fully understand everything, especially the speeches and the "adult talk" that would take place over the course of the evening. He does, however, remember having fun seeing his friends and relatives and enjoying a comforting sense of order and unity at the functions. He says,

My father liked to go to the So-Yuen-Tong association to socialize with friends and relatives from his old village in China. I always appreciated the values of family and community that the family association and its events promoted. And the food at the yearly banquets was always so good!

The Red Egg party, in brief, dates far back to the time in human history when high infant mortality rates were more rule than exception. If a newborn survived his or her first thirty days, chances were good that the baby was healthy enough to live and thrive. Gifts of *lay-see*, money in red envelopes and, in some cases, fine jewelry (often gold or jade) would be given to the child. The hosts would pass out red-dyed hard-boiled eggs to the guests. The red color of the *lay-see* envelopes and of the eggs symbolized good fortune and the happiness that came along with it.

There can be little doubt that Red Egg parties also appealed to Sherman's keen sense of family and community togetherness. Some were elaborate affairs, but many were celebrated in people's Chinatown or North Beach homes. Among the adults, grandparents, aunts, and uncles would pack themselves into typically small apartments or cramped flats to fawn over the baby. All engaged in animated conversations that centered on the baby, allowed participants to "catch up on the latest," or ended up as just plain gossip. The kids, all siblings and cousins, swarmed, ran, and jostled in lively play. Not even the steamy, moist, and deeply pungent aromas of boiled pickled pigs' feet or "drunken chicken" could stifle the joy and commotion. The latter dish is a whole chicken cooked in rice wine. It, as well as the pickled pig's feet, were specifically prepared for the new mother. She was to consume them over an entire month in order to benefit from the special powers they held for women who had just given birth.

While acknowledging that change is inevitable, Sherman nonetheless regrets that life today finds friends and family scattered, a lack of respect among people, and a sense of a social order in which it is a case of, *"everyone for himself and just me, me, me."*

My Parents Were Moonshiners

Looking back at his younger days in Chinatown Sherman recovered several things from deep within his memory. Among them was this story of his parents' home-based distillery,

I remember that when I was in grade school, my mom and dad made rice wine, or bok jiew, in the house. They had this big clay pot that held the mash which was made from fermented rice. Then, they poured it into a metal drum that could hold about five gallons and cooked it on the kitchen stove. They boiled it and they ran a long hose from the drum into jars and that was the alcohol. It really steamed up the whole house. There was moisture everywhere and on everything. I don't think they sold it. They just gave it away to friends or family and they kept some for themselves. I never asked questions about it. They were my parents, after all, so when they said that they were going to make rice wine, I just quietly accepted it. I think that they really only did it about once every year.

I Was Happy to Do What I Could

Even though my mother was far from her home in China and even though she had to work long hours, she always kept her cooking skills. She made all kinds of traditional dishes and they were all really good. Well, I didn't like the whole steamed fish. She would always pick a piece for me with her chopsticks and ask me to take it. I wouldn't, though, because I just thought the flavor was too "fishy." I like it now that I'm older and I order it a lot when I go to Chinese restaurants.

When I was in junior high, my mom would ask me to do the preparation work for dinner. She would be at the sewing factory until late, so she would tell me what I needed to do when I got home from school. I really liked to do it. It was what you might call an assigned chore, but it made me feel good to be helping the family and contributing. I always washed the rice. I put it into the pot that it would be cooked in – and we didn't have those electric rice cookers that everyone uses today – and swirl it around in water. I would pour off the water and do it again until the water was clear.

I don't do it like that today, because all the vitamins get washed out. My favorite part of the rice to eat after it was cooked was the hard and burned part from the bottom of the pot. It would be crunchy and have some flavor to it.

I also helped to slice or chop the veggies and the meat. We had a big circular chopping block that looked like a section of a tree trunk. The sides were wrapped tight with wire to hold it together. That thing was solid as a log, but it was really greasy. The chopping surface was porous and cracked so that grease and food residue would get into all the cracks and pits. It wasn't very sanitary, I guess, but we didn't get sick, and that's the way it was. I also would be sure to turn on the soup to boil and simmer at the right time. After dinner I would clear the table, wash dishes, and take out the garbage. The next step in my routine was to do homework and then go to bed. My mom would sometimes bring sewing home from work to finish. She would stay up until 10 or 11 at night with it, so I was always happy to do what I could to make things a little better or easier for the family.

Tommy L. Lim [10.]
They Didn't Want My Father's Money

Tommy Lim's parents and his eldest sister were all born in China. His second sister, also older than him was born in Napa, California where his parents had settled to start a grocery business. Tommy is the third of the family's children and he was followed by a younger brother. Tommy lived in Napa until his family relocated to San Francisco when he was 11.

Tommy is currently a self-employed optometrist whose practice, Berryessa Optometry, is located in San Jose, California. He finds fulfillment in being active in multiple organizations related to his profession. He also has a seat on the board of the Chinatown Community Development Center and serves as a deacon for the First Chinese Baptist Church in Chinatown's Waverly Place.

Although Tommy's childhood in Napa was generally a happy one, he did have to suffer pain and embarrassment from being picked on for being Chinese. He also endured a family tragedy before joining relatives in San Francisco in the summer of 1966. Upon arrival in the city as an eighth grader, Tommy was thrilled to be among so many other Chinese in school and in the neighborhoods of Chinatown and North Beach. His early brushes with racially based taunts had left him initially ashamed of his Chinese background, but several key experiences as a teenager and young adult helped to provide him with a foundation of purposefulness and contentment which has stayed with him through to the present day.

Like so many young Chinese men of the early 20th century, Tommy's father travelled to the United States in hopes of escaping what would have likely been a dismal future. By 1928 China had undergone years of political strife and a series of famine producing natural disasters. Great numbers of people suffered tremendous hardships. Once in the United
States, Tommy's father got together several other fellow Chinese in establishing a grocery store. The immigration laws imposed on the Chinese in those days barred any of these young immigrants from bringing their wives or children with them. Of his family's early days, Tommy said,

My father, Lim Sai Oy, and my mother, Huie Tai Oy, were married in 1928. He was 18 years old and she was 17. A year after the marriage, he left his young bride in China and came alone to America in order to seek a better life for himself and his future family. Little did he know that it would be eighteen years before he would be reunited with my mother. I often think of the love and fortitude that was required for them not to give up hope over those long years. It was not until after World War II that they were able to get together again. Their first child, Betty, was born in 1948 (after Tommy's father had travelled back to China). *When my parents moved to the United States one year later, they left their baby daughter in the care of my grandmother. In 1949, on their way to America, my mom was pregnant with their second child. They settled in Napa, California, where my second sister May was born. I was born in 1952 and my brother Jimmy was born in 1955. After a late start, my parents had a house full of children.*

In the late 1930s my dad had opened a grocery store in Napa with three partners who were also Chinese immigrants. The store was called "Napa Grocery," and it was a medium-sized supermarket. My dad was the produce manager, and he made weekly trips to Sacramento to buy produce for the store. My dad and his partners worked six days a week. They would open up the store at 9:00 a.m. and not close until 9:00 p.m. The store thrived through providing excellent value and service to its customers. However, Asians were not accepted in mainstream America at that time. My dad and the store faced racism in the predominantly white community of Napa. Barber shops would not cut my dad's hair. They simply told him that they didn't want his money. The Napa Register, the town newspaper, would not print the store's advertisements. When the store first opened, my father and the other Chinese partners and employees could not find housing. For months on end no one would rent an apartment or house to them. They slept on top of boxes in the warehouse. Fortunately, the store contained a small kitchen in which they were able to cook for themselves.

My dad and his partners were eventually able to purchase an old house around the corner from their store. This was where my dad and many of the others involved with the store lived. Over time the housing situation eased a little and the employees moved out. Our family eventually moved into that old house and that was where I lived during the first five years of my life. I am glad that after getting married I was able to bring my wife Bonnie to see my childhood home before it was torn down.

"Nay Huey Nai Thlay-ah?"

Tommy recently took a few moments to think back about his mother.

My mom, who I will always cherish as a very special woman, died in 2012 at over 100 years of age. Even when she was in her late 90s, she took walks (with a little help from a friend) six days a week from her home in North Beach to Chinatown to play mah-jong and buy dinner. My mom always stressed the importance of family values and hard work. Whatever positive values that I have today I owe to her. She was always there for me and she served as a great example of how to grow old gracefully. I will always love her very much.

Chinese as spoken in Chinatown during the 1950s and 1960s was heavily represented by Toishan dialects. One of them, *Thlay Yip* (or *Say Yup*) was the one spoken by Tommy's family.

Tommy says that he sometimes smiles when, in a quiet moment, one or another of his mother's old fashioned, but what he calls "cute," Chinese sayings comes to mind. These bring back good memories of a happy youth that Tommy holds dearly in his heart. These phrases are difficult to translate because, in addition to the literal meanings of the words, there are contexts, tones, interpersonal relationships, and the places in which they could be spoken to consider while seeking the truest meaning of what is said. Most speakers of Toishan *Thlay Yip* can probably appreciate the English translations fairly readily. For others, especially non-Chinese speakers, they can be challenging.

One saying of his mother's that Tommy enjoys remembering came in the form of a question. He spoke of it with a chuckle. If Tommy might have come home later than expected, his mother sometimes would demand, *"nay huey nai thlay, ah?" "Thlay"* carries several meanings, but in this case, it is "die" and the Chinese usually take great lengths to avoid speaking the word. The term or anything that even sounds like it bodes ill-will and serious misfortune. The number "four" is also pronounced "thlay" and is considered an unlucky number by more than a few. The difference in the tonal quality of *thlay* as *four* as opposed to *die* makes little difference to the many that are sensitive to its nuances.

The Toishan villagers' frequent and idiomatic use of expressions that include *thlay* was and remains distasteful to many speakers of Chinese. Its open and free use by those from the Toishan region has somewhat, at least to those from Toishan, softened its more dire connotations. The manner in which Tommy's mother (and a lot of others like her) delivered the query to him could be rendered as, "What? Did you crawl off somewhere and die!?" A mother's worry that something dire could have happened to her son was the true message, however. In everyday language, the question can be simply rendered as, "Where in the heck have you been all this time?" And the unspoken message would be, "I was very worried about you."

Another common saying using *thlay* that Tommy fondly recalls comes in the expression, *"ah thlay a-nay."* It was usually uttered out of a sense of mild frustration or irritation unaccompanied by any true anger. *"Ah"* in the expression means "hit" or "beat," so the literal translation would be "to beat you to death." A convenient American version of the phrase might be, "I'm gonna kill you," where actual homicide is never even remotely possible. An even more likely American equivalent would be, "You're gonna get it!" Since no serious anger or true irritation is involved, the words are deliberately not serious. In most Chinese households, true anger would be immediately shown through sharp blows to any exposed portion of a child's body. Whether by hand or with any conveniently nearby solid object, the blows would more often than not be delivered wordlessly.

In Tommy's case, his mother's love may have been expressed with some strange words, but it will always remain undying to him.

2.
A Kid's Chinatown
We Were Just Kids Being Kids

Before there were such things as day care or after school programs, Chinatown life revolved tightly around the concept of the extended family. If parents had to work, grandparents could be counted on to watch over those who were too young to care for themselves. Within Chinatown's limited space, aunts, uncles, older siblings or cousins, neighbors and even an occasional stranger could also be counted upon to help out. As they got older many kids just took it upon themselves to band together to go places and to help and look out for each other.

Judy Wing Lee
Fun on the Sidewalks

Judy spent many of her childhood hours playing on the streets near her home or her parents' business with her young friends. She and another Chinatown girl remembered some of their games and activities. Judy said,

My parents' sewing factory was on the 1300 block of Grant. It was 1348, I believe. It was located in the building owned by the Yick Family. My mom had previously worked for Chuck Wong on the 1400 block of Grant and he helped us to start up the factory. The 1400 block was a fun block to play on because we could run around the block from Grant to Green to Bannam to Union and back to Grant again without crossing the streets. We were street kids who played street games like tag, hide and seek, lining up playing cards against the wall and flinging other cards at them to knock them over, finding empty soda pop bottles to trade for candy, dodge ball against building walls, and tricycle races around the block on our trusty Bannam to Green to Grant to Union and back to Bannam circuit. We all knew to generally stay within this boundary. Sometimes we would go climb Telegraph Hill at the top of Filbert Street all the way to Coit Tower. We would also go fishing with drop lines at Muni Pier at Aquatic Park near Fisherman's Wharf. Kids being kids, we got into fights, too. I took part in my share of them, especially if anyone was picking on my sister. Some kid's mom would say to my mom that I hit her kid, but my mom knew I only hit them because they were bullying some other kid.

Another girl about Judy's age was Sheryl Chan. Sheryl was born in San Francisco and, growing up, spent a lot of time at her grandmother's. Her grandmother did not live in the heart of Chinatown, but just on its western outskirts on Mason Street. While Sheryl did not know Judy, she shared familiar memories about the games that so many of the former Chinatown kids played.

My older brother Ivan and I grew up in a typical Chinese-American family. When I was very young, my grandmother took care of me during the day while my mother worked. Grandmother lived on

Mason Street between Broadway and Vallejo Streets. I can still hear the cable car tracks and the clanging of the cable car bells outside the window, and I can still smell Grandmother's freshly cleaned coarse sheets on her bed where I took naps. My cousins and I would play jump rope, hop-scotch, or hide-and-seek in front of the house or go to the corner grocery store and buy candy and popsicles. I also remember eating the preserved plums (Chinese snacks called *mui*) *and stick jelly candies that came in colorful boxes.*[11.]

Deb Lem
I Was Born in 1949 and I Lived in Chinatown Until 1989

Deborah (Deb) Lem was born in 1949. Her maternal grandfather, Sam Ying Mock, arrived in the United States from China in the early 1900s. He settled in Palo Alto where he worked as a cook for Stanford University students living in the dorms. Deb's cousins on this side of her family all grew up in or close to Palo Alto. Their childhood experiences in the suburbs were far more American and far less Chinese than Deb's in Chinatown.

Having settled in San Francisco, Deb's paternal grandfather purchased the small building at 1046 Grant Avenue between Pacific and Jackson Streets. In the years prior to World War II, her mother graduated from Poly High in San Francisco and attended San Jose State where she majored in accounting. Deb's father graduated from Lowell High and was enrolled at USC where he majored in chemistry. Both of Deb's parents left college during the war and did not return. They met through being introduced by a mutual friend. Her parents were living at 1046 Grant Avenue when Deb was born in 1949. The building included a ground floor commercial space and one flat each on the second and third floors. Deb's grandparents lived on the second floor while her parents, Deb and her two siblings lived in the third floor. According to Deb,

My grandfather probably bought 1046 Grant in the 1920's and our family has owned it since then. Presently, my brother and I own it with our spouses. I grew up there, lived there while going to college, lived there while going to work in Redwood City, went away to grad school, came back again, lived in Italy and came back once again.

1046 Grant was my legal residence until 1989 when I started a business and bought my house in King of Prussia, Pennsylvania. Even then, I came back often to visit grandparents. In some ways, I sort of feel out of the loop, but I also feel as though I never left. Chinatown has changed more than I have.

While far removed from her native Chinatown, Deb's heart remains deeply entrenched there. The happiness she experienced as a child is abundantly evident in the memories that she shares about those halcyon days of the 1950s and 1960s. One can practically see the grade school-aged Deb skipping along Grant Avenue and its adjacent streets and alleys as she recalls the sights and flavors of her corner of 1950s Chinatown.

I would say that, in many ways, my childhood was idyllic. For living in the city on a commercial street, that is. It was safe, and it was pretty quiet at night save for the trash trucks and fish, pig, and chicken delivery people dropping off their supplies at night or in the morning.

I had my own room, my brothers shared. We had dinner together every night, sometimes Chinese, sometimes American food like roasts and fried chicken, and sometimes we went out. And we didn't always go out to Chinatown restaurants. A family favorite was Sabella's at Fishermen's Wharf. On Sundays, after church, we would often go for rides. My father loved to drive, so we might take a ride across the Golden Gate (which my father walked across when it opened in 1937) and have lunch in Tiburon or much farther north or south. Chinatown to me was populated by a cast of characters who all had their place in my small but exotic little world of growing up. We had an herb store down the block with walls made up of mysterious little wooden drawers that went from floor to ceiling. The shop owner would search among them for dried roots and who-knows-what with which to make the perfect concoction for whatever ailment you had complained to him about. Wrapped into a little paper packet these "medicines" would always taste terrible and bitter. Somehow, they never failed to work.

It was a real treat to me that, also just down the street, we had a store through whose windows you could see and smell those delicious roast ducks, faw-ahp. They were hung from black iron hooks behind the window. You could tell the freshest ones because their hook ends were shiny and slick looking. The ducks from earlier or even the day before had white gobs and drips of duck fat that was already cold. Those ducks were one of my all-time favorite family dinnertime treats.

And then there was the fish store! You knew that anything you bought from there was sure to be fresh because it was still swimming in a glass tank when you pointed it out to the shopkeeper as the exact one you wanted. The poultry shop across Pacific Avenue offered completely fresh products as well. I can vouch for that because I would wake up every morning to the sound of chickens that bawled, clucked and screeched as they were being slaughtered.

The Sam Lung Supermarket was just next door. It was a bright and friendly place. I remember a young man named Yam who would carry our groceries home for us. He would lug those big 50-pound sacks of rice upstairs and never complained. Most Chinatown shoppers were done with their rounds by mid-morning. All those fresh chickens and a lot of the fish would be gone before lunch time. Not all the shoppers were just from Chinatown. Sometimes you would see non-Chinese from other parts of the City buying things. There were always people from the Peninsula or across the Bay, too. These Chinese people liked to use their shopping time to meet with friends or relatives. They would walk together on their errands and chat to catch up or to gossip. Sometimes they went to have cha-gnow (also called yum-cha and currently referred to most often as dim-sum) if they had time.

Not all the shops were for food, of course. I remember how my brothers used to go to the souvenir shop on the next block for toys or gadgets or presents for some of their friends at Christmas or for a birthday. They were always followed around by the stern-faced and tightly coiffed lady who was probably the store's owner. She always wore her grey Chinese style jacket and quietly shuffled right behind the boys as they looked around. Of course, she was just *keeping a sharp eye on them in case they might steal something. I think I remember a lot of Chinatown shopkeepers being like that with us when we were kids. We were sometimes even afraid to just touch something because the old store lady would yell at us and make us buy it. All that for five-cent little toys or trinkets!*

A lot of these little stores were like mini-Costcos. They had anything you might ever need. They had American things as well as Chinese things. There was a place that I went a lot to for paper goods, usually school stuff. They had binders and ruled notebook paper for American school and they also had the blue booklets that we had to use for practicing our pen and ink characters in Chinese school. They even had Mother's-Day cards.

I eventually came to realize that Chinatown was not perfect. There were gangs that warred among themselves. There were thugs and demands for protection money from struggling business and shop owners. None of this was apparent to me as a child growing up. I always saw and remember the Chinatown of my youth as a compact, friendly and safe place to live and grow up in.

Saki Lee [12.]
Getting Lost and Being Taken to a Gai Chong

Saki Lee's maternal grandfather entered the United States in 1903 as a paper son. His original surname was Lew, but he arrived in the United States with his false father's name, Wong. Mr. Wong had taken advantage of the same key loophole in the Chinese Exclusion laws used by Sherman Wong's father in order to get Saki's grandfather-to-be to San Francisco. Mr. Wong ran an import-export business that was on Clay Street in Chinatown, and he applied to the immigration service for his teenaged "son" to be granted merchant status. He needed the boy to help in the business. Ironically, Saki's grandfather would grow up to become a restaurant owner, real estate dealer and stock market speculator.

Saki was born in the early 1950s. She grew up with an older sister and a younger brother. The three children were cared for by their divorced mother who was a first-generation ABC. The family lived on John Street and on the third floor of a four-unit building that was owned by Saki's maternal grandfather. John Street is narrow and modestly inclined. It measures just a single block in length, sits between Mason and Powell and runs parallel with Jackson and Pacific. Saki and her two siblings all went through school at Jean Parker, Francisco and Galileo.

When she was five years old, Saki had an adventure that opened her young eyes to the hard working yet kindly people who lived around her in Chinatown. The impressions made upon Saki in the span of a single afternoon would always remain with her. They would steer her onto a career and life's path filled with compassion for others.

One of my earliest memories of Chinatown was as a five-year old. One day my mother took my brother and sister to the nearby barber shop. She left me playing contentedly on our enclosed back porch. After a while I became restless and found out that nobody was at home with me. I fearlessly opened the front door, walked down the steps to John Street, and wandered out to look for everyone.

I walked along Powell for half a block and managed to cross Pacific Avenue. A kind and elderly Chinese woman approached me and spoke to me in my own native Toishan dialect, thlay yip. She asked me where I lived and where mama and papa were. She looked like an auntie I could trust. I answered that I did not know. I was beginning to find my adventure rather exciting.

The nice lady then took my hand and led me to one of Chinatown's many sweatshops (or 'gai-chong' for sewing factory) where my ears were assaulted by the clamor of loud women's voices competing with the din from foot-pedaled sewing machines rattling non-stop. All this was further punctuated by the shrill cacophony of Hong Kong music blaring from a record player somewhere in the background. As a five-year old I, of course, did not know that in those days similar sweatshops were everywhere in Chinatown. Poor immigrant women labored in darkened, crowded, and unsanitary rooms for long hours sewing garments for mere pittance wages.

The lady who had brought me shouted if anyone knew me or where

I belonged. For a few moments the sewing machines stopped. Shaking their heads, nobody could identify this stray little girl. I looked around and saw women who looked much older than my own mother who was 29. Mom, however, had a job that was much better than toiling away in a gai-chong. She worked in a large and modern building as a secretary for one of San Francisco's big insurance firms.

These immigrant women looked so grandmotherly to me. Even today I can still see their wrinkled faces etched with deep worry lines stretched across frowning brows. Some of them had bad looking teeth or even huge gaps where teeth should have been. With stooped shoulders the women sat huddled over their sewing machines intent on finishing as many garments as they possibly could. They would be paid by the number of completed pieces that they could deliver after a 10-hour day of work.

One of the women gave me a sweet pastry roll and, as I ate it, I sat in a big cardboard box filled with finished garments and peeked around. I felt at home among all these nice ladies all of whom closely resembled one or another of my own many aunties. I was completely comfortable. It was as if I belonged there. Of course, I could not stay there and one of the gai-chong ladies eventually brought me to the Hall of Justice and police station on Kearny Street near Portsmouth Square. Some hours later my very relieved mother came and fetched me.

A few years later the happy memories of the warmth and kindness that had been extended to her in the *gai-chong* to which she had been led as a lost five-year old encouraged Saki to visit other such sewing factories in order to try to make some spending money.

Later as a thirteen-year old I went to all of the neighborhood sweatshops. I was looking for customers to buy these brightly colored tinsel birds that my sister had woven in hopes of picking up some extra pocket money. In spite of the fact that all these hardworking women really needed all the money they could earn for the care of their own families, there always seemed to be one of them who was willing to part with a quarter or two for one of these little birds. I remember how the purchasers would gleefully show off their sparkling little trinkets to their co-workers before placing them beside their sewing machines. I wonder if this little glimmer of light reflected the brighter future that each of these women, laboring doggedly away in a semi-darkened workspace, hoped to someday deliver to their own children.

A Bit More About Gai-Chong From Judy Wing Lee

By the mid-1950s Judy Wing Lee's parents had established themselves as the owner-operators of one of Chinatown's numerous *gai-chong*. Although Judy, a self-described tom-boy while in grade school, had plenty of time to play, she also spent much more of her time helping out in her parents' sewing factory. Judy worked with her parents through high school.

We outfitted the sewing factory with used machines. My mom would 'pang yee' - separate and bundle the precut patterns sent to us by a clothing company for assembly with a ticket with the number of garments it would complete. Each sewing machine had two big boxes on either side for the 'yee'. We were able to get the boxes from the corner grocery store on Grant and Green. The completed 'yee' were tied in bundles and placed in a bigger box to await the buttonholer and button sewing machine operators. Finally, all was sent on to the ironer who packed the 'yee' into old banana boxes. The company we contracted from was Fritzi of California.

To recruit workers, my parents posted a help wanted sign in Chinese on a strip of red paper outside of the sewing factory. The workers also came by word of mouth, and they in turn provided referrals since they typically knew of others looking for work, too. The majority of workers sewed in the factory, but there were always a few who took the bundles and worked from home. All were paid in cash based on the number of garments they completed. When there was a legal crackdown on labor practices in the city my parents were required to have the workers fill out daily eight-hour time cards. The reality was that they were still paid by piece work. Since the time cards were just a formality, the workers were free to come and go and to work on whatever schedule was most convenient for each of them. They took their kids to and from school, shopped, cooked at home, put their kids to bed, and came back in between times to sew. The ladies were very hardworking and industrious. The factory opened from 8:00 AM to Midnight, Monday through Saturday to accommodate their schedules. The workers were eventually paid by check, and one of my responsibilities was to co-sign each check with my father.

The sewing factory was a nice social community for the workers also. There was a lot of talking – gossip even - sharing, caring, and every so often a little drama that could lead to the outbreak of jealousies. One of my duties was to flip the 78 rpm records on the big record player at the back of the work area. Music gave the gai-chong a small touch of human warmth. Later we got a Wollensak reel-to-reel tape recorder which played for an hour straight on each side. Many lifelong friendships were built in the sewing factory. My mom has stayed in touch with some of these ladies who are mostly in their late 80's to mid-90's now. Some of the kids I grew up with there, I still regard today as family.

Once, someone came to talk to my father about "protection." It was extortion, of course, and my father was angry about it and refused to pay. Not long afterwards a trash can stuffed with flammable waste was lit and placed against our gai chong's front window. The heat cracked the window so badly that it had to be replaced. My father gave in and made his regular payments. He was not bothered by again.

Eventually, my parents had to sell the factory to one of the workers to pay the IRS. My father had never filed income tax returns, and we were forced to liquidate to pay the back taxes.

Starting School and Subtle Changes

Prior to beginning school, Saki Lee's home life was one of bilingualism and dual social and cultural norms. She, as did all her cousins and adult relatives in her extended family, spoke both Chinese and English at home. Saki and her relatives could fluidly switch between English and Chinese and, in many cases, they would blend words from both languages into a single sentence. There were families, however, where none of the adult members had much English proficiency, so Chinese had to be their primary language. Television was still in its infancy so the impact that it would have on spoken Chinese or on the Toishan village social values brought over by parents and grandparents all through Chinatown was not yet apparent. In general, before starting school, Saki and practically every other Chinatown kid she knew were easily more Chinese than they were American.

From the first day of school onwards, however, the lives of Saki, her siblings, and all of her young neighbors, friends, and cousins began to change.

By the time I started kindergarten at Jean Parker on Broadway, I did not notice or think much about the fact that all of my classmates looked like me and everyone else in my world. We were all Chinese. But our teachers were pale skinned and talked and acted differently from the rest of us. My mother referred to them as "bok guey," or white ghosts. School was my very first encounter with The Other, or someone who was Not Me. I found this to be both fascinating as well as intimidating.

On one of my very first days in school, the teacher seemed exasperated because quite a number of the children would squint and look at her with blank faces as she talked to us. Many of my new schoolmates only spoke Chinese at home and didn't understand a word of English. Our teacher used a long pointer to indicate objects throughout the room in order for us to name their color in English. She also asked us to name each of her selected items. I finally managed to timidly whisper the correct answers. The teacher was noticeably pleased and asked if I could help by translating for the non-English speakers in her class.

Since we were bi-lingual at home, I was able to navigate between the familiar Chinese world and the new American world during my early school days. I clearly remember a moon-faced little boy who was sitting next to me. His cheeks flushed brightly red and he looked thoroughly miserable for not understanding what it was that his white ghost teacher was talking about. I, on the other hand, felt proud and special for being able to speak and understand English. I admit that I looked down upon the boy next to me and the others like him as dummies.

As time passed, I came to notice that not all Chinese students were really the same at all. There were two camps: those who did not speak English and those who did. The first group was hopelessly slow, not very bright, and generally out of place. The second group was somewhat elite and wanted to fit into the white ghost world. We carried on as if we were smarter and basically superior. I very much wanted to be a part of this second group. Teacher seemed to agree that those of the second group would be her preferred set of students. She even warned us not to speak Chinese or we would be penalized. This was the beginning of how subtly negative cultural discrimination began at a young age as we grew up in Chinatown.

First-Time Experience Out of Chinatown

While they were still students at Jean Parker, Saki and her brother were sent by their mother to spend a year in Ohio. Their maternal aunt Pat and her husband, their Uncle James, would care for the two siblings. Before going to Cincinnati, however, the two youngsters would first visit another aunt near Washington, D.C. for her medical school graduation. Saki and her brother would spend a couple of weeks with her and their grandmother who had been with their aunt for the entire four years of her schooling. It was the first time that either of the children had been out of Chinatown. Saki remembered,

My brother Jim and I were 9 and 10 years old when we boarded our first airplane flight. We were on our way to our Auntie Ida's graduation from medical school in Washington, D.C. What we did not know was that we were also going to be enrolled for a full school year in Cincinnati where we were to live with Uncle James and Auntie Pat. Before going on to Cincinnati we spent a couple of weeks with Auntie Ida in Takoma Park, Maryland. For two small Chinatown kids, the world suddenly expanded beyond our wildest imagination, and we were wonder struck with excitement at being plopped down into a strange and new world.

We suddenly found ourselves in a world bereft of jostling crowds of people constantly shouting in a variety of Chinese dialects. Takoma Park had none of Chinatown's unfriendly gray concrete streets where old men and women frequently and loudly spat out their disgusting phlegm onto the sidewalks. There were no dingy and darkened apartment buildings and housing projects like the Ping Yuens all up and down Pacific Avenue, and we were happily relieved of the odorous fish and poultry stores that lined Grant Avenue.

We thought we were in some kind of paradise! Takoma Park seemed to be filled with spacious green lawns with sprinklers and beautiful tree-lined streets. Jim and I could hardly believe our eyes. We thought that Auntie Ida's front yard was really a park. The only parks that we had ever known were San Francisco's Golden Gate Park and the one-block square of grass and trees that was Washington Square in North Beach. There was this huge and majestic weeping willow in the yard where Jim and I spent as many hours as we could to play under. There was also an ancient and gnarled oak tree from which we gathered acorns. We let our imaginations loose and used our acorns as play money.

Some neighborhood children came to play with us every afternoon in our huge park. We didn't notice that they were white, nor did they notice that we were not. One day, our grandmother, or paw-paw, who lived with Auntie Ida, asked us to invite one of the girls to stay for dinner. She first said yes, but shortly after seeing Paw Paw cooking in the kitchen, she reported back to me that she had changed her mind. "Ugh!" She screwed up her nose in disgust. "Your grandmother is frying tomatoes with meat!" I didn't get it. What was wrong with fried tomatoes? "We always eat them plain and raw," she said. "My mother would never think of frying them." I found out that Chinese food was pretty weird to my new friends.

Young Saki and her brother did not realize that their Aunt Ida had had to attend medical school all the way across the country from San Francisco because of racial discrimination. Although she had graduated from UC Berkeley with honors in zoology, none of the medical schools closer to home could "find a spot" for her.

Eventually, the handicaps of being non-white, female and poor turned in Ida's favor. She was accepted by Washington D.C.'s Howard University School of Medicine. Although popularly viewed as a "black university," Howard's broad and founding mission has always been to provide opportunities for socially and/or economically disadvantaged students of either gender and of any race. Prior to the Civil Rights era, which was the precise time that saw Ida studying at Howard, a vast majority of African American physicians were trained at Howard. Like Ida, they did not have a broad field of schools from which to choose.

As is customary of Chinese families, Ida's mother and Saki's *paw-paw* could not allow her daughter to live alone so far from home. As Saki has stated, her *paw-paw* lived with Ida during her four years at Howard. She refused to have her daughter do any chores or housework so that she could fully concentrate on her studies. Although she was very much a product of old China and all its deeply rooted cultural beliefs about girls and women, Ida's mother was filled with pride that her daughter was on her way to becoming a "*yee-sang*," or doctor. Saki continued her story,

Soon it was time to fly on to Cincinnati. Uncle James and Auntie Pat lived in a poor white neighborhood in an older part of town. They worked hard and, even though they were the only Chinese people around, it seemed to me like they were well accepted. The front entrance to their three-room home was where customers came to drop off or pick up their laundry. Piles of bundled laundry -- washed, dried, hand ironed, and folded -- were neatly stacked just behind the front desk. The laundry for pick-up was wrapped in brown paper and tied with some string. A little bell would ring whenever the front door opened, and either Auntie Pat or Uncle James would attend to their customers with a cheerful smile. Uncle James spoke with a heavy Chinese accent. Auntie Pat was born in San Francisco so her English was perfect.

Jim and I were happy there. The living space was just behind the laundry counter. It was a single but good-sized room that was partitioned with some cheap paneling to create a bedroom for Uncle James and Auntie Pat that gave them some privacy. We had a bunk

bed in an opposite corner of the room. There was also a rectangular dining table where we were treated at least twice a week to non-Chinese food which delighted us greatly. The second room held the stove for cooking and a big barrel-shaped washing machine that chugged along all day and every day. The third room was Jim's and my favorite. It was the drying room - a small space where little burners on the floor dried the wet laundry hung up wherever there was space. We had hours of winter time fun playing there when the heaters were off. The room would still be somewhat hot and very comfortable and cozy.

At school I was amazed that my 10-year old fellow students were physically so different from the kids I knew in Chinatown. They were so physically big. The girls already wore nylon stockings and lipstick, and they had boobs big enough to require support of a bra! During recess, I would even hear talk about who had their periods already at the age of 10 or 11! Like me, Jim was small for his age, but it was to his disadvantage as a boy. He felt picked on. Jim told me that Uncle James had advised him to say that he was not Chinese, but Hawaiian. I'm not sure how this might have helped, but since Jim had a little darker complexion than I did, I suppose it made sense. Uncle James also encouraged Jim to defend himself and fight back. We all shared lots of practice sessions wrestling and tumbling around with each other, but I'm not sure that really helped Jim all that much.

Melody Chan Doss-Wambeke
The Flower Fields of Sunnyvale

Melody remembers her first-ever time away from Chinatown. Melody, her brothers and her mother left the city to spend a summer working together at the Sunnyvale flower farm where her father was employed.

The land was about six acres in size and was leased to a Chinese farmer. He was acquainted with my father and also needed a cook for the summer. My mother was hired to cook three meals a day for him, the 10 field workers, and us. She also helped in the fields.

58

It was a miserable summer because we were crammed into a small trailer. We were literally transported into a strange world. There were no familiar tall city buildings, no Chinatown, no familiar playground, and no local library. All we could see around us were fields filled with rows and rows and rows of different colored asters and chrysanthemums. My parents did not have time for us and we did our best to entertain ourselves. In a child's mind, a summer season is a very, very long time. I remember that the landowner and his wife were blondes and that made quite an impression on me since my sole contact with non-Chinese people at that time was restricted to the Caucasian teachers from school and a few Italian neighbors.

My parents and the other field hands were also prolific gardeners. They tended to their small plots at the end of the day. I noticed that my parents grew large green vegetables. Maybe it was Bok Choy. When I looked at the rows of corn, I couldn't help but think of the song from the then-popular musical, OKLAHOMA! It really looked to me that it grew as tall as an elephant's eye. My parents instilled many things in me, but the passion for gardening was not one of them. I do not have the patience for it.

At the end of that summer, my brothers and I returned to Garfield Elementary School a bit taller and very tanned. My mother later asked if we would consider spending the next summer helping my father and others at the flower fields. We quickly vetoed the idea.

Sherman Wong
Cameron House, Chinese Playground, and Part-Time Work

Sherman started school by attending Commodore Stockton which sat in the heart of Chinatown and was popularly referred to by its students as "Commodore." At a time when children were assigned to the school nearest to their home address, Sherman should have been assigned to Jean Parker which was barely two blocks from his Salmon Street home. The sewing factory where his mother worked, however, was much closer to Commodore. Planning ahead for the easiest way to walk to pick their son up after school, Sherman's parents listed the sewing factory's address as that of their home. Although he does not remember a lot about his first years in school,

Sherman states that there was just one Chinese American teacher at Commodore. Her name was Miss Shirley Lee and she was his favorite teacher.

By Sherman's fifth grade year, crowding had become a problem at Commodore. The school's highest two grades, fifth and sixth, were bused to a previously all-white school in the not too distant Marina District. Oddly enough in Sherman's case the school was (and remains) called, Sherman. Commodore remained the students' home school. They assembled there in the morning to board buses to Sherman, and they were dismissed from Commodore after being bused back in the afternoon.

I really liked it. It was an adventure. It got me out of Chinatown and into the world. Until then all I knew was Chinatown and it was crowded and kind of old and even dirty. I remember going to the Ping Yuens [13.] *to visit family and friends and the elevators that took you upstairs always smelled of old urine. Chinatown was closed in. Sherman was very different for me because there were a lot of white kids there. It was exciting to me that some of them came from Alcatraz. They were the kids of the prison guards and workers and the warden. They came first by ferry then in buses. There were also kids from the Navy base at Treasure Island, or TI. The base was out in the Bay and was connected to the City by the Bay Bridge. Those kids came on buses like us. We got along well. I had friends from among those kids, and it was just a great experience to get to interact with white kids and to learn about things that were not all Chinese.*

Like practically every kid who lived in or near Chinatown, Sherman enjoyed making the short walk from home to Cameron House located on Sacramento Street between Powell and Stockton. It offered youth activities and Presbyterian spiritual guidance, and Sherman participated in them all the way through high school. Of Cameron House, Sherman said,

We could go to Cameron House after school or on weekends. Friday nights were always popular because it was the start of the weekend and more of my friends would show up and we could stay late. We

were assigned to groups depending on our school grade. Each grade was divided into two designations: low and high. If you were in the Low Third, for example, it meant that you were in the first semester of that grade. High Third was the second semester of the year. We used to show our grade level on our schoolwork by writing L-5, or H-5, for example. When you went up to "high" you felt special or a little better than the kids who were "low."

Anyhow, we would have our Cameron House leader and then we could pick a name for our group. I remember a couple of groups: The Buffalos, Golden Eagles, and the Mohawks. I can't remember any of my group names, though. One of the things I liked a lot about Cameron House was the six-week day camp that they had over the summer. We were organized by groups and I remember that we had fun making a group flag. You had to pay, but I don't think it was that much. One summer they offered a scholarship or something like that so my parents encouraged me to participate and I did.

When we were older, like in the 11th or 12th grades, we went on retreats. It was the first time I ever used a sleeping bag and there were no bathrooms where we went. If you had to do your business you had to go into the bushes to do it. One of the directors was Reverend Dick Wichman, and he would invite us to a facility that the Presbyterian Church had in Mill Valley for sleepovers. He was really personable, outgoing, and fun. He was like a father figure to a lot of us. He usually greeted us with a big hug, and he also had a little thing he did which was called "the whisker rub." He would hug you and give you a big friendly rub on the cheek with the stubble on his chin. His wife's name was Lois and she was always very nice to us also. She treated us like she was our mom.

If I didn't go to Cameron House, I liked to play at the Chinese Playground. The slide and swings were fun and there was this circular thing that you pushed to either make yourself get really dizzy or to try to make your friends who would sit on it without holding on slip off. There was also a game room that was decorated like a Chinese house and it was fun to play ping-pong there.

One of our PE teachers at Francisco Junior High was Mr. Kim who was Chinese. He was a great tennis player and we used to watch him practice on the court at Chinese Playground. He was a tough teacher and we were pretty intimidated by him. At that time there were some kids that formed a gang. They wore black jackets and black pants. Their jackets had purple trim and they called themselves "The Immortals." I don't think they were really that bad; they just needed to have a sense of belonging or something, so they hung together. We regular guys were a little scared of them, but they didn't really bother you if you didn't bother them. But, Mr. Kim, he wouldn't take anything from those, guys and they never gave him any problems, either. Later, his son Richard also became a teacher at Francisco,

After some 40 years of service at Cameron House, the Reverend Dick Wichman was denounced by one, then several additional former Cameron House boys for sexual misconduct and abuse. He was dis-ordained by the Presbyterians. Very few, if any, of the Chinatown youth who spent time at Cameron House knew of any such occurrences until it came out in the news in the late 1970s. Most of those who were children at that time agree that Wichman's violation of their trust and that of Cameron House and the Church is deplorable. Few would go so far as to condemn or criticize Cameron House itself, however, as the institution's value to the community remains unquestionable. According to Sherman, Dick's son, Johnny, is currently in the ministry at the Westminster Presbyterian Church in Northern California which he finds admirable.

Sherman's parents did not want him to work while growing up. They were far more interested in seeing him do well in school. They felt that time at work would take away time for study. Sherman states that his parents reiterated to him that if he ever needed money, they would give it to him whether it was for clothing, recreation, or school supplies. Sherman spoke about the two times when he was briefly employed as a teenager.

In 1962 I got a brief summer job as a busboy at the Universal Café in Chinatown. It was on Washington Street between Grant and Kearny. It was during the summer and my friend, Alex Wong, who was the regular busboy, wanted time off to go on a vacation with his family. I agreed to take his place. Universal was a pretty big place. There was a downstairs dining room and there was an upstairs for the big banquets. It could get really hectic and you really had to move it. Sometimes it was quiet, but my boss didn't want me to ever stand around doing nothing. He would tell me to help make won-ton if I didn't have tables to clear. To make a won-ton, I would take the flat square egg-noodle wrapping and have it in front of me. Then there was a big bowl filled with the meat filling. I had to take a spoonful of it to place about in the middle of the wrapper. Then I would use the edge of the spoon to wet the corners of the wrapper with a little water. This would help all the edges stick together when it was time to fold the wrapper together. I did one after another that way.

My favorite thing about working at the Universal Café was the communal dinner at the end of the day when we would close up. The cooks would go out of their way to make good dishes from fresh ingredients. Everybody from cooks to waiters to busboys and dishwashers would then sit at one of the big back tables to eat. It wasn't too different from eating with a table full of people like there would be at a banquet. Chinese really like their banquets.

The other job I had was at the YWCA. I was a busboy for the dining hall. The YWCA was on Powell Street between Clay and Sacramento. I worked there for just a short time when I was in high school. I went to work after school from about 4:30 until 9:00. At six o'clock all the residents would come to the dining hall for dinner. They were all youngish women who were single, and the resident population was pretty well mixed between Chinese and white. I earned $1.50 an hour. I would get home pretty tired, and I would be too tired to get any schoolwork done. That's when my parents told me that it was a bad idea for me to work and that if I really needed any money, I should just ask them for it.

Chinese School

I went to Chinese School for five years. It was at Hip Wo.[14.] Since I was more used to my parents' village dialect of Chinese, it was sometimes hard for me to understand the teachers who taught in Cantonese. I was there for five years but, I really didn't learn too much.

For a test, I would just memorize things and get it all down by rote. I would be ready for the tests, but once it was over ...pssst! ... everything would be gone. In the beginning it wasn't too hard to learn how to write. The words were pretty basic, so I could do them. Later the writing became more complicated, and, even though I could write an individual character pretty well, I could never put them together to make a sentence. It was sort of like that in speaking also. When they started in with Mandarin after I had been there for a few years, things got really bad. I couldn't understand any of it at all.

Even though I wasn't in the Hip Wo marching band, I got to march in some parades. There were two big ones for Chinese holidays. One was for 10-10 Day which is the 10th of October.[15.] The other parade was for Chinese New Year. The student body would dress in white shirts and march in formation behind our band. Well, we didn't really march and it wasn't much of a formation. We just walked under the direction of a leader who kept us in order. At the end we got paid a little bit. I think it was a quarter,

Deb Lem
Commodore Stockton School

My school was Commodore Stockton in the middle of Chinatown. No one knew who Commodore Stockton was (a former military governor of California during the Mexican-American war)*, but it didn't matter. We just called the school "Commodore," anyway. I could have gone to Jean Parker school, but my mother had a very sound reason for having me go to Commodore. The two schools were about the same walking distance of about four blocks from where we lived, but in case of rain there were more shop awnings that I could stay dry under between home and Commodore than between us and Jean Parker.*

The teachers were kind. I enjoyed learning how to read, write and do arithmetic. Otherwise, school was daunting for me because I could not make very many friends there. Before I even started school, I grew up in a household where we spoke a lot of English. At Commodore virtually none of the kids in my classes spoke English at home. It was hard for me to get to know anyone too well. Even with the schoolmates that I had fun with, I would only get to know them as well as our time in school allowed. There were no such things as play dates or going over to someone's house after school. Everyone I knew had parents who were eking out a living for their families by working in sewing factories or as busboys. These jobs required long hours away from home. Everyone my age was a latch-key child. We all rushed home after school and got ready to quickly turn around and go back out to attend Chinese school.

I remember feeling a little out of touch during Halloween of my second-grade year. We made paper masks in school that we were going to use for a parade around the schoolyard. Well, my mother made a ballerina costume for me that I wore to school. I was the only one in my class that had a costume. All of my classmates were from families that had not been in the United States long enough to know about American customs like Halloween. I guess that I was really the one who was different. I was Chinese, but I didn't really speak the language all that often. It was hard for me to express myself or understand what other people would say to me. Looking back at Halloween again, it's sort of funny in a way, but I will always remember Trick-or-Treating along Grant Avenue. The China Pharmacy always set out a popcorn maker for the kids, and Winky's was one of my favorite stops because they always gave out great candy. I think it's too bad that Grant Avenue just isn't like that anymore.

A Little of Dad's Chinatown

My dad enjoyed fishing in his spare time. We always enjoyed whatever he brought home after a day of fishing up on the Sacramento River or around San Francisco Bay. I remember the fish he would catch. Striped bass, or stripers, from the Bay or freshwater bass from the Delta. He would often take his fresh catch *along with us for a meal at KK Gardens. The restaurant was on the second floor of a building on the south side of Jackson Street. The larger tables were separated from the main dining room by lacquered wooden partitions. I will always remember the spittoons outside of each of these dining spaces. Dad would hand his catch over to one of the cooks, and before long, we would have a meal fit for royalty! The centerpiece, of course, was fresh steamed fish garnished and flavored with ginger and scallions. Yum! Those are among my most vividly remembered meals of my youth.*

My father would sometimes take my brothers and me for a walk through Chinatown to visit some of his friends. If we would visit Jimmy who owned a small dry-cleaning shop in Waverly Place, he would give us some change to buy ourselves ice cream cones at Eastern Bakery on Grant Avenue. He and Jimmy were always sure to admonish us to look both ways before crossing the street.

Another of Dad's friends owned a noodle factory in the alley behind our house. I can see Charlie Soo-Hoo so vividly to this day. He seemed to always be completely coated in a fine white powdery dust from the flour used for the noodles. I never understood how he could see through his glasses!

Irene Dea Collier
I Was Snoring So Loudly That I Drowned Out the Teacher

Irene was enrolled at St. Mary's of the renowned all-girl drum and bell corps for both American and Chinese schools. Unlike many Catholic schools of today, St. Mary's was not a costly private school. Rather, it was established for the broader purpose of bringing Christianity to a population at risk of perdition for its ignorance of God. Until 1958, it was a mission school that required no tuition. Young Irene spent a bewildering and overwhelming first year in America learning in English from nuns during mornings and early afternoons before going to her late afternoon Chinese lessons with a young woman who had formerly been a teacher in Hong Kong. According to Irene her lessons in English went far better than those given to her in Chinese.

I couldn't understand a word of my Chinese schoolteacher's mainstream Cantonese. The girl sitting next to me spoke both Hoi Ping and Cantonese, however, and she explained that I would need to buy school supplies that included ink, calligraphy brushes, and an ink box. I didn't know it, but the ink box required a cotton pad onto which I was supposed to pour some of the ink and my parents assumed that the pads were to be supplied by the school. The next day, with no cotton, I poured ink into my ink box, stuck it into my pocket, and hiked on off to school. Before long, I had ink all over my hands and face, my coat and dress, and on my desk and school paper. After being yelled at by my teacher just as my poor younger brother who was only four years old was being yelled at in a different classroom for the same thing by his teacher, I walked home to extra yelling on the part of my parents. I escaped the various forms of typical family corporal punishment such as the knuckle rap to the head or the ear twist, but I had to take even more yelling for ruining my new coat. My family couldn't afford to replace it or even to have it cleaned. I spent the next three years using a black spotted red coat.

I don't know how or why, but at school I was able to grasp English pretty quickly. I really struggled with Chinese, though. I think that maybe it was something about the influence of my own dialect with its particular tones and vocabulary that made it so hard to try to pick up Cantonese. The sounds of the Hoi Ping village dialect that I was so accustomed to made it difficult for me to clearly hear or produce proper sounds in Cantonese.

My Chinese school classmates and I were so frustrated with our Chinese lessons. Our teacher was very nice and she tried her best, but we didn't know what was going on and we just became increasingly inattentive, unruly, and disrespectful. Our teacher was a very pretty woman, and she could not believe how terrible we were. Our behavior would have been unheard of in Hong Kong or China, and it bothered our teacher so much that she could barely manage the classroom. Even I (who would go on to become a dedicated middle school teacher) *became a rogue student. I remember sleeping through many class sessions, and I am sad to say that I clearly remember a time when I was snoring so loudly that it drowned out the teacher. I woke up with a snort and everybody was laughing at me. Throughout the school year we were ranked by class order of achievement. The highest I ever got was eight out of 35. By the time I was in my second year, though, I was ranked last in the class. My parents couldn't afford to pay for me to learn nothing, so they took me out of Chinese school. I took advantage of all my new-found free time to stay home to read books in English.*

As difficult as things were for me, I cannot say that there weren't certain things that I liked about Chinese school. What I liked best about it was the camaraderie with other students. Although I didn't learn a thing, we had so much more fun in Chinese school than in American school. Over the years I would run into classmates, and we loved talking to each other. This type of friendship did not happen in American school and I never could figure out why. Perhaps the differences in our social standings were not as great in Chinese school. We were all equally poor. There was certainly no such thing as one of us being from a wealthy family.

I also liked the artistic side of Chinese school. I liked using a brush and dipping it in ink. I enjoyed the challenge of keeping my wrist rigid as I would try to keep the motion of my forearm fluid. I enjoyed trying to apply the different types of pressure that you had to employ just so in order to create graceful strokes that would leave neither too much nor too little ink on the paper. In my mind's eye I compared brush calligraphy to the fanciful Chinese sword fighting movies where woman warriors would float and glide around their enemies in a ballet of blocking and parrying more than of slashing or stabbing. I also liked the smell of the newsprint booklets that you slid the practice character masters into. I liked the funny pictures in each lesson. Although I loved everything aesthetically about Chinese school, I didn't learn much for not understanding much of what the teacher would say. I guess that it was for being far more imaginative in Chinese school than I was attentive that helped me like it as much as I did.

Of course, like so many former Chinese school students today, I wish I had paid attention or made a greater effort in class. I regret losing the opportunity to be more fluent conversationally in Chinese, be it

Cantonese or Mandarin, and I really feel that I missed out by not learning how to read the language.

Tommy Lim
Culture Shock

While still living with his family in Napa, life changed greatly and suddenly for Tommy Lim in 1961. He was in the third grade when his father, just in his early 50s, suffered a severe stroke. After many months of rehabilitation and therapy, Tommy's father regained some strength in his arms and legs and began, albeit with difficulty, walking again. Tommy's oldest sister who was 14 was allowed to learn to drive and carry a special operator's license in order to help her family get around. Everyone understood that Mr. Lim would remain seriously impaired for the rest of his life. They simply hoped that he would survive long enough to see all of his children reach adulthood. Tommy said,

My father suffered a second stroke and passed away when I was in the seventh grade. He was only in his mid-50s. My mother felt that once the adult male figure was gone, some people would have less respect for us and the family would become more vulnerable. I was 11 years old at the time, and as the oldest boy in the family, I felt that I needed to grow up fast.

Our family moved from Napa to San Francisco nine months after my dad passed away. We had visited relatives many times in San Francisco but I never thought that I would be living there. Since my now widowed mother still only spoke Chinese and had four children to care for, it made sense for us to move. We would be closer to family and there would be far more Chinese people around us. Talk about culture shock! I had never seen so many Chinese in my life! It was there that I realized that I was really Chinese, but now I had my chin up; I was proud. And best of all, I wasn't alone any longer.

Through the many years of work and saving in Napa, Tommy's family was able to afford to purchase a building in North Beach. The dwelling was on Jones Street adjacent to the opening of the two-block long Valparaiso Street at about mid-block. The east-to-west streets on either side of the Lim's portion of Jones were Greenwich and Filbert. The neighborhood was mixed between whites who were largely of Italian descent and Chinese. Tommy, who was used to the openness of Napa, found it strange to see houses and buildings squeezed tightly together in San Francisco. He also missed having a back yard and being able to ride his bicycle anywhere he wanted to. The sidewalks where Tommy lived were not dangerous to play or walk on at any time of the day, but the streets themselves were a different matter. There was simply too much car traffic and everyone had to be especially vigilant. Few Chinatown kids owned a bicycle.

In 1966 when Tommy arrived in San Francisco, he was about to begin the eighth grade. His new school would be Francisco Junior High which was an easy six block walk from his home. Even closer by were the North Beach playground, public swimming pool, and branch of the San Francisco public library system. Washington Square Park, the Palace movie theater, Telegraph Hill, and Chinatown were also all close by. Tommy enjoyed going to the Chinese martial arts movies that played in the Chinatown movie houses. He recalls that his mother liked it that he went to see such films as she believed that they would provide him with some form of connection to the Chinese culture. Tommy was happy in San Francisco and said,

It was, as I had anticipated from the very beginning, a relatively smooth transition to my new environment. I quickly made new friends. Francisco Junior High School was a great time in my life. I was practically in shock to see that at least 75% of my classmates were Chinese like me! Things were going to change very positively for me.

Life was simple and fun, and things seemed easy. Even though I spent only two years at Francisco, eighth and ninth grades, I really loved my time there. I was in homeroom 218 and the school had organized intramural sports that pitted homeroom against homeroom. These, in fact, were called "homeroom games," and we played them during our lunch period. We had an hour for lunch, so we would eat as quickly as we could and then hurry the two and a half blocks from the school to the North Beach Playground. We would meet whichever homeroom team that was assigned as our opponent and play slow pitch softball against them. There was no grass and no infield dirt. We played on a hard blacktop surface with white painted bases and base paths. Our outfield would back up into the outfield of the softball space across from ours. We sometimes caught a fly ball while facing the outfielders of other teams. Long rolling hits sometimes made it all the way to the batting area of games across the playground. Those usually wound up being home runs. I think we just took the crowdedness for granted since the neighborhood of Chinatown was always crowded anyway. The games lasted until the end of lunch period and whoever was ahead was the winner. Sometimes in a tie or very close game we would get a warning, "Time's up! One last pitch!" If the batter might make a difference in the score if he got a hit, the pitcher would just throw one way out of the strike zone. The batter would then move quickly way out of the batter's box and take a wild swing. Sometimes guys would actually get a hit doing that. We would go back to the playground on weekends to play more softball and basketball. It was so much fun. Those were really good times for us.

.

Optometry School in Chicago Got Pretty Lonely

Following high school, Tommy attended City College of San Francisco in part to make up for some of his less than stellar high school grades. Before finishing the two-year undergraduate curriculum at City in 1973, Tommy had decided that he would like to become an optometrist. His own optometrist, Clifford Chang, whose practice was on Clay Street in Chinatown, provided Tommy with a letter of recommendation for his applications to optometry school. According to Tommy,

I started optometry school at Chicago's Illinois College of Optometry in September of 1973. It was a little strange to be so far away from home and, once again, among a student body that featured just a handful of Asian Americans. There were two other Chinese students and one who was from a Japanese background. There were a lot of farm boys from places like Iowa and Nebraska among my fellow optometry students. Those places were as strange

71

to me as San Francisco and Chinatown would have been to them. I did not share much in common with them outside of school. I was not a drinker and I did not smoke weed which were fairly popular off-hours activities. The other students would often go home on weekends, so it got pretty lonely in the dorms those first two years. My mother sympathized to such an extent that she told me that if I just wanted to return home, it would be alright. She knew that I was lonely and not particularly happy, but I was determined not to quit. I would stick the program out come hell or high water. I really appreciated my mother's gesture, though.

At the end of my second year in Chicago I returned to San Francisco in the summer of 1975. On June 28, 1975 Bonnie and I got married. I was twenty-three years old and Bonnie had just turned twenty-one. A local Chinatown group, Jest Jammin' of which my buddy Norman Fong was (and still is) *a member, played for our wedding. Another member of the band, who, like Norman, was an original and ongoing member, was my brother-in-law, Ed Toy. He is the group's drummer. We moved back to Chicago shortly after our wedding. I left the dorms and Bonnie and I rented an apartment. Bonnie worked as a secretary in a civil engineering office to support us and I graduated on time in June 1977.*

Jack Woo [16.]
Being an All Chinese Group Did Not Create Any Difficulties for Us

Jack Woo was born in a village in Canton in 1949 and soon afterwards was left behind with his mother while his father, already an American citizen, returned to the United States. Jack and his mother remained in his father's native Cantonese village for a year or two before moving to Hong Kong. It would not be until Jack was five that his father could send for him and his mother. The small family – to which two daughters were soon afterwards added – settled into a house on Mason Street not far from the Cable Car Barn. Jack's mother continues to live in that same house to this day.

Jack values his years in Francisco Junior High School as among his happiest as a young boy. He cites the many friends that he made at the time and how the bonds forged some half century ago have persisted into the present day. Because he had some buddies who were already in it, he was readily persuaded to join the Chinatown American Legion Cathay Post's Drum and Bugle Corps in 1964.

I joined in 1964, but I wish I had done it in 1963 when the Drum and Bugle Corps got filmed for the movie "Flower Drum Song." The Corps was dressed in its Chinese style uniforms, and when I saw the film, I was thinking, "Wow! Those guys have gained immortality!" I could see some of my buddies marching in the very front row. That was the last year they used the traditional Chinese uniform. I think they wanted to be more modern because none of the other drum and bugle corps had Chinese outfits. We got a green-colored army looking uniform (former Drum Major Roger Fong says that these uniforms were officially called "cadet style") *complete with shako hats. I was a snare drummer and some of the Corps' best featured songs included the popular hit "Where or When" as well as the theme from the lion movie, "Born Free." We also played "Frenesi."*[17.] *We never played Chinese tunes because we wanted to get away from being identified as a Chinese band. We wanted to be accepted as an American corps just like the rest of the corps in California. We even incorporated a patriotic song, "Americans, We,"*[18.] *into our repertoire.*

Then there were those times that the Cathay Post Drum and Bugle Corps would be invited to perform at half time for the 49ers at Kezar Stadium. That was a long time ago! The 49ers left Kezar and played at Candlestick Park for almost 45 years before recently moving to their new stadium outside of the city. Playing at a pro football game wasn't like the extravagant productions that they have at halftimes during today's games. Still, it was a really big deal for us in those days.

The three years that Jack was with the Cathay Post Corps were not only fun, but an eye opener as well. Road trips for competitions and parades took him and his friends out of Chinatown for the first time. Among his fondest memories are the food for its quantity and variety that the Corps enjoyed on the trips and playing and swimming in motel pools where they lodged. Jack recalls trips to

Yountville to play in the Veterans Day parade there and to Stockton where Cathay finished second in the Northern California Regionals to a perennial power, the Richmond (California) Hawks. Except for a group from Los Angeles and another from Sacramento called the Mandarins, Cathay was the only all-Chinese D&B that Jack ever encountered or knew of.

Being an all-Chinese group did not create any difficulties for us. It was quite the opposite! We liked to mingle and socialize. Even though we were
in a competition, we could get together with other groups and talk about things like long-practices and hard marching. It was fun to just mess

Around with them. Being out of Chinatown, it was the first time I could see girls other than Chinese ones. Wow, those white girls were really nice looking. Blonde hair and blue eyes. Boy, oh boy! They really got my heart thumping! Even though I was really shy, inexperienced, and naïve, a friend and I asked a couple of Hispanic girls to a party one night. At first, they didn't seem too sure, but after a little bit they surprised us and accepted. It was a fun time, but there was no kissing or anything like that! We were all just a bit too young!

I Was Always in the Bottom Half of Chinese School

Jack says that he was always a good student in school. He always did his homework, paid attention, and tried to get good grades. Yet, as good a student as he tried to be in American school, Jack considers himself to have been a "bad" student in Chinese school.

I was always in the bottom half, and looking back at my old report card, I would consider whiting out or erasing my old grades before I ever let anyone see it. I didn't like Chinese school because I resented having to spend all day in American school only to have to rush off to do it all over again. I originally started out at St Mary's, and since I came from Canton, I did not have much trouble with the language. After a year or two my father moved me to Chinese Central High. I'm not sure why and I never was comfortable enough to ask. I just did what he told me. Looking back, I think that the move was made because the tuition might have been lower than at St. Mary's and that one of the teachers at Central was somehow related to my family. My one regret is that I did not pursue Mandarin. I think back now and feel bad, but back then I really didn't want to take any more classes than I had to.

Aside from being inattentive in class, Jack and his friends tended to cut Chinese school. They would usually go to the Commodore Stockton schoolyard to play basketball.

I was always careful not to do this on Mondays because that was my father's day off. He liked to pick me up after school on those days, and the family would go on down to Chinatown for dinner. To my surprise one Tuesday or Wednesday, dad must have switched days off. When I saw him, I was really scared. I thought that he would punish me for sure. There was going to be the old conk on the head – the ling-gok – with his knuckles, but he didn't say a word. Maybe he just thought that "boys will be boys."

Jack's time at Central was not a complete loss as he joined its marching band as a bass drummer. He and another student were the only two boys in the entire unit. Being young, shy, and naïve by his own account, Jack did not take advantage of the availability of potentially "eligible" female company.

I Looked Up My Old Francisco Year Book

By the time he reached the seventh grade, Jack had become a very good swimmer. He took his abilities in the water to the North Beach public pool where he volunteered to help give swimming lessons. Jack remembers that,

The public paid a dime to get into the pool and it was a nickel to rent a swim suit. The suits were grey cotton and they were loose and baggy. You had to be careful to tie it on really good or else you could get embarrassed in the pool. Francisco students used the pool at no cost for the weekly swim sessions they had for P.E. The whole class always had to hurry up to do everything on swim day. We boys would run to the locker room in the gym after our previous class let out. The gym was across the street from the rest of the school. We put all our school books in our PE lockers. Then we had to line up for roll call. After that we marched in formation the three blocks to the pool. The gym teachers, I remember Mr. Bluth, Mr. Kim, and Mr. Simpson, would get mad at us if we talked because we weren't supposed to bother the people in the neighborhood. Mr. Kim was Chinese and he was a pretty good tennis player. We would sometimes see him practice at the Chinese Playground on weekends. Mr. Simpson was really fit and athletic. There was a rumor that he was once a circus performer. He could do tricks with a basketball like the Harlem Globetrotters.

When we entered the pool, they just handed us a grey cotton swimsuit and we took it to the pool locker room to change into. We ran out of the locker room as soon as we were changed and had to go through a long shower room that had running shower nozzles on both sides. Some of them had hot water and some had cold water. We got about twenty minutes to swim and then the gym teacher would blow his whistle for us to get out. Then we had to run through the shower again, get a towel from one of the towel monitors, change, line up, and march back to the school gym. I don't think we were ever late for our next class, but our clothes were always messy and our body was always still kind of wet. The worst was when water still dripped from our hair. Then it would get our desks and notebooks all wet. There was also always somebody who would sit for the first few minutes of class shaking his head and hitting his ear to get the water out.

Jack stated that he enjoys looking back to the days of his youth. He consistently states that his junior high and high school days, close to a half century ago, were among the best of his life. Taking time to revisit those happiest of times, Jack recalled some of his old teachers.

I remember a few of the P.E. teachers at Francisco. Each had his own personality and character. There was one named Mr. De Soto ... he was really big and overweight. We always wondered how he could be a P.E. teacher if he was so huge. Nobody was brave enough to ask him! I heard that some of the guys in one of his other P.E. classes used to call him "Jelly Belly" behind his back. I bet they never dared say it to his face!

I didn't see this, but I sure can believe it. One day Mr. Simpson got so mad at a kid that he knocked him down and then kicked him before he could get up. Mr. Simpson had some serious muscle on him, like a pro body builder, and I'm really glad that I wasn't there to see it. That kid could have gotten killed. No teacher would get away with it nowadays, but that's just how it was for us back then.

Even though Mr. Simpson and Mr. Kim were so intimidating, we still had our moments of misbehaving and doing silly things in their PE classes. We used to run around and play a game called "far-guy-hoon" which was like tag. You would sneak up to a guy real fast and flick your fingers on the bottom of his chin and say, "far-guy-hoon!" which means "turkey ass." He would be stuck with the name until he could get someone else. We would all keep an eye out for the guy, and as extra precaution we cupped a fist under our chin so that we couldn't get caught. We usually did this at lunch time or in P.E. class because we would have room to run away from the guy who was the turkey ass trying to get us.

Shortly before retiring from his career as a pharmacist, Jack was surprised to recognize one of his former teachers from Francisco who had gone to fill a prescription at Walgreen's.

I think in the mid 90's while I was working at the Walgreen's on Geary Boulevard in the Richmond district, Mr. Diamond happened to drop in to fill his prescription. He was a Social Studies teacher at Francisco. On test days we would call him "Mr. Demon." I recognized him immediately...he hadn't changed much, so I introduced myself to him and told him he was one of my favorite teachers back in Francisco in the '63 class. He was so taken aback that someone from that early part of his teaching career remembered him!

We talked about his grading methods and that I figured out how to get good grades in his class ... just write (copy) long and detailed

77

reports and turn them in! He graded our homework by using exponents from algebra (x to the 2nd power, x to the 3rd, etc.). That was our first introduction to algebra. I did pretty good in his 7th grade class because my father bought me a set of Encyclopedia Britannica which I used a lot for my class papers.

Mr. Diamond was a pretty neat teacher. He was young, confident, and pretty friendly. He was always relaxed, too. One day his wife dropped in to say, 'Hi.' She was really good looking like a Hollywood actress. Well, she came in and he grabbed her and planted a kiss on her lips. Boy! The whole class was shocked and we all started giggling. I don't think any of us at that age ever seen anyone kissing someone on the lips in real life! Later one of my classmates said that she was a model for one of the big downtown department stores.

School kids have been carrying backpacks for so many years that I can hardly remember it being any other way, but back in our days, in the 60s we would all use a "grip." It was a type of travel bag that we used to carry our school books in. It was made of cloth or canvas and had handles. The top zipped up. I remember mine was a PanAm airline one. Also, I used to be right on the cable car line, so when I used to go to school or coming home after school, I would hop on and hop off of a cable car while it was slowing down. I never waited for it to stop, and since the driver could see me, he wouldn't bother to come to a complete stop. It was just quicker and easier for everyone. It was fun and kind of like a challenge to your athletic abilities because sometimes if you were late, you had to sprint full speed after one of those things. Nowadays they won't let you get off the cable car until it comes to a complete stop because the city is afraid of lawsuits. Imagine, we were getting a "San Francisco" experience back then without even knowing it! And the tourists of today are paying up to $10 for that experience!

3.
Cabaret Dancers: Two Chinatown Teenagers
"Chinatown, My Chinatown"

Native San Franciscans Cynthia Yee and Pat Chin are present-day members of the *Grant Avenue Follies*. Performing for fund-raising or charitable events, the *Grant Avenue Follies* is a revival of the type of dance troupes that ruled and dazzled in night clubs all across America from the 1930s through the post-war period. Hollywood films of that time period, whether drama, comedy or musical, often included scenes that represented just such clubs. Well-appointed sets, many in the Art-Deco style, depicted dinner and dancing places packed by ladies in opulent gowns and gentlemen in shirts, tails and top hats out to enjoy the evening. The revelers would be entertained by big bands playing upbeat numbers and leggy chorus girls high-stepping it on a floor that barely separated the musicians and diners.

Racial separation had been the rule for American society dating back to well before the 1930s. The culture of race-based discrimination led Chinatown, like African American Harlem, to foster its own "home-grown" and locally owned late-night hot-spots. If Harlem had the *Cotton Club* and the *Apollo,* San Francisco's Chinatown could boast of the *Forbidden City,* the *Chinese Sky Room,* the *Lion's Den*, *Club Mandalay*, *Kubla Khan* and *Club Shanghai.* All were Chinese owned and operated. If Hollywood featured Cab Calloway, or Fred Astaire and Ginger Rogers, it also featured Chinatown's Dorothy Toy and Paul Wing.

Pat performed in the *Chinese Sky Room* and other venues in the 1950s. Cynthia danced with Dorothy Toy in both the *Forbidden City* and the *Chinese Sky Room* in the 1960s. Both women also traveled with road productions. Pat was a member of the *China Dolls Revue,* and Cynthia was with the *Toy and Wing Oriental Playgirls Show.*

Cynthia Yee [19.]
Influenced by the Best

Cynthia Yee is an ABC whose family name was Fong. She was born in 1945 at Letterman Army Hospital in the Presidio of San Francisco. Cynthia's father, who had been born in China, was in the army when Cynthia was born. Cynthia's mother was an ABC whose family lived in Vallejo as her father worked in the Naval Shipyard at Mare Island.

When she was in school at Commodore Stockton, Cynthia's family moved to a residential building at 959 Powell Street on the corner of Clay Street. The multi-story building where she lived was owned by Dorothy Toy and her second husband. Dorothy lived upstairs and was friends with Cynthia's family. Cynthia remembers that Dorothy was always kind and generous to all the kids who lived and played nearby.

Dorothy was a professional dancer who had toured the United States, performed at the London Palladium, danced on Broadway and been in the movies. She had been called "The Chinese Ginger Rogers" and many who had seen her dance would agree with the comparison. It was not at all the case that Dorothy either imitated or patterned herself after the famed American performer. That she was labelled "the Chinese Ginger Rogers" was merely a high compliment and testament to the stunning skills that Dorothy brought to the stage and the screen. Numerous Chinese or other Asian performers who passed themselves off as Chinese were given the flattering nickname, "The Chinese ...." Among these were the Chinese Frank Sinatra, Houdini, Fred Astaire and Betty Grable. As in Dorothy's case, all the names were simply open acknowledgement of the Asian performers' own set of skills and talents that made them equals as performers to their white American contemporaries.

Dorothy, born in the United States, was of Japanese heritage. She had changed her family and birth name of Takahashi to Toy because it was simpler to pronounce and remember. This also made it all the more appealing to the world of show business. At the height of her popularity and success, using a Chinese name helped keep Dorothy out of the internment camps to which many American-born Japanese were forcibly relocated during those World War II days. By the mid-1950s Dorothy had left Hollywood behind and was spending a good deal of time on tour. She was always sure to send postcards to Cynthia and the other neighborhood kids back in San Francisco. Whenever she returned from one of her performance tours, Dorothy was sure to hand out little prizes and souvenirs to her young friends. They adored her for this.

Knowing that Dorothy was in show business inspired young Cynthia to want to learn how to dance. Some of her friends were already taking dance lessons from former Chinatown club performer Tony Wing. Tony, who was born Filipino, had also changed his name many years earlier for show purposes. Like Dorothy, he reasoned that if he were to perform in Chinatown's dance and dinner clubs, he needed a Chinese sounding name. By the time Cynthia was a child, Tony had retired from the clubs and tours in order be a dance instructor. Several generations of Chinatown children share memories of learning to dance from Tony. Most of them actually thought he was Chinese. Rather than follow her friends and neighbors by automatically sending her daughter to Tony Wing, Cynthia's mother asked Dorothy for a recommendation. Dorothy suggested Sergei Temoff, a former member of the Bolshoi Ballet.

Since Temoff's studio was not in Chinatown, Cynthia would spend the next seven years taking the bus to and from her classical ballet lessons. Cynthia remembers the time that she spent with Temoff was hard and very disciplined. She was grateful, however, because it was during her time with Temoff that she secured the best possible foundation for her future dancing endeavors.

Another early influence on Cynthia's early interest in dance came about when she was 10 years old. Her parents were entertaining house guests and decided to go for dinner and some dancing at one of Chinatown's most popular nightclubs, the *Forbidden City*. The club was not in Chinatown proper, but on Sutter Street between Grant and Stockton just a block from Chinatown. Dorothy was performing there. No babysitters were available so Cynthia was allowed to tag along. Cynthia remembers that her father's small group got tables at the very front of the dance floor and that she was allowed to sit at the center so that she would be sure to be able to see everything. Just like in the movies the bandstand was at the far end of the club and the dance floor was between the band and the diners. Cynthia recalled being awash in giddy sensations as she watched the show. She says that she was mesmerized and that there could be no way for her to describe the depth and intensity of the production's glamor.

There was an extra treat in store for Cynthia that night. In addition to Dorothy's inspiring dance numbers, there was a magic act. The magician, Ah-Hing, like Dorothy, also happened to be an upstairs neighbor of Cynthia. Cynthia loved the trick that Ah-Hing, dubbed as the "Chinese Houdini" back then, did with doves. Cynthia remembers that Ah-Hing, the only name she ever knew him by, kept his doves on the back porch of his Powell Street flat. Cynthia says that she enjoyed standing on her own porch a floor or two below to listen to the gentle and melodic cooing of Ah-Hing's birds. The bird trick delighted her just as it had several years earlier when she had seen it for the first time. Ah-Hing had been the entertainment for a children's birthday party that was celebrated at a nearby and rival nightclub, the *Chinese Sky Room*.

The Forbidden City and The Chinese Sky Room

Cynthia graduated from Galileo High School in 1963 and planned to enroll in San Francisco State that fall. She wanted to save some money over the summer, so she found a salesgirl job at one of the Grant Avenue souvenir shops. She worked at *United Art Company* next door to Eastern Bakery for a dollar per hour.

By the time she graduated from high school, Cynthia's family had moved from 959 Powell Street, and she had not seen Dorothy for a while. One afternoon, however, Cynthia's mother Mildred ran across Dorothy while doing errands in Chinatown. The two women got to talking and when Dorothy asked after Cynthia, Mildred told her about the progress her daughter had been making with classical ballet. Dorothy was then the producer of *Toy and Wing and the Oriental Playgirls* who were booked as one of the acts at the *Forbidden City*. According to Cynthia, Dorothy chose the name "Playgirls" because the *San Francisco Playboy Club* was an extremely popular venue in the early 1960s. The club was located on Montgomery Street almost right on the intersection of the Financial District, Chinatown and North Beach. It was also near Jackson Street, one block from Portsmouth Square and just two blocks from Grant Avenue. "Wing" was Dorothy's old partner and former husband, Paul Wing (no relation to Tony) from their hey-day as a dance team that captivated audiences and movie fans from Hollywood to New York and London.

That evening Dorothy called the Fongs' number. According to Cynthia,

We were at home and my mom answered the phone. She called out to me to say that it was Dorothy. She then said that one of Dorothy's chorus girls was sick and would miss work for the whole summer. She said that Dorothy wanted to know if I would be interested in going down to the club to try out to be a substitute. I was ecstatic. I remember hearing myself saying, over and over; '...yes, yes, yes, yes!"

When asked if she felt nervous at all about her pending audition

Cynthia responded by saying,

I was not nervous. I was really happy, but I wasn't nervous at all. I was confident from my seven years of ballet training. Over the years I never really got nervous about performing at all. Except if I knew that there was somebody in the audience that I knew. Like a friend or someone in my family. I hated it whenever that happened. I think it's natural, though. A lot of performers and dancers that I knew felt the same way. They only got nervous in front of family or friends.

Cynthia reported to Dorothy at the *Forbidden City* the day after the phone call. She does not remember the details of what Dorothy wanted to see from her, but that after a brief audition that she breezed through she was told that she would go on that very evening. There would be about five or six numbers, but Cynthia would dance in the chorus line with five other girls for just one of them. She and the *Oriental Playgirls* were to open with *Grant Avenue* from the play and movie *Flower Drum Song*. The song was written by the famed and accomplished duo of Rogers (music) and Hammerstein (lyrics). Cynthia said that it is her favorite song from the production. More than a few Chinatown residents from then down to the present time continue to enjoy the song's words which include,

> *"A western street with eastern manners,*
> *Tall pagodas and golden banners:*
> *Throw their shadows through the lantern glow.*
> *You can shop for precious jade or teakwood tables, or silk brocade or see a bold and brassy night club show; on the most exciting thoroughfare I know.*
> *We call it Grant Avenue, San Francisco, California, U.S.A!"* [20.]

The movie version shows characters in traditional style Chinese costumes who quickly break into a song and dance number that reflects those of a typical Broadway performance through and through. So it was at the *Forbidden City* and the other Chinatown clubs. Audiences, curious about Eastern culture, flocked to the clubs with very little notion of what to expect. They always loved it, however, when Chinese musicians, singers and dancers boomed out snappy and lively numbers just like those made famous in Hollywood's song and dance films dating back to the 1930s.

Cynthia remembered that the *Grant Avenue* song would evolve into a medley of other *Flower Drum Song* numbers. As there were three shows that night, Cynthia appeared on stage to dance to the medley three times. Despite her complete lack of show-business experience, Cynthia never found learning any of Dorothy's rich and varied choreography to be overly difficult. Cynthia's ballet training really paid large dividends for her. Cynthia earned $65 per week which she felt was a good amount and much more than what she would have made peddling tourist trinkets back at the *United Art Company* on Grant Avenue.

The general routine at the *Forbidden City* as well as at the other Chinatown clubs was to offer three 45-minute shows a night at roughly 8:00, 10:00 and 12:00. The performers were all Asian and they often wore Chinese or Japanese inspired costumes. Almost all of their acts, like the *Grant Avenue* and the *Flower Drum Song* medley were cabaret style as on Broadway or other supper and dance clubs throughout the USA. Very few were not in English. Cynthia said,

Even though we did acts that were popular in movies, on Broadway or in any other nightclubs in the country, people came to see us because we were Oriental. That's the word we used back then. It would be Asian today. We were very popular because we were unique. The Caucasian audiences liked us because we were exotic to them.

The clubs offered dinner followed by dancing before each show. The menus offered either Chinese or Chinese inspired fare or American food.

According to a menu from the *Club Shanghai* of the late 1940s and early 1950s, the Special Chinese Dinner included "relishes, Mandarin soup, chicken chow mein Chicago style, fried prawns, green chow yuke, pork egg foo young, Canton fried rice, Chinese

tea and almond cookies." The $2.75 dinner was served from 6:00 –
11:00 PM. [21.]

By her third day with Dorothy, Cynthia was performing with the
Oriental Playgirl chorus line in a second group number that featured
a unique version of *Never on Sunday*. The song from the movie of
the same name had become popular through frequent radio play. In
order to fit some of that coveted "Oriental mystique" into her acts,
Dorothy had translated the song into Japanese for the Playgirls to
sing. Cynthia said that her mind was quicker back then and that she
was able to memorize songs and routines, including the Japanese
version of *Never on Sunday* without too much difficulty.

At just 17, Cynthia was the youngest dancer in the troupe. All the
others were, as Cynthia recalls, at least ten years her senior. Cynthia
remembers them all as kind and helpful. As a novice performer,
Cynthia needed their help the most in those very early days at the
Forbidden City. She was especially grateful for all the dressing
room assistance with make-up and costumes that they gave her.
Photos from the club's most active years show that the dressing
room at the *Forbidden City* was little more than a glorified closet.
Dancers and furnishings were piled up practically on top of one
another. However uncomfortable or inconvenient, crowdedness was
a way of life in Chinatown where there was never enough space for
its far too many residents. Everybody simply adapted. Cynthia says
that she remembers with great fondness how the other chorus line
performers often took her in hand to learn choreography on the fly.
She said, "They were a band of older sisters."

Cynthia recalled several of her favorite *Oriental Playgirl* acts. One
was what she referred to as a "cowboy" number complete with ten-
gallon hats and toy six-shooters. Among the act's songs were *Deep
in the Heart of Texas* and *Don't Fence Me In*. Dorothy regularly
brought her group to San Quentin prison across the Golden Gate
Bridge from San Francisco in order to entertain the inmates as well
as the guards and staff. Concerned with security and levels of
morale, prison officials required the "guns" for the act to be left
outside the prison. The group was also told to drop the song *Don't
Fence Me In*. Besides its problematic title the song features a

mournful melody and lyrics that refer to things denied to the inmates such as "starry skies above," "wide open country" and the ability to "wander over yonder 'til I see the mountains rise."

Another of Cynthia's favorite acts was a striptease that involved three performers, one of whom was often Cynthia herself. The characters bore the names Miss Uni-Na (pronounced *uni-nay* as a play on the "United Nations"), Miss Hong Kong and Miss Tokyo. The three dancers would enter together with Miss Uni Na, a part that Cynthia never had, fully clothed in robe and gown. Her companions, Miss Hong Kong and Miss Tokyo, both of whom Cynthia has played, appeared in a leotard and fishnet stockings. Miss Uni-Na would slowly and seductively strip off her outer garments. As she removed items of her wardrobe she would let them easily slip from her fingertips onto the stage. Her fellow dancers would glide over to them, gently lift them from the floor and, smoothly wrap them over their shoulders. By the end of the number Miss Hong Kong and Miss Tokyo would each be fully covered while Miss Uni-Na would be quite exposed. Of the act Cynthia said,

It was graceful and tasteful and there was never any true nudity. We drew the line at that. It was nothing like the acts in the clubs that came to Broadway soon after.

The Playgirls Hit the Road

In 1963, Cynthia's first year as a dancer, the *Forbidden City* was still owned by its original founder, the famed, if not legendary, Chinatown entrepreneur Charlie Low. Low was a self-taught businessman who grew up as the son of an immigrant shop owner in a small Nevada town. Armed with an adventuresome spirit, Low moved to San Francisco in 1922. Forbidden to rent housing by laws steeped in racial prejudice, Low managed to purchase a pair of adjacent lots that had been empty since the 1906 earthquake. He built what became the Low Apartments at the corner of Powell and Washington Streets. One of the apartments would become Low's home for life. From then on one business venture led to another and success built upon success. In 1936 Low built and operated the first cocktail bar in Chinatown. It was named the *Chinese Village* and was located at 702 Grant Avenue. Not one to sit still, Low soon hit upon the idea to create a night club. His vision became the *Forbidden City* which opened in 1938. Of his idea and of the club itself, Low said,

The idea came to me after visiting all the other Caucasian or Spanish or Italian night clubs in San Francisco. They were all doing good business, and I said, "Why can't I do it? If they can do it, I can do it." San Francisco, as well as other states and other cities, had never seen a Chinese nightclub with an all-Chinese floor show and the time was ripe for something like that.[22.]

Cynthia was not employed by the club or by Low, but by Dorothy. Dorothy being the producer of her own group, show and acts contracted independently to Low and the *Forbidden City*. Cynthia, as well as many others in and out of show business, always found Dorothy's acts and productions to be impressively innovative. Low had once said that overcoming barriers had caused him to "Always try to think faster than the next guy." [23.] Dorothy, responding to the same set of challenges or obstacles faced by Charlie, added, "We found that we had to be much better than the American dance team, the Caucasians, or else we wouldn't get the booking. We had to be ten times better, not just a little better." [24.]

Shortly after Cynthia started at *Forbidden City*, Low sold the club to Coby Yee, a popular and successful Chinatown dancer and businesswoman. Dorothy then moved her act to the nearby *Chinese Sky Room*. Cynthia does not know the particulars for the move as, "I was young and didn't really know about any of those kinds of things." It was late 1963 and Pat Morita, who would soon gain national popularity as "Arnold" on the *Happy Days* TV show and as "Mr. Miyagi" in the *Karate Kid* movies and Samee Tong, best known as "Peter Tong" the houseboy on television's *Bachelor Father* were also performing there. Cynthia says that all the performers did three shows a night on Fridays and Saturdays and two shows on Sundays and during the week at the *Chinese Sky Room*. Mondays were off. Even though the height of the clubs' popularity had already passed, Cynthia remembers that the *Forbidden City* was almost always full on the weekends. She added,

"You know how much the Chinese love to dance!" As for weekday crowds, Cynthia estimated that they were "always pretty good." Audiences continued to include Chinatown regulars as they had since the earliest days, but Cynthia guessed that 80% of the clientele was Caucasian. In Cynthia's time many of the clubs' audiences came on Gray Line bus tours. Gray Line had a ticket office at nearby Union Square where many of its tours started. The buses offering night club tours had a regular route that made three stops in the following order: *Forbidden City*, *Chinese Sky Room* and *Finocchio's* which was on Broadway and featured lively female impersonation acts. By the end of 1964, however, the *Sky Room* closed, and Dorothy took her *Toy and Wing Oriental Playgirl Show* to play exclusively on the road.

During Cynthia's first two full years with it, the act ranged the length of the West coast. They went to Bakersfield in Southern California where they performed in what Cynthia remembers as "a classy and upscale supper club." They went from Southern California to Oregon and pushed further north into Washington. Cynthia was in awe of Dorothy's tireless nature. The group's producer was also one of its singers and dancers and, on top of that, its choreographer. She was constantly seeking to push her group beyond "good" or even "better." As the booking agent, she was an energetic and very personable networker. One lucrative find for Dorothy and her troupe was the Western Fair Convention held in Fresno. Getting on with the fair circuit enabled the show to range the length and breadth of Canada as well as the United States. Cynthia recalls dancing on the main outdoor stages at county fairs and that the group was often the opening act for fairs that headlined "big names" that included the likes of Red Skelton, the Smothers Brothers and Nelson Eddy and His Orchestra.

The group traversed Canada from Vancouver to Halifax, Nova Scotia and back. They originally drove the entire round trip in two station wagons, one following the other. One afternoon they got lost in a snow storm around the town of Medicine Hat in western Canada, and the driver of the car carrying Cynthia slid off the road and into a heavy bank of snow. Nobody was hurt, but the car was damaged beyond repair. From then on, they used a single vehicle: a nine-passenger limousine purchased from a San Francisco taxi company. Dorothy's sister, Helen, who was the group's featured vocalist, became the regular driver.

The road show normally included Dorothy, six dancers and Helen. Sometimes Paul Wing would accompany the group. Dorothy had married Paul during their "Toy and Wing" days, but the couple had since gotten divorced. They were married in part to avoid scandal whenever they travelled and roomed together back in the highly conservative days of pre-World War Two America. Cynthia says the group would pack up their props, costumes and personal clothing and pile it all on the car's roof to be tied down under a canvas sheet. Cynthia always felt that the limousine was roomy, comfortable and safe.

Cynthia does not remember any racial confrontations in those days of the Civil Rights Movement. One time in North Central Canada, however, the group was in a parade and some people yelled insults at them, the loudest of which were calls of "Jap!" Cynthia says that it did not much bother her as she assumed that the comment was related to animosities dating back to World War II. Cynthia also says that, being young, she was simply not particularly sensitive to such things. "We were not so politically correct in those days. A lot of things just were not a big deal. Maybe they weren't nice, but things were like that in those days. People are so much more sensitive today," she said. She believed that they, as an all-Asian group, were viewed more as something "exotic" or "a novelty" than anything else. She added, "The places we went to in Canada and even the United States there were hardly any Asians." Once, in Montreal during *Expo 67*, the 1967 World's Fair, a father brought his very young daughter up to Cynthia.

He was very polite and said that they enjoyed our show. They had never seen Chinese people before. He wanted to know if it would be alright for his little girl to touch my hair. I did not mind at all and I said, 'OK.' She ran her hand through my hair and seemed to enjoy it. The father thanked me and they said goodbye. I was not offended. In fact, I actually got a kick out of it!

Cynthia commented that touring was hard work with travel, rehearsals, nightly shows and living out of a suitcase. There were benefits, though. Whatever town they went to seemed to always have at least a few Chinese residents. It was almost always the case that they owned restaurants. The Chinese, probably as eager to see the act for its "novelty" as anyone else, were sure to show up. Often, after the last show, these restaurateurs would invite the troupe back to their restaurant. They would open up, fire up the kitchen and make all manner of real Chinese food that was, of course, very good and very welcomed. The food was also plentiful and free. Meals also were provided by the clubs in which the group performed. Like the old clubs back in San Francisco many were supper clubs. After the last show Cynthia and her companions would be invited to eat with the club's staff. They dined on the same food that was served to the paying public, so it was always good. Although Cynthia does not recall specific details about their accommodations, she clearly remembers them as usually being in hotels with clean and comfortable rooms. Their engagements usually lasted several weeks at each stop, so there was time to relax a little and even to play tourist when the group's hosts would take them sightseeing or on local outings for fun.

Cynthia recalls that the first time she was ever in a private plane was during a stop for the London, Ontario Fair. The fair manager invited her for a ride in his two-seater which gave her a thrilling aerial tour of the city. Another opportunity for fun and free meals came about in Rockford, Illinois near Chicago. One of the troupe had been dating one of the sons of the Hunt family of ketchup renown. Saying that there would be "safety in numbers," some or even all of the girls would cajole their friend into getting a date with the young Mr. Hunt that would include all of them for dinner. Although the girls had ample opportunities to spend time with the local gentlemen, Cynthia says that Dorothy kept a good watch over them and would never permit anything to get out of hand.

Chinatown, My Chinatown

After leaving the *Oriental Playgirls,* Cynthia ran a jewelry business on the third floor of the Grant Avenue building that was shared by the *Empress of China* restaurant. She stayed in the jewelry business until retirement at which time she and a friend, Ivy Tam, decided to take a senior dance class at the Chinese Recreation Center just west of Chinatown and by the cable car barn.

Ivy, like Cynthia had been a dancer. She, in fact, got into performing in part because she had been married to Charlie Low in the early 1960s. As Mrs. Low, Ivy would go to the *Forbidden City* to watch rehearsals and shows and to help with whatever things needed doing from arranging dining tables to helping the dancers with their costumes and jewelry. At one point there was such a shortage of dancers that Ivy was convinced to try a little dancing to see if she would be able to join the *Forbidden City* show. She learned quickly and was added to the troupe. She says that she had a lot of fun and really enjoyed her time doing it. [25.]

Ivy was some 20 years Cynthia's senior and they did not know one another during their years performing. They met because Ivy had first been a long-time friend of Cynthia's husband-to-be who used to live in Vancouver. He would visit San Francisco from time to time on business at which time he had met and befriended Ivy. She was sympathetic that he had to travel such a long distance to a city in which he did not know anyone. She took it upon herself to invite him to her place for home-cooked Chinese meals whenever he was in San Francisco. One evening, while they were dating, he invited Cynthia to meet "a wonderfully nice girl." From that time onwards, Cynthia and Ivy became life-long friends.

Cynthia and Ivy enjoyed the Rec Center dance class so much that they spoke to other friends about it and eventually two others, Pat Chin and Isabel Louie joined them. The four friends had all, at one time or another, danced professionally in one or another of Chinatown's now closed clubs.

Cynthia has long been active in Chinatown. One time, while she was the president of the Chinese Hospital Auxiliary, the hospital was looking for ideas for a fund raiser. Cynthia proposed that a group of former Chinatown showgirls made up of herself and some old friends from her days as a dancer could put on a performance for the sake of the charity. The hospital immediately took to the idea. The performance was a success. Among those attending were friends, acquaintances and some who had once seen the women perform in the Chinatown clubs. Many who watched them at the Chinese Hospital benefit praised the dancers and even asked if they would consider performing in future events. Cynthia and her friends were flattered and pleased by the positive reactions and concluded that they should stay together as a group and work on a repertoire of dance numbers. They adopted the name *Grant Avenue Follies* and, looking ahead to future benefit and charity events, established it as a not-for-profit organization.

Cynthia retains nothing but deeply fond memories of her years with the *Toy and Wing Oriental Playgirls*. She holds dear the memories of friends and companionships forged and made forever fast in the dressing rooms and stages of the *Forbidden City* and the *Chinese Sky Room* and on the road in the Toy and Wing limousine. She just keeps dancing with friends new and old as a member of the *Grant Avenue Follies*.

I just love our costumes, so bright and so colorful from our top hats down to our tap shoes. And I also love the props we use in our numbers. I am so happy when our audiences watch us and I see them smile and I watch their eyes, all aglow, as they follow our movements. We dance to the music of the forties and the fifties; the sounds of our audience members' younger days when they also danced along to the very same songs. We perform to show tunes and two of our standards and must-sees for the public are the medley from "Flower Drum Song" and that long-time oldie, "Chinatown, My Chinatown." I loved it when I was 17 and I love it now. I cannot think of one single regret for having been a performer. Not one. And now, every time I go out with the Follies to dance I am happy and I am gratified to know that I, we, bring such joy to those who watch us. It's that simple. I am happy because they are happy. It makes life so great.

"Chinatown My Chinatown" [26.]

"Chinatown, my Chinatown;
Dreamy, dreamy Chinatown;
When the lights are low.
Almond eyes of brown.
Hearts that know no other land;
Hearts are light and lights are bright;
Drifting to and fro.
In dreamy Chinatown."

Pat Chin [27.]
The Chinese Sky Room and The China Dolls Revue

Like Cynthia Yee, Pat Chin was only 17 when she was first hired to perform in a night club act. While Cynthia joined the *Forbidden City* for her debut, Pat got her start through Andy Wong's *Chinese Sky Room* after responding to a newspaper ad seeking dancers and stating, "no experience necessary." Andy was born and raised in Chinatown, served in the US Army during World War II and his wife, Penny, was crowned as the first ever Miss Chinatown in 1948. Andy also served as the post commander of the American Legion's Cathay Post through which many of Chinatown's youngsters passed as members of its renowned Drum and Bugle Corps. Andy started his first night club with an uncle in 1937 and maintained *Andy Wong's Chinese Sky Room* until he lost his lease and closed down in 1967. The *Sky Room* was located at the corner of Grant Avenue and Pine Street in an upper floor of the *Grand View Hotel.*

Andy's club, as well as all the others in traditional and conservative Chinatown, often skirted parental oversight or concerns by hiring young women only as waitresses. After a few weeks the servers would be asked to take a few dance lessons so that they could substitute or fill-in for the regular performers on an as-needed basis. Most, of course, would wind up as regulars in the shows. After he left the entertainment circles, Andy remained active in Chinatown organizations and retired as a top salesman for a Cadillac dealership.
[28.]

Choreographer Walton Biggerstaff was another key player in the Chinatown night club scene. He was a dancer in both ballet and modern dance, a dance instructor and a choreographer who moved to San Francisco in 1929. He established a dance studio on Jackson Street. It might have been from that very location that Pat was hired for the *Sky Room*. Walton was quite an accomplished artist who studied and performed in both New York and Europe in the 1930s. When he returned to San Francisco in 1940, he began an association with Charlie Low and became the long-time choreographer for the *Forbidden City*. Walton was free to take his expertise to other clubs and that is how Pat Chin became one of his proteges. [29.]

Some of the more accomplished performers in Chinatown as well as choreographers, Walton among them, were disconcerted by what they saw as poor dancing skills from young and inexperienced hires such as Pat. They were critical of these dancers' "two left feet," inability to walk in high heels without having to look down or without falling down steps or twisting an ankle, or being "clumsy." [30.] Many girls, Pat among them, bore through it all and gradually acquired the skills that kept audiences coming back for more. More often than not, the average club patron was a poor judge of true dancing ability anyhow. As Cynthia Yee has noted, many customers who had never before seen an Asian face were more taken by the exotic nature of the Chinese girls than by their actual dancing skills.

Andy's shows did not just perform in the *Sky Room*. According to Pat's best recollection she believes that Andy put together road acts as a way to earn more income and possibly to promote his San Francisco club. Pat said that the troupe to which she was assigned as a chorus girl after her original hire was sent on the road to play in as many venues that would have them. Pat recalls,

We traveled up to The Cave Supper Club in Vancouver for a three-week engagement. This was my first road company job and it was very enjoyable for me. The customers were very hospitable. They invited the whole cast to dinners and when we went to the Chinese restaurants, we were treated like celebrities. On our days off, Sammee Tong, who was our emcee and stand-up comedian would cook a big pot of stew in his motel room to feed us all! Sammee later became a national celebrity for his television role on the show "Bachelor Father." Unfortunately, there were no ongoing road contracts after our time at the Cave, so we returned to San Francisco. Without anywhere to send a travelling act, Andy no longer needed me.

I was lucky that the manager at my prior job with E. F. Hutton liked me enough to take me back. I stayed with Hutton for a while, but when I saw another ad in the papers with pretty much the same wording as the earlier one from the Sky Room, I went for an interview at the St. Francis Hotel where I had been an on-call hat check girl and, like before, I was hired pretty quickly. The job was for the China Dolls Revue that was based in southern California.

I went to Hollywood for my training. It took place in the show-room of a night club and restaurant and the experienced dancers did the training of us newbies. When we were able to get our routines down we performed one show in Los Angeles. Then we were on the road with me being one of the chorus girls. We travelled up and down the coasts of California, Oregon and Washington to perform Las Vegas-style variety shows. We never knew there so many Elks clubs! We then left the coast and performed at several casinos in Nevada. Just as before with the Sky Room, we ran out of contracts and the road show ended. After six months of touring I was once more without a job.

I stayed with friends in Los Angeles that I had met as a road performer. Because of my prior experience, I was able to find a job at another branch of E. F. Hutton & Co. It was on the corner of Hollywood & Vine. One of the brokers would bring a hibiscus every week for me to wear in my hair! So far since my short time in the Grant Avenue art goods shop, I had been living a pretty exciting and good life.

Once she had left home to seek her own way through the world, Pat became generally happier and more content. She had grown up in an ambience devoid of warmth or affection and had endured, at best, years of benign neglect. Once out working, especially with the *Sky*

Room and *China Dolls Revue*, Pat was able to meet people who offered genuine friendship, support and caring. She also says that she gained a lot of confidence and in-depth understanding about the nature of professional entertainment. She continues to regard her fellow dancers and entertainers from those days as her best and most true family. Pat remembered some of her *China Dolls Revue* companions and their acts.

There was a couple with us who did modern oriental-style dances. The man's name was Don Keigo Takeuchi who went on to have his own show troupe. It was called the Imperial Dancers, and they wound up dancing all over the world. We had a singer named Florence Ahn who the China Dolls Revue billed as "the Korean Nightingale." Before I met her, Florence had taken a two-week contract to sing in Havana, Cuba. President Batista (whom Fidel Castro would replace in 1959 during the Cuban Revolution) *liked her so much that she was held over in Cuba for a whole year. She came to the China Dolls Revue when she returned from Cuba. She also sang at the Forbidden City and with the Flower Drum Song* (Broadway) *Road Company. We had a Japanese ballet dancer named Chio Kadamatsu whose big trick was to spin around on pointe for very long periods of time. There was also Ming and Ling who were a father and son singing and comic act. Finally, I remember an acrobatic team called the Asia Boys. They became very successful and played in many of the top clubs all around the country. I saw them on television on the Ed Sullivan Show and I saw them live in the San Francisco at Bimbo's 365.*

After about a year and a half working for *E.F. Hutton* in Los Angeles, Pat received a telegram from Andy Wong. It was sometime in 1955 and the *Sky Room* had an opening for a regular performer.

Undivided Attention from Frank Sinatra!

The entire time that I was at the Sky Room was as a chorus girl. It was a time of fun, hard work and always staying busy. The hardest part of the work was spending all day rehearsing and learning new shows before going back to do three shows every night. We were only off on Thursdays. Still, I can say that we were like a great big family. Most of us girls lived in the same apartment building on Bush Street. It was just down the block and around the corner from the club which was at Grant Avenue and Pine Street. One of our most fun activities outside of work was whenever we would celebrate one another's birthdays.

A lot of big-name celebrities visited our club. I met Bob Hope and Bud Abbott and Lou Costello there. We would chat a little, mostly small talk, and it was fun to take pictures with each other. I also saw Duke Ellington, Louis Armstrong, the Treiniers, Tito Puente and many other famous popular performers of the day as customers of the club. I remember how Ellington always sent out Christmas Cards in April. Of course, some of our own Sky Room performers that worked there at the same time as I became famous themselves. Some also worked at least for a while at the Forbidden City. Four of them were Jack Soo, Sammee Tong, Pat Morita and James Hong.

Of the four performers named by Pat, all appeared in both film and television. Two are Japanese Americans and two are American born Chinese. Sammee Tong was born in San Francisco and is best known for his role as Peter Tong, the houseboy on the television show, *Bachelor Father.* Some viewed his role as a servant as demeaning to Chinese Americans, but Sammee himself said that he enjoyed the role because he did not simply play a subservient character. He elaborated that he felt that he was given substantive dialogue and that he was allowed to create comic situations and funny lines to draw laughs for the show. James Hong, from Minnesota, may not be known for major roles, but he has been in movies, television and served as voices for animated movie characters.

Jack Soo was born aboard a ship in transit from Japan to the United States. His family name was Suzuki and, because of it, he and his immediate family were interred in a concentration camp for Japanese and Japanese Americans during World War II. Jack passed some of his camp time performing and entertaining his fellow internees. He eventually garnered a great number of professional credits over his lifetime, but he is probably best known for his roles in *Flower Drum Song* (both the Broadway play and the film) and on the television show *Barney Miller* in which his character was notorious for making bad coffee for his companions to drink.

Pat Morita was born in Isleton near Sacramento, California. He was well-liked as the character who became the owner of Arnold's drive-in in the television show *Happy Days*. He also starred as the Karate Kid's mentor in the movie *Karate Kid* and its three sequels. He has numerous other credits for television and films, among which was *Midway*, about the World War II naval battle in which he played a Japanese admiral. His dialogue in that film was all in Japanese that was sub-titled in English.

If not busy meeting celebrities or working with soon-to-be celebrities, Pat and her *Sky Room* co-workers were usually free between shows. Their exotic dancer was married to the owner of the nearby *Macumba Club,* so the girls would often dash on in between sets to sit back, catch up on their girl-talk, maybe flirt a little and just watch a show. The best part was that it was free. Pat recalled,

Two other famous persons we met were Herb Jeffries,[31.] *a singer who was performing at the Macumba and Johnny Mathis. Herb was very friendly and invited the whole gang of us to his hotel suite at the Holiday Lodge for drinks after our shows. He was most famous for the song "Flamingo" and was married to the world-famous exotic dancer, Tempest Storm. Johnny was just starting out and, if I remember right, one of my former schoolmates, who was a nephew of one of the club's owners and a good friend of Johnny's, brought him to the club so that he might sing there. Johnny was very good, of course, but he did not stay too long. It was very early in his career, and he moved around to any place that would have him. I bet that Andy Wong regretted not signing him to a management contract!*

Pat continues with her Sky Room memories:

After working at the Sky Room for a few years a certain young man began to keep coming back to enjoy our shows. It turned out that he was most interested in seeing me at the club. I was flattered and we gradually got to know each other. It was so strange to meet a person my own age instead of the older men you were always meeting at the club. He and I hit it off quite well. It felt like there was a good dose of Karma involved because it turned out that he grew up in a store right across the street from me on Stockton and Clay Streets. Now, Chinatown is not really that big, but we somehow never got to know each other until 1956! We were married January, 1957.

About March or April of the year in which I was married, Columbia Pictures came calling. They wanted to use the Chinese Sky Room as backdrop for a scene in the movie, "Pal Joey." It was interesting, fun and exciting even as we worked all day on a movie scene then had to go straight back to do our regular three shows later in the evening. One day during a break in the filming, the star of the film, Frank Sinatra, paid undivided attention to me. After my part in one of the takes, he helped me off the stage, lit my cigarette, and made a lot of small talk. He expressed his desire to see me again, so I invited him to the club that night to see our show. He came with a producer type man and a starlet and sat through our first show of the evening. I greeted his party after the show and he did not want to leave. His party had to go to a reception at the Fairmont that evening, so they more or less dragged him off. Lucky for me! There I was, a newlywed, tempted to be led astray by the glamour of Hollywood! Darn! After all that, our scene was cut from the movie, but I will always cherish the memories!

I remained at the Sky Room for about a year after I got married. When I left I returned to Hutton where I picked up where I had left off as a board marker. I stayed in the financial district for a while and my supervisor at Hutton even helped me get a job at the Bank of America. I worked there until it became time to raise a family which brought a lot of satisfaction and happiness to both my husband and me. In the 45 years that we were married, my husband became a very successful and well-liked businessman. I was happy that he enjoyed the company of a great many friends as well as associates who became friends from all walks of life.

4.
Coming of Age
We Were Left to Pretty Much Figure Things Out by Ourselves

Former Chinatown kids recall the at times difficult transition from childhood to adolescence and adulthood. The consistent parental admonition was, "study hard and be good" where "good" was given to mean "reserved, respectful and obedient." Chinese custom, however, makes neither time nor allowance for explanations or reassurances about the expected path to goodness. The Chinese tradition merely called for children to quietly observe their elders and carefully emulate their behavior. Childhood's uneven path, with all its unexpected curves and obstacles, often resulted in confusing or difficult times for Chinatown's youngsters. Parents who had to work long hours or who did not speak English or understand American culture were of scant assistance during these trying years.

Melody Chan Doss-Wambeke
My Mother Would Cry for Days After I Eloped

Communication in the Chan household among Melody, her two brothers, her mother, and her unhearing father grew ever more challenging as the children got older. Although initially fluent in Chinese, the three siblings very readily adapted to English which they had begun to learn at their grade school. From their early years at Garfield Elementary, through Francisco Junior High, and Galileo High, their primary language was English. Melody and her brothers continued to speak Chinese when at home, but their fluency in it declined quickly and steadily. In the meanwhile, Melody's mother had never had either time or opportunities to pick up any English and her unhearing father relied on notes, handwritten in Chinese, by his wife. For the elder Chans, it could only be Chinese or nothing. According to Melody,

During family conversations my mother began to slowly realize that we did not truly understand the meaning of her words. She would speak simpler Chinese to get her point to us when we were in our teens. My father continued to speak in Chinese but, due to his deafness, the vocal quality of his words was strange. I recall my father's attempts to sound out some English words. The sounds were harsh and very difficult for us to understand. In some ways he lived in his own world. My mother and our other relatives continued to communicate with him by writing.

Because I studied formal Chinese (in Chinese school) *longer than my brothers, I became the occasional interpreter for them with my parents. I was always happy to interpret for my mother, but I felt personally frustrated that I could not speak conversational Chinese with greater fluency. Fortunately, in North Beach, Chinatown, and even San Francisco people were familiar with the fact that many Chinese immigrants spoke very little English. People were patient and understanding when they saw children like me explaining things to their parents in their native tongue as we went about chores and business outside of Chinatown.*

My mother was often frustrated that she had not learned English. I never recall that she asked any of us to teach her, though. By the time we were in high school, she probably felt that she had gotten too old to learn. My parents were very traditional and rarely spoke to us children about their inner frustrations or problems. We were the children and we were expected to be obedient and studious. It was not our place to ask questions about anything. This Confucian tradition of filial piety lasted with me until I left for college. I have always felt that my mother was maybe born at the wrong time. If fate could have been kinder to her, she might have had a chance to learn English after she arrived in Chinatown. Her life would not have been so hard.

Despite her great love and respect for her parents, Melody could not resist falling in love with a man who was not Chinese. She tells of her journey away from her family's centuries old traditions and values to enter the realm of *fahn guey*: the foreign devils.

I met Ted, my non-Chinese husband to be, through a woman with whom I had once worked as a waitress at a family restaurant. Ted and my former co-worker were dating at the time, and we spent the next three years as friends. I was not aware that they had broken off their relationship when one afternoon Ted invited me out for a cup of coffee. I did not drive at the time and, rather than see me take the bus home when we were done, he offered me a ride. Before too long, we were dating and progressed to the point of falling in love. From that time forward I could not imagine life without Ted, but I kept him a secret from my family. My parents continued to hold Chinese traditions and values dear, so I knew that they would completely forbid the relationship. Their old country beliefs were so firm that I dismissed all possibilities of trying to explain my feelings for Ted with them or to attempt to plead with them for understanding. I had seen television shows and movies where a young American woman might argue a case such as mine before her family, but the traditions and expectations of my family offered no such recourse to me. The mere thought of me talking back or getting into a yelling match with my Chinese parents was preposterous!

Ted and I eloped to Reno.

I returned as Mrs. Ted Doss to the Chan household in order to retrieve my clothes. You can imagine the fireworks! There were tearful, loud, and drawn out expressions in Chinese of dismay, shock, anger, and that granddaddy of all Chinese admonitions: the child's disrespect of her parents' wishes. My mother was sure that it was all a foolish mistake that I would soon miserably come to regret. My mother wrote in Chinese calligraphy to my father about what I had done. He just responded with an expressionless nod. Ted reached out to my father and shook his hand. For my part, that day at the house proved to be the most dramatic and the scariest time of my life. My mother would cry for days and blame herself for my actions.

In my traditional Chinese upbringing, family was everything. Although I was determined, it was still a great challenge for me to learn and to understand that my allegiance was no longer to my Chan family, but to my husband Ted.

It took nearly two years for the dust to settle. During this time, Ted began to build a demolition contracting business and I resumed my college studies. My brothers and one of my cousins worked very hard to smooth the ruffled feathers. Their efforts eventually opened the way for Ted and me to finally return to the Chan house in order to participate in the family celebrations of Christmas and Chinese New Year. It was going home, but so different because I was no longer one of the household. The Chan family was neither verbally nor in any other way outwardly affectionate. The family seldom offered praise or compliments and there were never any hugs given out. My uncles and aunts were polite and they smiled at Ted and me. My relatives spoke very little English and most of what they could say usually came in broken form. Ted spoke only English. I served as the interpreter between my mother and Ted.

My mother was a most fantastic cook who prepared all of our family meals. The traditional Chinese way of serving chicken was to chop it into pieces that were neatly arranged, bones and all, on a large platter. After sitting through a couple of my mother's family dinners, Ted told me privately that he was afraid to eat the chicken because all the bones were still attached. I related this concern to my mother. At the next dinner, my mother served a small plate of breast meat without the bones just for Ted. She also added a fork and knife along with a pair of chopsticks at his place setting. The rest of the family continued to just dive in with our chopsticks and eat away. I believe that small step was the beginning of my mother accepting him into the family as the Chan son-in-law. Through Ted my relatives learned that not all non-Asian men drank and, in the end, he was fully accepted into the Chan family. Over time I taught Ted a few basic polite Chinese phrases such as" good morning" and "how are you." My mother always smiled whenever Ted would greet her in his broken Chinese!

Ted and I were married for 34 years and I lost him to cancer at age 80. As I am recalling my life as Melody Doss, I always felt that Ted's best quality was that he had a good heart. Despite the cultural and linguistic challenges he faced, he was always an empathetic and understanding man. He was my husband, my best friend, and my right arm.

Saki Lee
Losing My Chinese Identity

Except for their one year stay with her aunt and uncle in Cincinnati Saki, and her siblings spent their entire growing up lives in the John Street flat that was owned by their maternal grandfather. While Saki and her brother found life far away from Chinatown to be enlightening and fun, there were times when it proved difficult. Saki recalls some of her Cincinnati experiences,

Overall Jim and I got along pretty well at school and around the neighborhood. There was a cute boy named Doug who was my boyfriend. One day, riding on the back of his bicycle, my foot got caught in the wheel spokes and we tumbled down onto the concrete pavement. My knee was scraped and bleeding, and someone picked me up and took me and Doug to the laundry. When Uncle James saw the mess that I was, he began to scold Doug. Uncle James was a pretty big man, and when he was waving his arms around in excitement, I am sure that he looked pretty scary to 10-year old Doug.

And then, it happened. Maybe because he felt intimidated or maybe for some other reason I won't ever really know for sure, Doug got angry and spat out some words I had never heard before in my life. He yelled, "You are just a Ching Chong Chinaman!" and he dashed out of the laundry. Although the words were new to me, I intuitively knew how nasty they really were. Doug never came around or played with me again after that. I was heart-broken and did not understand any of this. But Auntie Pat and Uncle James who were always so gentle and so kind tried their best to console me. They tried to explain to me that, "some people are just not too smart." I caught them as they looked meaningfully at each other. I couldn't be sure, but I just thought that perhaps they knew something that I did not.

Another time, one of the big-breasted girls named Sheila saw a bracelet I had on and said that I had stolen it from her. I told her she could ask my Uncle James if this was true, knowing that she was just trying to bully me. So off she went and rang the bell of the laundry. I had already told Uncle James about her false accusation. Being rather overprotective of me, he was already on the warpath in preparation to defend me. He came to the front desk menacingly and waved his arms as he loudly stated to Sheila in his heavily accented English, "You don't know anything. We gave her this bracelet. Go home." And then, like Doug had earlier done, she also said the same words as she slinked out the door, "Ching chong Chinaman..." Despite my young age and general naiveté, I clearly recognized that she meant to be harsh, unkind and cruel. Sheila never bothered me again, though.

Later, when I tried to ask Uncle James what Sheila's and Doug's words had really meant, he and Auntie Pat dismissed my questions. They wanted to be reassuring and said that I should not even think about it. They wanted me to believe that anyone who said the types of things like Sheila and Doug would be best ignored. They were simply stupid people who were unworthy of any attention at all.

In the innocence of childhood, protected by the fierce love of two much trusted adults, I readily accepted their wisdom and their reassurance and felt safe. It would be many years before I could finally understand how intense a struggle Uncle James' and Auntie Pat's reality had really been. They struggled for all their years in Cincinnati in painful alienation living in what I had never recognized as a poor and largely hostile white ghetto. They were far from friends or family. They were completely deprived of the familiarity and closeness that all Chinese communities strive to provide. They absorbed the taunts, disdain, disrespect, and even hatred that they were always so careful to deflect away from me and from Jim.

Several years after Saki and Jim had returned to San Francisco, their aunt and uncle followed suit. Their uncle opened a laundry called "James' Laundry" on the corner of Powell Street where the Hyde Street cable car tracks turn away from Chinatown. They did well enough to purchase a nice home at California Street and Fifteenth Avenue to which they eventually retired. By now Saki was in her teens and resettled into familiar surroundings. She was not as comfortable as she had once been in Chinatown, however. She recalled some of her thoughts and feelings from that time,

The extent of my exposure to Chinese things while I was in high school was limited to just a small list of things. Whether at home or at a relative's there was always some form or another of Chinese food. Some of it was pretty disgusting to me. If I could get away with it, I would discretely avoid the things that I least liked. I would even experience unpleasant feelings walking along the sections of Stockton or Grant where fresh foods were sold. The vegetables were usually harmless enough, but some of the big melons and root things made me feel uncomfortable. The smell of cages stacked one atop another and filled with clucking chickens and all their droppings turned my stomach. Equally nasty were the pans and basins packed with live fish; gills flapping desperately, mouths agape, and eyes bulging.

There were things that I quite enjoyed as well. Chinese New Year

was always a nice time for me. The nervousness that I felt as kids tossed firecrackers all over the place was diminished by the bright colors of storefront window decorations plus the general sense of happiness all around. I loved all the colorful lanterns, dancing lions, and long, elaborate, and beautiful dragons. There was also the joy of lay-see, good luck money, cheerfully handed out by a smiling auntie or uncle with a loudly cheerful "Gung Hay Fat Choy!" or "Happy New Year!"

One aspect of the Chinatown-wide New Year festivities besides exploding firecrackers that I did not enjoy was the screechy Chinese music blaring from street corner shops that hurt my ears. My teenaged inclination towards western music, whether rock 'n roll or classical had already long been firmly established. Chinese musical instruments and the chromatic scale that they were played in along with female vocals let loose in long falsetto blasts might have been familiar to me when I was very young, but not anymore!

Despite trying to be polite, well-behaved and getting good grades in school, I had to endure being scolded too often. Even though they were all bi-lingual my mother, and any other adult relative with a mind to do so always yelled at me in Chinese. Somehow, that experience always seemed especially menacing. I think I would have been much less intimidated or frightened had I been chastised in English instead.

Perhaps the most enduring aspect of the ever-diminishing facets of Chinese life and culture still within the teenaged me was hearing over and over again from the disapproving lips of Chinese people: "What kind of Chinese are you? You don't speak Chinese!" I harbored strong feelings of being ostracized for years thereafter.

Still, I wanted most of all to fit in with my white American friends who seemed so confident and articulate and did daring things like smoking marijuana and listening to loud rock music. I remained very shy and introverted, however, so I still wasn't all that comfortable with non-Chinese friends and their ways of thinking and doing things. I enjoyed classical music and spent every morning before school walking our family dog, Tiger, in the beauty of Russian Hill Park just to be alone with myself and my thoughts about who I was, what I wanted, and where I might someday go.

Jack Woo
My Buddies and I Could Always Find Something to Do or A Fun Place to Go

Except for trips around California with the Cathay Post Drum and Bugle Corps, Jack Woo spent all of his growing-up life in Chinatown. In his adult years, Jack pieced information and events together to surmise that his father was in all likelihood a paper son. Jack, however, ever mindful of his place and his manners, never worked up the courage to ask his father about his status. Jack describes himself in the past as a "good boy whose main concern in life was to be a good son."

Chinatown was a small, intimate place ... you could easily walk to a friend's house and then, together, easily walk and quickly arrive at any number of places: Portsmouth Square or Washington Square, North Beach Playground and pool, the schoolyard at Commodore Stockton, the Chinatown YMCA, Cameron House, and lots of other places. My buddies and I could always find something to do or a fun place to go. We could walk all over and never worry about anything bad happening ... not like today. I know that life goes on and change is always bound to happen, but I really regret that of the Chinatown I knew when I was young, only 30 or 40% is still like it used to be.

Jack also has warm memories of some of his favorite teen activities.

There were three pool halls near Cathay Post. The pool places were all within easy walking distance. There was Jack's, Johnny's, and the L and M. Jack's and Johnny's weren't really pool halls. They were just small and dark places that had a couple of tables and maybe one or two of the old pinball machines. Some of us liked to go for games of pool or pinball before or after practice at Cathay Post. Jack's and Johnny's were quiet and clean places that I enjoyed. You were supposed to be 21 to get into a place that had pool tables, but the owners never said anything to us about it. I learned how to be pretty good at pool and had a lot of fun learning how to do some of the trick shots. Of course, I was no Minnesota Fats or anything like that.

I was pretty bad at pinball. It was a dime for three balls, but I got frustrated because I would always wind up tilting. I just didn't like wasting dimes on something I didn't enjoy. Even though it was illegal because it was a form of gambling and we were all minors, Jack's or Johnny's would give small payouts of cash for high pinball scores. Even though I never played, I sort of enjoyed the thrill of knowing that I was in a place where illegal things were going on.

The third pool hall, the L and M, was a little farther from the Cathay Post than the other two places. It was near Kearny Street and it was kind of a tough place. I was in junior high school and high school guys or even adults liked to hang out there. They were always smoking and using bad language. Back in those days guys who wore black jackets and black pants were considered real bad asses. They were gangsters and the type of guys who would carry a switchblade or even a gun. I didn't ever see any weapons; it was just what I thought. Of course, I didn't go there very often. Whenever I did, I was always with an older friend.

There Wasn't Any Danger and We Never Worried About Anything Happening

Jack talks about Friday nights, weekends and school breaks when he would stay out late with friends at a time when playing in the city's parks and streets was completely safe.

I clearly remember the Limbo Rock song by Chubby Checker in 1962-63. On Friday nights the year that song was popular we would go to North Beach Playground to play softball and hang out. Sometimes we would get a stick and practice the limbo rock with the girls there; it was great fun to 'see how low can you go?' I guess that was the beginning of us guys flirting with the girls!

I also had a lot of fun at Playland By the Beach. It was right across from the Great Highway that was part of the old Highway One that ran all along the California coast. The amusement park was a

110

couple of blocks long and it had a small roller coaster and rides like the Rock-o-Plane, Tilt-a-Whirl, and Caterpillar. There was also a Fun House and lots of booths with games like at a carnival or fair. It didn't cost anything to go to Playland. You only paid for whatever ride or attraction you wanted to go on. I think everything was ten cents or maybe a quarter at the most. Sometimes on weekends a few of us would find our way from Chinatown out to the beach and go for roller coaster rides or bring our slot cars there to race against other contestants. We guys would go in a group by bus and sometimes we would run into a group of girls that we knew from school who also rode out in a group on the bus. We would mingle with them to talk, buy snacks, and go on rides or play games. Then we would just get the bus home separately.

One last activity I fondly remember is that once a year the YMCA clubs would organize a ski trip up to Lake Tahoe. We were one of the lucky ones in Chinatown to be able to get out of the neighborhood and up to Lake Tahoe and experience SNOW! We actually learned to ski, too! To this day, I'm still a pretty good skier, thanks to the Y.

I didn't get into "fashion" much, but I did a little bit when I was in the 8th grade. Peer pressure influenced me into dressing more like the crowd. Before then, my mom was the one that was buying all my clothes. I didn't think anything about it until the 8th grade when most of the guys started wearing certain shoes or clothes. They were into Converse All-Star "Chuck Taylor" canvas shoes. Before I knew any better, I went to Flagg Brothers on Market Street and bought a pair of generic canvas shoes that looked just like the Converse ones. Boy, did I lose face when I wore them to school! There was nothing I could do about it and since money was always tight in those days, I just had to keep on wearing them until they were worn down. I also got the genuine Derby jackets when they got popular. The big things were the three-quarter trench coat and the car coat. We would go to the Derby distributor on First Street and Market. We just walked upstairs to a showroom where they had all their jackets and coats on racks ready for shipping. We would pick what we liked, try it on, and pay wholesale prices in cash. Chinese kids were always welcome there because a lot of Derby's clothing was made in

Chinatown gai-chongs by our mothers, grandmothers, cousins, and aunts. Those were really good quality clothes and they lasted forever.

We really enjoyed going to Washington Square after dark for games of hide and seek. There wasn't any danger and we never worried about anything happening. Nowadays, though ... I don't think kids could do what we did. Sometimes an older friend with a car would drive us younger guys over to Oakland for mini-golf since there weren't any courses in San Francisco. We also did organized activities at the Chinatown Y. They had lots of basketball there and we had a lot of fun playing in tournaments. After the games we would walk around Chinatown and end up at one of the restaurants that stayed open late to get chow mein or something like that. That was called going for "siu yeh," or midnight snacks. You got a lot for just a few dollars back then. It makes me think of the George Lucas film, "American Graffiti," where the kids hung out all night at Mel's Diner. We didn't get home until very late, but our parents didn't say anything.

During the winter holiday season, the Y sponsored Christmas caroling in different neighborhoods in the city. One time the Chinatown Y teamed up with the Y from Concord. That Y had lots of non-Chinese girls and, wowee, they were so pretty! I don't mean that the Chinese girls I knew weren't attractive or nice, but those girls from Concord were not what I was used to seeing all the time. Of course, I was too shy to ask any of the non-Chinatown girls out. I wasn't even that confident with the Chinese girls. I had too high expectations, I think, and I always picked the prettiest one to ask out. They didn't accept, and after a while, I got tired of rejection and kind of would give up.

My friends and I enjoyed fishing along the piers of the Embarcadero that were not far from Chinatown. In those days you could just walk out onto them and nobody ever bothered you. The Municipal Pier at Aquatic Park was another good place for fishing. We used droplines, rods and reels, and even climbed down on the old wood pilings to toss spears at the fish. Sometimes, if we felt like going someplace different, we would take the bus all the way out to Lake

Merced that was pretty far from Chinatown or North Beach. It's out past Stonestown and SF State and that was quite a daring adventure for us. They stocked the lake with trout and we usually caught something to bring home for dinner.

There was really only one time when something kind of bad happened to me. It was during 7th grade when a buddy and I went fishing at Lake Merced. A group of older white kids approached us and started to mess with us. They tried to take our fishing poles from us, but we didn't let them. Then they started to ask for money. Before anything could really happen, a uniformed park employee heard the racket and came over. The older boys began to try to blame us. They said we were the ones who were trying to get money from them. Then my friend who was from a rich family pulled out a wad of twenties as if to say, 'why would we try to steal money that we don't need?' That convinced the ranger and he let us go. You know, if this was the worst thing to really happen to me when I was young, I would have to say that my days of growing up in Chinatown were good and a lot of fun.

Chinatown Bands and Road Trips Meant Some Easy Hook-ups

When I was in Chinese school and about 13 years old, I became close friends with a classmate named Louis Lew. Back then we used to cut Chinese classes a lot to go play basketball in the Commodore Stockton school gym that was very nearby. Sometimes I would go over to his family apartment on weekends and hang out. I remember that Louis loved Elvis and James Brown, the King of Soul. Louis would take out all his albums, show them to me, and sing a few bars of his favorite Elvis songs. He would also get up and do a few James Brown dance moves for me. Little did I know that Louis would soon form his own band and be singing and playing at all the school dances. Louis formed his band when he was a student at Galileo and named it the Illusions. They were really good.

By then I was a little less sheltered than I had been growing up, but I was still amazed that Chinese (people) could sing and move like that ... especially Louis! I thought that only Whites could play in a band and that only Blacks could be soulful lead singers!

113

The Illusions would perform mostly at events within our community at places like Victory Hall which was in my Chinese school on Stockton Street, Chinatown night clubs, and school dances. Sometimes I would drive Louis and the Illusions to Sacramento where they would play at a place called the Confucius Hall where a lot of the local Chinese kids would hang out. Some of the band members (including Louis), and some of the guys who followed after them would meet Sacramento girls and manage some pretty easy hook-ups. It was pretty exciting for everyone to be meeting new people of the opposite sex from different Chinese communities! As we all started college people went to different schools so it was hard for the band to stay together. After college one of the old Illusions members, Victor Ng, joined up with Jest Jammin.' He, Ed Toy, Brad Lum, and Norman Fong are still performing together today.

Jest Jammin' and other Chinatown Bands

Norman Fong,[32.] the current executive director of the Chinatown Community Development Center, is also the lead vocalist and sax player for the long-lived and sole surviving Chinatown Soul Band, *Jest Jammin.'* According to Fong, the group first got together informally as five musically inclined friends who wanted to play at a house party. It was 1968 and a mutual friend to each of the group's members had been drafted and was on his way to Vietnam. Fong, a 1969 graduate of Galileo High School, recalled,

We weren't really a group or a band at that time. We just got together to play at our friend's farewell party. From that point, one thing led to another and we became one of the many, many Asian American groups that were popping up all through Chinatown during those days. We've been together for almost 50 years now. I would say that the thing that has kept us united and so close is our friendship. We were all Galileo guys, and we always liked each other. There has been nothing bad enough or strong enough to break us apart. Now, 50 years is a long time and the band has changed since 1968, but three of the original five guys are still together. There's me, and I am lead vocal and I play the sax, Ed Toy who is

114

our drummer, and Brad Lum on bass. We have added members over time and we now have ten people. We also have a brass section now.

We still play pretty much the old standards like Motown hits by performers that include Smokey Robinson and Gladys Knight. We really like Earth, Wind, and Fire, too. We are trying to keep up with the younger generation and have added things by people like Bruno Mars to our repertoire. I think of us as the "Chinatown Soul Band" and we have been at it for more than 40 years. Our current (2016) members are: me, Norman Fong, vocals and sax; Joellen Chew, vocals; Brad Lum, bass; Victor Ng, guitar and vocals; Gordie Jeong, keyboards; Ed Toy, drums; Jan Yonemoto, sax; Huey Wong, sax and flute; Bill Keast, trumpet; and Phil Wong, Congas and percussion.

Jest Jammin' gets bookings throughout Northern California. The group can be heard at places that range from large public functions to college campus festivities. Locally they play at New Year's Eve parties, the Chinatown Moon Festival, the Chinatown Street Fest (in Oakland's Chinatown as well), weddings, and private parties. According to Norman,

We can't quit. Too many of our friends and even our friends' now grown kids want the band!

The names of just a few of Chinatown's bands that were contemporaries of *Jest Jammin'* include *Majestic Sounds, the Persuasions, Enchanters, Eclipse,* and *the Illusions.*

Competition was stiff and finding gigs was not always easy. Norman laments that back then he and his group would face racially motivated bias whenever they applied to play at venues outside of Chinatown. Usually turned down by non-Chinese related clubs, *Jest Jammin'* resorted to staying in their own backyard for performances. One drawback of that was that the close quarters of Chinatown made practicing difficult. Neighbors were quick to complain about noise, and they rarely waited until very late before doing so.

The Bands and Their Fans

In some ways the bands contributed to the coming of age process for many Chinatown youths whether they played or sang in one or if they just listened or danced to the music. With the explosion of mainstream music during the 1960s that included the Motown Sound, Rhythm and Blues, Rock-'n-Roll, and the British Invasion geared towards teen listeners, the youth of Chinatown, searching for its identity, could now feel that it had grasped the knob of a door leading towards their inclusion into a significant part of popular American culture. According to Jeffrey Chan who was just 13 when he saw his first Asian American Chinatown group perform, the emergence of Chinatown bands …

… broke us out of a stereotype. We weren't just waiters, bus boys, or guys who worked in laundries … that's how people viewed us until we started playing music …You should have seen us – a bunch of Chinese guys up there playing James Brown … I guess we got into soul music because a lot of us grew up near the projects – North Beach, the Fillmore, Japan Town – and that was our circle. They listened to soul music and so did we. Plus, it was the time of civil rights and the Third World movement. That united us with Black music. [33.]

A former brass player for one of the groups added,

It was an awakening for our generation of Asian Americans. The music inspired a sense of community, and it brought Asian Americans together to voice themselves against the Vietnam War and to fight for civil rights.[34.]

A former band member, Tim Leong, remembered looking out at his audiences. He said,

They were dressed to the "T"s – guys in shirts with 4-inch collars or "hi-boys" so heavily starched that they scraped necks raw. You would wear your hair in a pompadour to appear taller, add

rhinestone cufflinks, alpaca sweaters, and black pointed shoes with pimp socks. All you needed was a splash of Jade East cologne to complete the ensemble. The girls weren't to be outdone, ratting their hair into monumental bee-hives to match their dates' hair-dos. 35.

Jeffrey Chan remembered one girl's tall hair-do.

Her hair was so high she looked five foot-eleven. The next day at school she was only four feet! 36..

There were not many girls who performed with the groups, but Cookie Wong was an exception. She was most likely the first Chinese female jazz singer to be part of a band in those days. Remembering the short skirts, eye-liner and frosted lipstick, Cookie who was 18 when she started singing, added,

I was very studious, but I liked music. So, I just hung around with the guys. But, my mother never worried. She knew a lot of their parents. They weren't bad boys. They didn't even smoke! 37.

There Would Be Mean Stare-Downs

As the good friend and trusty driver for the *Illusions,* Jack Woo remembered that large groups of teens packed closely together did not necessarily mean that a love fest was imminent.

Although I've been recounting the good moments of my experiences during the Chinatown band years, things were not always perfect. We were kids coming of age into our teens and with that a lot of hormones were surging within our young bodies. Going to those dances was like a rite of passage for some of the Chinatown ABCs.

Chinatown was not that far from a large block of public housing projects on Bay Street near Fisherman's Wharf. Filipino kids would find their way to where the Chinese were and the feeling among the ABCs would be that the project boys were invading or muscling into their territory. Neither "turf" nor female honor could be allowed to be violated. It was a time when many of the guys felt the need to show off their machoism (sic); especially in front of the girls. Most of the time there would be mean stare downs or toe-to-toe stand offs between the alpha ABCs and their adversarial counterparts: young Filipino boys.

This was kind of ironic because when the dances were in Sacramento's Chinatown, the Sacramento boys would consider the "Frisco Boys" as the intruders and the whole stare down drama would take place there. It was scary back in that period of time during those confrontations, but all was usually settled with talk downs or fist-a-cuffs. It was very scary for the innocent by-standers, but it is pale compared to today's hip hop/rap concert events where they settle this macho posturing or disrespect with hand guns!

Our Main Goal Was to Learn How to Be "Bad Asses"

Jack did not communicate that much with his father while growing up. He didn't want to ask too many questions out of respect. Today, he looks back with a sense of admiration for his father whom he refers to as a "forward thinking man."

Back in 1964 my father decided that I should attend high school at Washington instead of Galileo. He wanted to keep me away from what he saw as a problem with hoodlums or gangs. Among those groups at the time were the Junior Raiders. They were nothing like the really bad gangs like the Wah-Ching, Joe (Fong) Boys, Hop Sing, and Jackson Street Boys that came up later in a few years. Those guys were violent criminals. The Junior Raiders and some other groups like them were mostly just a bunch of ABCs who would act tough and do small stuff. It was probably a wise move by my father, though. I was really pretty much a good kid who went by the rules. I did my homework and tried to do the right things. Still, I was resentful that I got separated from some of my Francisco buddies who mostly went to Galileo. I also did not enjoy the long ride on the #2 Clement bus every day. I had to get up extra early for that!

While Jack was in high school, the martial arts film craze was in full swing. Bruce Lee, who spent considerable time in the Bay Area and Chinatown, was everyone's hero.

A couple of buddies and I went to the Y and we all signed up for Karate classes. Our main goal was to learn how to be "bad asses." Since we were already Y members, we got a discount on our lessons. After the first year, our instructor left the Y to form his own studio. I liked Karate enough that I followed him. I stuck with it from the ninth grade through the twelfth, and I earned a black belt. Once I started college, I sort of lost interest. I never really did anything with Karate after high school. Some of my old friends that I really became very close to while we were Karate students still call me from time to time to go watch a local tournament. As strong as our bond still is, I never go with them. I just don't think I could sit through a whole Karate tournament! I've been there and done that and the interest is just gone.

After High School I Just Went Along with Everyone Else

Jack followed the crowd of ABC high school graduates who almost all automatically signed up for admission to City College of San Francisco. One attraction of City for Chinatown families was that it charged no tuition. Also, many of Chinatown's high school graduates lived at home, worked in a family business or had part-time jobs nearby and could thus continue contributing to their family budgets. Once an ABC finished his or her two-year college core curriculum requirements at City, he or she usually transferred to State or Berkeley. While these four-year schools charged tuition, they, especially State, were not particularly expensive. As with City College, they were also close to home.

I didn't know where to go or what to study, really. I just went along with everyone else. I knew that the usual Chinese immigrant family would want their kids to be a lawyer, a doctor, or an accountant, so after City I went to Berkeley. I took science and biology classes so that I could get into medical school. After about a year, a friend who had applied to pharmacy school asked me to do it with him. I didn't even know what pharmacy school was, but I applied to UOP (University of Pacific) in Stockton. I was sort of surprised to be accepted. I graduated in 1973 to a fairly open job market in which pharmacists were in high demand. The small corner drug stores from when I was young were all giving way to the big chain stores

119

the likes of CVS, Rite Aid and Walgreen's. They all needed pharmacists and I wound up getting hired by Walgreen's. I stayed with them for forty years until I retired.

Judy Wing Lee
I Had the Freedom to Go Out with Friends

Like Jack Woo, Judy Wing Lee was always mindful to be a good daughter and be helpful to her parents in whatever ways they asked. Still, she recalls that she was able to have fun whenever she wanted to. She spoke about some of the teen activities she shared with her girlfriends in Chinatown and North Beach.

It didn't bother me to work for my parents in the sewing factory. It was just something I did because I grew up in a social environment where children naturally did what they could to help their families. I didn't get paid or an allowance, but if I needed something within reason my mom would give me money. Seeing how hard my mom worked, I was willing to help and never felt deprived. Sundays were set aside to sweep out the threads and fabric fragments in the factory. I hated sweeping underneath the sewing machines because I had to do it individually with a whiskbroom and on my knees. It wasn't mandatory that I had to work. I had the freedom to go out with friends once in a while, too.

After a long week at school and helping out at our parents' businesses and maybe even after having to go to Chinese school right after regular school and still helping our parents either at home or at their business, we were pretty ready to just have fun. I remember "fun" as mostly meaning that I didn't have to be somewhere or do something for anyone but myself. I would get together with my girlfriends and, having no responsibility, we were always laughing and acting silly. We went to a lot of dances around Chinatown. Victory Hall on Stockton Street, right where Jung-Wah Chinese school was, is a place that I remember had a lot of dances. We girls liked looking at the boys and talking about them, but a lot of the times we would just dance together - girls with girls. It was kind of a big deal to be asked to dance by a boy. It was even a bigger deal if we would actually accept. The International Ballroom seems

120

to be another place that I remember as a place that we went to for dances. More often than not, we would just go to someone's garage or basement, too. Even though many were popular back then, I was not familiar with the Chinatown bands or any of their members. My friends and I mostly danced to records or prerecorded music rather than live bands.

I recall that we used to go downtown to a store called The Music Box to buy the records. It was on Market Street and not too far from the Powell Street cable car stop. We could take the cable car for a nickel from Chinatown. A lot of times we just walked because we wanted to save our money. Like a nickel was such a big deal! Still, we learned to be frugal, or gu-hon, through the day to day behavior of our parents.

Anyways, at the record store you would take your record choices to a little booth and listen to them so that you could decide if you really liked any enough to buy. We often went to each other's houses with our 45 RPM records for 'jam sessions' and to learn and then practice the latest dances. I don't remember all the dances we taught each other but the Twist, Calypso, Jerk, Mash Potato, *and the* Bear Hug *or* Slow *stand out. Once we could manage the steps pretty well, we pretty much applied them to any of the then-current popular hits. One of my friends, Jean Lew (the one who was married to John Lum), was a great dancer, and we took many of our dance cues from her. Another friend, Irene Lau, used to bake cookies for us. I recall that my family was in the last stages of moving out of 1347A Grant Avenue and the entire flat was empty. We had a really nice jam session there with all the free space to do our moves in. When not dancing or hanging around together, we girls would talk for hours on the phone. We even crank called the cute boys! The last time I saw Jean was almost forty years ago. She had just given birth to a daughter. I still see Irene. She lives around the corner from me in San Francisco.*

I Was Able to Hold My Own

Judy remained in Chinatown until adulthood at which time she moved into the City's Richmond district. Working at California

121

Pacific Medical Center (formerly Children's Hospital of San Francisco) she found herself in a racially diverse environment. Although she did have to put up with some discomforts related to ethnicity or race within the neighborhood or at work, Judy does not consider any of them to have been especially significant. She does, however, mention that she sometimes used the stereotypes of Asian females as being "quiet", "smart", "hardworking", or adverse to 'troublemaking' to her advantage.

Coming across as a non-threatening Asian female had its advantages in my adult work life. The black patients (at Children's Hospital) *would frequently pull the race card when things didn't go their way although it very rarely came up when I was working with them. The black patients tended to treat me better than they did my white colleagues. I would also like to think that my colleagues always had a good impression of me because of the old stereotypes, and I used that to my advantage many times. I would shock them whenever I would break out of the mold to speak my mind.*

I didn't really feel much discrimination growing up as I didn't have much opportunity to venture out of the Chinatown/North Beach area... (and) I pretty much got along with the Chinese kids ... whether they were the new immigrants or American-born.

As an adult, moving out into the Richmond District, I did encounter a few racial bullies who used verbal attacks on me when they could not win an original argument. It never became physical ... I was able to hold my own to beat them down with my words, but I did pick and choose my battles for my own safety. In my later years, I decided it was best not to waste my time to stoop down to such a level, unless the bullies were picking on someone weaker.

Judy spoke about an incident that appears familiar to many a former Chinatown Kid whenever they find themselves any meaningful distance from San Francisco or the West Coast.

I remember about 40 years ago, my hubs and I were in Maryland trying out a restaurant a friend had suggested. When we walked in, all eyes were upon us as if they never saw a Chinese before. I felt uneasy. After we sat down, a scary thought crossed my mind ... These people could have killed us and fed our bodies to the crabs and no one would be the wiser! (Judy laughs aloud) - *we ordered, ate quickly, and left!*

As Judy has stated, living within the socially comfortable environment of Chinatown kept her sheltered from any but relatively benign racially motivated unpleasantness. Two other ABCs recall growing up away from Chinatown "in the avenues" as the Richmond and Sunset Districts are commonly called. Of the two, one endured some degree of racial taunting while the other did not. A third ABC who spent his entire childhood in Chinatown talked about some of his mother's attitudes towards non-Chinese people when he was in grade school. This ABC also revisits the time when he felt like an outsider while serving in the Marines Corps.

Flo Chin is about the same age as Judy and like so many of San Francisco's Chinatown Baby Boomers, she was born at the Chinese Hospital. Flo remembers moving from Chinatown to the Sunset District which is adjacent to Judy's Richmond District. She tells about an unexpectedly unpleasant encounter, much like those described earlier by Saki Lee, that took place when she was ten.

As a child I lived with my family in the heart of Chinatown on Sacramento Street. Without a formal education my father had to work as a waiter in Chinese or American restaurants. This eventually took a toll on his legs since he had to stand all day. As a result, in his later years he would suffer very painful leg cramps. My mom did her share by working in a sewing factory. Back in those days one was paid by the piece, and not very much at that. My mom scrimped and saved wherever she could. My parents worked every single day, seven days a week. They never had any leisure time. After I finished Kindergarten, my parents had finally worked long and hard enough to save enough to buy a house in the Sunset district.

For the next four years we lived among Caucasian families. The only person who drove was my brother-in-law; everyone else had to take the bus or carpool. I was in a carpool to get to Chinese school in Chinatown. One day when I was ten years old, I was waiting at the corner for my ride. Some Caucasian junior high boys riding on their bikes called out at me, "Ching Chong Chinaman, Ching Chong Chinaman." These derogatory remarks – which I certainly did not deserve – left me in tears. Years later I read books by authors that included Gus Lee and Amy Tan. In reading these books I was able to see that what happened to me when I was ten years old was part of a larger picture of prejudice.[38]

Virginia (Ginny) Owyang grew up in the Richmond District. She attended and graduated from Presidio Junior High and Washington High. The two schools are barely two blocks apart between 29th and 32nd Avenues and separated by Geary Boulevard. Presidio is now classified as a middle school. As a young man Ginny's father worked in his father's laundry in Redwood City. The laundry has been preserved and is today an historical landmark. Ginny's mother came to the United States in 1938, six years behind her husband. She spent a brief time in detention at the Angel Island immigration center out in San Francisco Bay.

Ginny's description of childhood life in the Richmond District does not include any of the type of racially motivated behaviors spoken about by Flo and Judy.

When my siblings and I grew up in the Richmond District in the 1950s and 60s there weren't too many Chinese families. Most of our friends were Caucasian until we got to high school. We had a wonderful time with our neighborhood and school friends just biking, skating, chatting, and having fun. We participated in after school sports and student government. Even though we didn't have much money, we never felt deprived. Of course, it was not all fun and games. We always helped out after school at my parents' grocery store and did household chores. As I became older, I also had many part-time jobs, one of them working as a gift wrapper at the Emporium Department store, and another at the San Francisco Opera House as an all-around helper. [39]

Harold Lee
"You Shouldn't Associate With That Kind of People, They Aren't Even Chinese."

Harold Lee [40.] spent his entire childhood close to or in Chinatown. He remembers a few of the earliest times where racial matters cropped up. They were not always directed at the Chinese by non-Asians.

When I was in the fourth grade, I sat next to one of the few Caucasian kids in our school. I don't remember his name, but I think it may have been Richard. I also think he was only in our school for about one year. He transferred in during fourth grade and by fifth grade he was gone. We sat at tables instead of individual desks so Richard and I worked, talked, played together and became friends. He was not from San Francisco. He lived with his younger brother and his divorced mother. His mother was always at work. She was gone to work every day before the boys got up, so she would leave them money for lunch and dinner. It was interesting to me that Richard and his brother could be alone until late every day. All my Chinese friends and cousins usually had extended families and were almost never left by themselves.

Richard told me that he and his brother lived near the produce market that used to be by the piers and the Ferry Building. They liked to play around the old piers on the Embarcadero because some were abandoned. Back then, abandoned places didn't have locks or gates or fences and kids from everywhere would find them and play there. Richard thought that one of the piers was haunted. He said that some old guy drowned there a long time ago, and his ghost was still around. They asked me to go one day after school, but I told them that I would have to ask my mother's permission. They said that they never had to ask their mother anything.

When I asked my mother about going to play with Richard and his brother after school, she commented, "He isn't Chinese." She then wanted to know where he lived and who his parents were and what their jobs were. I didn't know too much. I just told her what Richard had told me. She then declared, "No. You shouldn't associate with that kind of people. They aren't even Chinese." So, I didn't get to play with Richard.

Another time when I was still in grammar school, I said that I thought the lone African-American girl at school was cute and that I had a sort of a crush on her. That was met by loud expressions of surprise and derision from all my Chinese friends and classmates. "She's a 'hok guey' – a black ghost (as in not a real person)!" "Eeeewww, how could you!?" "Oooh, you like a 'see-you-gai!' (chicken cooked in soy sauce and, therefore, dark brown in color). Even though I have long forgotten her name I very much recall that she was always well-dressed, polite and friendly. I hope that the Chinese girls were nice to her because I think that she would have been a good friend to any of them.

Less than ten years later, Harold joined the Marine Corps. He would find his youthful idealism severely tested during his two tours of duty in Vietnam.

I admired President Kennedy, and by the time I finished high school the war in Vietnam was in full swing. I suppose that my strong sense of patriotism or my feelings of wanting to support the causes of my country led me to join the Marines in 1966. I just kept thinking about President Kennedy's famous quote to not ask "what your country can do for you but to ask what you can do for your country." Maybe being in ROTC at Galileo influenced me, also. I served two tours in Vietnam.

It was during my enlistment in the Marines and while I was serving my country that I had some first-hand and up-close experiences with racism. It was during my two tours that I really came to realize how others could feel so negatively about Asians. Fighting in an Asian conflict made it even harder for me to present myself as no different from any other American. I'm not totally sure how I made it through both tours in Vietnam because the second one wasn't too different from the first where my being Chinese or Asian was concerned. Well, it wasn't easy and it's still very difficult for me to think back to that time. Mostly I would have to look the other way, just take the heat, and play along with everyone. Keeping everything inside was painful. I was there just trying to do for my country, like President Kennedy had said, and I was being treated as an outsider. I didn't see that I could do anything about it but accept and tolerate it. I ask myself many times why did I ever join the Marines? I was naïve, I guess. I wonder what I would have done if I could have known before joining up how I was going to be treated.

Although Harold is reluctant to offer specifics about the words or the incidents related to race that most bothered him, there was a very common term applied to Asians throughout the Vietnam era: *Gook*. The term originated as a pejorative to use against the Vietnamese enemy who was also called VC or Charlie (for Viet Cong). Such usage typically served to belittle the enemy and thus could provide a slight psychological boost for meeting him in potentially life-threatening situations.

Practically all Asian American servicemen of the time have had the term used in their presence. In many cases apologies were quickly offered. *"We didn't mean you; you're one of us,"* or *"Hey, you're a good gook (or our gook), man."* A pat on the back or the offer of a cigarette often followed. The consolation was small, but it usually cornered the Asian American into quiet acceptance. Still, *Gook* was a unique term of prejudice that carried a double load of animosity for men such as Harold. It was the only word that, on top of being racist, had the power to imply disloyalty. Being outside the circle of the white majority for being Black or Latino was one thing. Those servicemen, despite a generalized disrespect by their white comrades for their differences of appearance and cultural behaviors and values, were nonetheless still allowed to be American. *Gooks* were primarily the enemy, so the Asian American, however subtly so, in addition to being "different," was also a possible "traitor."

Unlike the Black or Latino service members, Asian Americans were few and far between. The old strategy of "go along to get along" as adopted
by Harold was about the only recourse left to the targeted individual of Asian descent. Men like Harold, who were motivated by a sense of loyalty to the country of their birth, and inspired by a greatly popular and beloved president, were often left embittered,

frustrated, and deeply wounded.

Irene Dea Collier
"You Two Need to Go Back to Chinatown"

Irene Dea Collier remembers a trip to downtown San Francisco at the time when she was a student at Francisco Junior High and about 12 years old. It would have been in 1960 or 1961 when Irene and a friend from school went to the Woolworth's at the corner of Market and Powell. They both worked in a Chinatown curio shop and wanted to spend some of their money. Irene remembers,

We were hungry and thought that we would like to get burgers. We knew that there was a lunch counter in the Woolworth basement, so we went and took seats. Well, we waited and waited for service, but the waitress ignored us. Eventually an older man, maybe the manager, came over to us and said, "You girls need to go upstairs. You can't eat here." We weren't too sure of what was going on ... we were pretty young. So, we just got up and went on upstairs. There was a popcorn machine there and since we were hungry, we got some. We sort of thought that we had been told to leave because we were just kids. Years later I asked my friend if she thought that we had been kicked out because we were Chinese. She did not remember the incident at all. I tried to get her to remember, but she just couldn't.

Irene remembers another trip downtown with the same friend. They had taken the Number 30 Stockton Street bus through the roughly three-block long Stockton Street tunnel. Each end of the tunnel opened onto a vastly different world. At the Sacramento Street end was Chinatown. At Sutter Street was the bustling All-American center of commerce that was (and remains) San Francisco's downtown. The girls rode a few blocks further beyond the tunnel before getting off in the vicinity of Macy's. Irene says,

We were looking for a birthday card for one of our friends so we went into this little card shop. We were just looking over the cards when the proprietor came up and asked us what we wanted. When we told him, he said," You two need to go back to Chinatown for

that." At first, I thought it was maybe because we were kids, and he thought we were too young to do any real shopping. My friend understood, though, and she was pissed. She wanted to talk back to the guy or yell at him or even to cuss him out. I just pulled on her arm and told her that we should just leave. I also asked her about this when we were older, but she could not remember any of it.

Many Teachers Lacked Understanding about Chinatown

Irene found that racist attitudes towards Chinese youth continued even among some of her teachers at Galileo High School. She sensed that more than a few of the individual teachers' rants about the relative ignorance of teens and their generally limited worldview were more racially charged than might at first meet the eye. It was during the mid-60s and many Galileo classes were predominantly if not entirely populated by Chinese Americans, the majority of whom lived in or near Chinatown. According to Irene,

We were the first large group of Chinese students to attend Galileo. Until we arrived (in the fall of 1963) *the school was mostly white with many students being of Italian descent from nearby North Beach. Some of these teachers thought we were dumb or lazy, but we were from poor backgrounds. Even though our parents valued education they were so busy working or such limited speakers of English that they could not help us. The resources in Chinatown were also limited. We had the Chinatown Branch Library, but it simply did not carry the types of books and journals that would help us in a literature course where we had to read Kafka, for example. The teachers felt that we lacked initiative for not taking it upon ourselves to go find the resources necessary to support our studies. They also would yell at us to speak up in class: to participate. I think they assumed that our silence came from not knowing anything. There was no understanding that Chinese kids are taught to be quiet and to listen and to follow what adults or authority figures guided them towards. We weren't deaf or dumb; we were actually being respectful. I think that too many of our teachers at Galileo lacked any understanding about the limitations of Chinatown, our families, and our economic positions. A lot of us helped in the family by working or by doing things for the household while our parents worked really long and hard hours. There was no empathy from so many of our teachers. We were left pretty much to figure things out by ourselves.*

More overtly there was the drama teacher who never cast any of the Chinese students in the school plays. He claimed that we couldn't be cast because "we couldn't look the part." We might have been 10th graders from a closed community, but we weren't dumb. We knew what was happening. A lot of the Chinese kids began to grumble and complain and make open comments. The teacher finally seemed to feel pressured into accepting a Chinese actor. I remember it because the student was one of our brightest classmates. He was given a lead role although I don't specifically remember as which character, in "Witness for the Prosecution." *Maybe he was the cast as the judge.*

Then there was the case of the Homecoming Queen. The teachers who sponsored or supervised the homecoming events were surprised and upset when we voted one of our Chinese classmates for the role. To top it off, she was just a 10th grader. There were just so many of us Chinese in our class that there was no way this girl could get outvoted. The poor girl didn't even want to do it. She was embarrassed, I think. I don't blame her for feeling as awkward and out of her element as she did. You could tell by the way the teachers acted and talked that they weren't at all pleased.

On the other hand, there were teachers who were good about us being Chinese or non-white. There was one woman who always came in with her hair all a mess and her clothing disheveled, but she seemed to really care about us. She told us that we needed to broaden our horizons and to get out into the world. She knew that most Chinatown high school graduates would start college at City College because it was free. They would then transfer for their junior and senior years to SF State where a whole semester's tuition was $50 the first year I went there. If someone had money, they could go to Berkeley. Well, this teacher had graduated from Stanford, and she did not think that we needed to limit ourselves to City and State. She got a bus one day and packed us all on a field trip to Palo Alto. Some of us hadn't ever been that far from San Francisco in our *entire lives. Well, we all loved the Stanford campus. Inspired and encouraged by our teacher, a whole bunch of us applied for admission. None of us got in.*

I Was So Captivated!

Whatever disappointments she might have endured, life was not always disconcerting or harsh for Irene. She still enjoys reliving the joy of bus rides to baseball games at Candlestick Park 50 years ago. These happy memories occur most often during the baseball season as she has remained a life-long Giants fan.

Since I was comfortable staying home, I didn't go out very often which was fine with my parents. I did have a friend, Diana whose parents were pretty comfortable whenever the two of us would hang out with one another.

Diana's mother was pretty Americanized and she was a really big Giants fan. She always seemed to have tickets, or she always seemed to know how to get them. I think that lots businesses throughout the city, Chinatown included, always had cheap tickets for people to buy. Sometimes they were even free. Well, I remember that on a Ladies Day Diana and I got bleacher seat tickets for 25-cents. Then, for a nickel, we took the Number 15 Kearney bus that went from Chinatown all the way to Hunters Point near Candlestick. This was the first time I had ever been to a baseball game. I didn't know anything about the sport, but because Diana went a lot with her parents, she understood it really well.

So, we got off the bus before its stop at the Navy Yard which was still active then. We had to walk up this really long hill to the ballpark. It was, and still is an African American neighborhood and we had to walk by a lot of people's houses. I remember seeing these black men washing their cars with such pride as we walked by. These were the early 60s so the cars were big American models with lots of chrome and long bodies with tail fins and white side-walled tires. I still love that kind of car. Anyway, these gentlemen would always seem to be concerned for us: two little 12-year old Chinese girls walking with their brown paper bags of snacks up this big old hill. They'd ask if we were lost or where we were going. When we would tell them that we were OK and that we were going to the ballgame, they would seem to relax and they would smile at us and tell us to have a good time. I liked seeing these men and their families out by their houses. I sensed that they were being protective of us and that they kept an eye out so we wouldn't make a wrong turn or have anything happen to us. I just felt very safe.

My first view of the inside of Candlestick was so inspiring! It was beautiful! I had never seen such an expanse of grass as was on the field. It was so green and so neat and so perfect. It took my breath away. I loved all of it. And Diana was so helpful. She understood the game and would explain things to me. I came to really appreciate the subtlety and the nuances of baseball. There was the deception or the conspiracy between the pitcher and the catcher to do whatever they could to have an advantage over the hitter. And there was the strategy about all kinds of things like stealing bases or not, switching pitchers, using pinch hitters, moving fielders in certain ways. It was fascinating and it was lovely. I was so captivated whenever I would go to ballgames that I have even remembered to this day what the sky beyond the outfield looked like or how the sun would cast its light and create shadows on the field and into the stands.

Whenever I got home from a Giants game, my mother would ask where I had been. I would answer that we had gone to the park because I knew that she would think I meant Portsmouth Square or Chinese Playground in Chinatown. I knew that she would unquestioningly accept that because I had gone with Diana. Had she ever known that the park I'd gone to was actually Candlestick ... boy, she wouldn't like that!

Every Week Mom Would Take Us to The Movies

As children, you kind of don't understand why it was difficult; you just know that parents are always really tired. My mother's work as a seamstress took her to "che-yee" every day, and after dinner she would go back to the sewing factory and work until 10:30 or 11:00. But every weekend she would take us to the movies.

We would watch all kinds of movies: Cantonese operas on film, people in modern clothes, and "the Monkey King," But the thing she loved the most was the (classical Chinese) *opera. When the opera came to town, it was so special for her. She would talk about it; she would talk about "hai ai-hay"* (watching the grand opera). *I still can remember that five-year old child, going to the opera, and just the buzz and excitement.*

And people in the audience were eating melon seeds, and they were tossing melon seeds all over the place. They really loved to eat chicken wings, too. They would be sucking on those chicken wings and just watching the opera. They were so enraptured and captured by the storyline. Men and women both went, but I think these stories touched the hearts of the women the most because these are stories about suffering. These are stories about things that our mothers and grandmothers had all lived through in China. They were about things that are beyond your control and how the individual can rise above it and how the individual can be a hero or a heroine. And I think this is what captivated them.

In the Chinese movies there was always high drama. Everything was always going wrong for people in the movies. Landlords were ruthless. People had no voices in their government. And all kinds of terrible things would happen to all these perfectly nice people up on the screen. I remember watching all these women sobbing in the audience. And it did have a great effect on me. We always felt for our parents. We feel what they feel.

Tommy Lim
From Name-calling in Napa to Happiness and Love in Chinatown

It wasn't hard to spot our family in Napa. The ethnic makeup of the town back then was about 90% white, 8% Hispanic, and 2% other. My siblings and I were in the "other" category. In school we were usually the only Asian kids in the class. In fact, I never even had an African American classmate in any of my schools until I was in the 7th grade. Life for me in a small town wasn't too bad as long as I

133

wasn't noticed. I just wanted to fit in and be like the rest of the kids.

I will never forget an incident in the 4th grade when I was misbehaving and a male teacher called me a "dumb Chinaman" in front of the entire class. To this day I remember that exact situation and how I felt so terribly embarrassed. The other kids were laughing; all I could do was look down at my desk and awkwardly try to laugh it off. This type of situation, fortunately, did not happen often. However, during my youth I was called "Chinaman" more often than I would like to admit.

Practically all Chinese in America consider the term "Chinaman" to be among the vilest of slurs. They do not much differentiate it from other terms which include "chink," "gook," or "slant-eyes." All are equally and intensely offensive. Tommy could not understand why not being white or merely looking different in Napa could lead to such offensive name-calling. Such incidents left him wanting no more than to blend in and not be noticed. Tommy also remembers strong feelings of *"not feeling proud to be Chinese."*

Sports and Girls

Franklin Hom, [41.] currently a member of Tommy's church, the First Chinese Baptist Church in Chinatown, shares a few memories of his own youthful athletic and other endeavors in the North Beach and Chinatown neighborhoods. Although he is four years older than Tommy and had already graduated from Francisco by the time Tommy arrived at the school, Franklin describes some of the activities that Tommy and his circle of teenaged friends most certainly also enjoyed.

Franklin was born at the Chinese hospital in 1948. He remembers moving into one of Chinatown's *Ping Yuen* housing complexes with his parents and his younger brother when an apartment became available to them in the mid-50s.

We had a two-bedroom apartment on the fourth floor. I shared a bedroom with my only sibling and younger brother. The bedroom was not large enough for two twin beds so we shared a bunk bed, with me sleeping on the top since I was the oldest.

The *Ping Yuen*, or "Peace Garden" housing project, referred to simply as "the Pings" by Chinatown's ABCs, came about because by the end of World War II Chinatown's dense population was in dire need of adequate housing. The City had responded to calls from the Chinatown Community's leaders for new and affordable housing within the neighborhood. Their pleas were supported by their neighbors in the adjacent Nob Hill neighborhood who simply preferred to have the Chinese remain in Chinatown rather than to spill over into their part of the city. By the early and mid-1950s, three block-long multi-story public housing complexes had been completed in Chinatown. A fourth unit was finished in the early 60s. Applicants for the one to four-bedroom apartments were accepted based on family size and income level. While Chinatown's housing shortage remained a chronic problem, the Pings went a long way in meeting the area's housing needs. Franklin continued with his memories,

The backyard of our Ping Yuen consisted of a large concrete courtyard. On weekends and sometimes on weekdays I played kickball, baseball, football, and handball with the other kids. We never had any problems getting enough kids to play these games because there were more than 100 families living in the project. A lot of times friends who did not live in the Pings would come join us in our games. From this experience I discovered a lifelong love for playing sports.

I stopped going to Chinese school when I started high school. I finally had enough time to participate in school activities. I tried out for the school's light-weight basketball team during my junior and senior years and I was fortunate enough to start every game. In order to improve my basketball skills, I practiced whenever I could at the Commodore Stockton gym and at the Chinese Recreation Center where I also played for the basketball and volleyball teams. We played against teams from other recreation centers and playgrounds in the city. After high school I continued to play on various basketball leagues for a number of years including the Chinese Christian Union Basketball League. I finally quit playing competitive basketball at the age of 40 after I tore my left Achilles tendon playing in the church's 3-on-3 basketball tournament.

Franklin does not say if he ever played or practiced basketball at the Chinese Playground. The central Chinatown spot was renamed *"Willie 'Woo Woo' Wong Playground"* in honor of one of Chinatown's best known and beloved athletes. Willie Woo Wong played on the University of San Francisco Dons men's basketball team that won the 1950 National Invitational Tournament, or NIT. In those days the NIT was more prestigious than the NCAA tournament that has become such a huge event today. Wong was only five-foot five-inches tall, but former teammate and one-time UCLA head coach Steve Lavin said of him, "Willie was easily the most complete player we had on our NIT team in 1950." His nickname reportedly originated from the fans who would call out, "Woo! Woo!" whenever he scored. Lavin added, "He was scoring from everywhere, shooting from inside, outside. It became clear to me that he was very good in transition. He could stop on a dime and shoot that long set shot." His coach from 1948 stated that he was "… one of the finest passers and floor men ever to step up to college competition." Willie died in 2005 and was posthumously selected to the USF Athletic Hall of Fame. [42.] The playground eventually fell into the hands of gangs who disputed it in "turf wars" in the late 60s and early 70s. Even in the present-day vestiges of criminal and gang activities persist there.

In general, an athlete possessed of the prowess of one such as Willie Wong is a rare person. Many, like Franklin, are skilled, dedicated and enthusiastic, but few rise to true and broad fame. Mark Zannini, a close friend to many ABCs and a frequent visitor to Chinatown, remembered the following about organized sports at school and in the neighborhood.

When I arrived at Galileo in 1963, I entered a scene that was different from what existed in junior high. The infusion of White kids from the Marina and Pacific Heights and the African American kids from the Western Addition and Potrero Hill created quite a different social atmosphere than what I had experienced at Francisco. Cliques became more ironclad and sports, particularly football and basketball, became more important for establishing social standing and recognition within the school.

Because a large percentage of students at Galileo were Chinese, the student body was hard pressed to supply the school's sports teams with tall or bulky athletes. As a consequence, the varsity grid and hoops teams lingered near the bottom in the City-wide won-lost standings. On the other hand, many of the ABC young men were very talented athletically, and they made Gal's 130 and 110 basketball teams very competitive. There was a great deal of pride in Chinatown for the athletic standouts. The athletes could be seen working out at Chinese Recreation Center. I liked to play basketball but was a poor athlete. Another 'bookworm' type guy named Patrick lived in the alley next to Chinese Rec, and he invited me over to play pickup there. We played a few games of two on two. Needless to say, we got our clocks cleaned badly by the super quick guys who hung out there, many of whom played on the Gal lightweight teams. [43.]

Cameron House Where My Whole Life Would Be Changed

When it was time for Tommy Lim to move on to high school, one of his teachers at Francisco, Miss Fusco, recognized his strong academic potential. She encouraged him to attend what then as now was San Francisco's elite public high school: Lowell. Although Galileo was not far from Chinatown and the preferred school of most Chinese kids, Tommy took his teacher's advice to go to Lowell.

Although Tommy admits that he was well aware of Lowell's status as a very serious college preparatory school, he also admits that he got distracted. He did not apply himself to his schoolwork and his grades slipped. He missed the neighborhood ambience that he would have found at Galileo. Lowell was almost an hour away from Chinatown by public transportation and Tommy's commute involved taking a bus or cable car through Chinatown to Market Street. From there, he had to transfer to the M streetcar for a ride to the far western end of the city. Even after getting off the M car there was still a lengthy walk down Eucalyptus Avenue to the school.

One of the two highlights of Tommy's time in high school was when he got his driver's license as an 11th grader. Getting to and from school was no longer the ordeal it had been during the previous year. There were, of course, other automobile excursions unrelated to school that undoubtedly abetted Tommy's shortage of academic ambitions. The second highlight of his high school years came when he joined Cameron House. He and a friend decided to join at the same time and for the same reason: to meet girls.

My friends and I usually hung out at a gung fu club located at 880 Pacific Avenue, across the street from the Ping Yuen Housing Project. We were known as the "880 Boys." Our sifu, or master, was Wong Jack Man who supposedly once fought a challenge match against Bruce Lee. For a few years my social circle evolved around the gung fu club and going to youth dances around the Bay Area. That all changed in 1968 when a couple of friends and I decided to join Cameron House. This was the place to be at that time, especially if you wanted to meet girls. Little did I know that my whole life would be changed. At Cameron House, I was introduced to the Four-Square Program, emphasizing physical activity, Bible study, prayer, and service to the community. It was there that I was introduced to Christ. I saw the Holy Spirit in action in people who were serving the community as club leaders, summer day camp leaders, and community activists. It was also at Cameron House where I met Bonnie Toy. She was the only sister (the family has five boys) *of my friend Edmond, who belonged to the same Cameron House club that I did, the Sentinels. The Toys lived in one of the Pings and, thanks to Ed, my first date with Bonnie was on December 23, 1970. If there is such a thing as "love at first sight" then this must have been it.*

When we first met at Cameron House, Bonnie was still in high school and I had just started at City College. The youth leaders were typically high school aged members of Cameron House like Bonnie. There were not many college aged members like myself in that role, but I was designated as a youth leader nonetheless, and Bonnie was assigned to serve as my "mentor." Cameron House's was the largest day camp in Chinatown, and I quickly felt very special to have the young kids count on me as I led and guided them in a variety of activities. Bonnie, who was a veteran at all this, helped

138

me to learn the songs, games, and other things that I needed to know. Bonnie and I helped the young campers with arts, crafts, games, day trips, and talks about helping people. It was especially gratifying to put my own faith into action as well as to help the younger kids learn to appreciate how to be caring and giving as well. Bonnie and I worked well enough together that we gradually developed a strong mutual attraction that led us to our very happy marriage of 40 years and counting.

Tommy also met another individual at Cameron House, a student his age: Norman Fong. The two have remained close friends ever since. Norman grew up to become a Presbyterian minister and the current (as of 2018) Executive Director of the *Chinatown Community Development Center*. Tommy is on the board of the CCDC, and he and Norman continue to share passionate interests in the welfare of Chinatown and its residents and both remain strongly centered in Christ.

Years into the future, Tommy and Bonnie would often leave their daughter Kelly, then in the second or third grade, in the care of Tommy's mother-in-law. Bonnie's mother, who continued to live in the Ping Yuen housing project, would take her granddaughter to Cameron House where Kelly, like her parents before her, would make lifelong friends. Tommy is particularly proud that his now grown daughter has returned to Cameron House as a member of its board.

Sherman Wong
I Won Quite Frequently

Like the great majority of Chinese Americans his age, Sherman's junior high and high school years would find him increasingly influenced by mainstream American culture. While many had rarely or even never ventured far beyond the familiar and generally safe confines of Chinatown, 1960s America would come, blasting daily at them in the form of AM rock radio. The two stations most popular with youth throughout San Francisco in those days were KEWB (910, or, as it melodically advertised itself, "Channel 91!") and

KYA (1260). Those were the days of friendly and gabby DJs and call-in radio contests.

Sherman recalls the Woolworth lunch counter in a better light than did Irene Dea Collier, the *Music Box* listening booths that Judy Wing Lee and her friends also enjoyed, and good times with night-time radio contests.

When I would go downtown, I would go down Powell Street until it ended at Market. There was a big Woolworth's right by the cable car turntable and it had a long lunch counter. After having a Coke or a snack I liked to stop in at the Music Box. It was just around the corner from Woolworth's on Market. They had listening booths so you could test the records you wanted to get to make sure they didn't have scratches or that they weren't warped. They always had the KEWB and KYA lists of top hits, the Top-Ten, I think, taped in the window. They were mainly advertising lists to encourage people to buy certain records.

There was a contest on KEWB called "Name it and Claim it," where the DJ would play just a little snippet of a record, and if you could get through by phone to tell the title, you would win that record. I would have the radio turned down while I did my homework at night, and when time for the contest came, I would take a break and see if I could win. The trick was to know what time the contest was going to be, and it was usually at the same time every hour. I would pre-dial the number except for the last digit. You could leave the phone off the hook for a long time like that, and whenever the DJ announced the contest and played the bit off a record, I would dial that last number. If the line was busy, I would hang up and redial. I would repeat this until someone else got into the contest or until I got through. I got through a lot and I won quite frequently.

Once there was this contest where they played three bits of different songs for just the shortest time: maybe barely a second. The caller had to get all three to win a cash prize that got bigger the longer nobody could win. It was at more than $300 when I got through to the station. I knew two of the songs, but missed the third one. Off the air the DJ said, 'I shouldn't do this, but I'm going to tell you what

140

the song you missed is. If you get through in the future, you can win.'
A couple of nights later, I got through and won $330!

Another fun contest I remember was when one of the stations gave
away a car. I was old enough to drive by then and my family didn't
have a car, so I thought that I should try it. I remember asking my
dad why he wouldn't get a car. He just said that he couldn't do it
because "I'm too nervous to drive." So, the idea of the contest was
that over a whole month one caller per night could win the right to
get a car key that might start the car. I called in and I won the
privilege to a key. After the month, we all went down to the
dealership on Van Ness Avenue, or auto row, as it was called then.
We each picked a key at random from a box and whoever's key
started the car would get it. I didn't win, but it was fun to do. It was
a blue Dodge Demon, a sort of ugly car, but I guess I would have
taken it if my key would have worked. My parents didn't want me to
have a car while I was in high school, so it wasn't until college that
I got my first one. It was a VW Beetle.

Shame and a Deep Sense of Failure

Sherman met his first wife, an ABC, while they were both in college.
He was studying at San Francisco State, and she was attending City
College. They met through a Chinese student organization that
Sherman remembers as the CSIO, Chinese Student International
Organization, the primary function of which was to sponsor social
events such as dances, picnics, movie nights, and bowling outings,
among other activities. There was another group, the name of which
escapes Sherman, but he says it was more involved with community
affairs, Asian-American student concerns, and was even prone to
activism. Neither Sherman nor his wife-to-be were too keen on it,
however. When they announced their engagement, both families
were immediately enthusiastic. Sherman recalls the excited
anticipation shown by his parents at the prospect that grandchildren
would surely be not be long in coming after the wedding.

The wedding ceremony was a traditional Chinese one. Although
Sherman offered few details, theirs was a small affair attended by
few but the immediate families. The bride and groom simply

exchanged words, or vows that they wished to become husband and wife. After these mutual pledges, the tea ceremony was performed in which the couple knelt before the parents to offer their respect and obedience in the form of cups of tea. After they drank the tea, the parents offered blessings and gifts in the form of *lay see* and, for the bride, jewelry. In his brief comments about the wedding, Sherman said,

My first wife wore a Chinese dress, a red cheung-sam. [44.] *Even though the ceremony was a traditional Chinese one, I wore a rented tuxedo. The wedding banquet was held at the Four Seas restaurant and included 30 tables.*

Chinatown wedding banquets have varied greatly between being purely traditional and thoroughly Western. It would be reasonable to assume that in Sherman's case, it was a combination of both.

The marriage lasted six years and resulted in no children. Although divorce was neither as common nor openly discussed or acceptable in American society back then as it is today, it was, for the Chinese, among the most calamitous of fates that a family could be made to endure. Sherman recalls,

It was especially hard for me to have to split up my marriage for what I knew the family reaction would be. There would be shame and a deep sense of failure for my parents. Their lives had been devoted to bringing me up to be good son and my repayment to them was this shattering disappointment. As I expected, everybody felt terrible about it, but there was no yelling or screaming and no casting of blame onto me. The Chinese way is to be stoic and to internalize pain and suffering. Back then I didn't know of anybody else who had gotten a divorce. I felt very unique in the worst way possible. My dad had to go into work every day, and it was hard for him to see his coworkers and his friends. It was like he had a mark on him. He was stigmatized.

Through all that, I think we were at least a little bit lucky in one way: my wife and I did not have kids. At first it was a burden on the family. The tradition and expectation are that right after you get

married you should start making grandchildren. And it would be the absolute best thing if your first child was a boy. This grandson would be the one to continue the family name into the future. If we had had kids, I would have hated the problems and the hassles of things like custody fights and visitation rights and all of that. That would have been just one more thing to remind everybody about how terrible things were. So, it was ironic that during the marriage, something wasn't quite good or right because we didn't have kids, but after the divorce, it was good that we were childless.

The lingering shadow of the divorce's shame was finally removed when Sherman eventually remarried. Of his second marriage Sherman says,

My second wife is from Hong Kong and she originally came to the United States as a student. Her older sister was already enrolled in a biochemistry program offered by the University of Wisconsin, so when it was her turn to attend an overseas college, she also went to Wisconsin. It was convenient because she didn't know anyone anywhere else in the United States, and the two sisters could be together to help each other with daily living. There wasn't a lot of Chinese food available in Oshkosh, for example, so their family sent packages with all kinds of things that they could cook in their apartment.

Before finishing her undergraduate work at Wisconsin, my wife (to be) transferred to UCLA. By then she had found out that there were some other Hong Kong people that she knew in Southern California. I think that the cold winters of Wisconsin bothered her a lot. Anyhow, I met her and eventually we told my parents that we wanted to get married. This was in 1981. All of her family was in Hong Kong so, in those days before the internet and e-mail, she had to write a letter to tell her parents about it. Since this was my second time, we toned everything down and had just a few close friends and family for a small banquet at the Golden Dragon restaurant. The only family members on my wife's side who attended were her parents and sister. My new in-laws came to San Francisco from Hong Kong and my sister-in-law came from Canada where she had gone to work after graduating from Wisconsin.

It wasn't too long before the first of my two kids was born. Both were boys, so I think that once my first son, the family's first grandson, was born, my parents were so happy and so proud that it sort of made up for the whole divorce thing. The traditional red egg and ginger party for celebrating the arrival of a new child was held at the Celadon restaurant for my first son. The Celadon is located where the old and very popular Joe Jung's used to be on Stockton Street.

My Parents Preferred That I Be More Chinese Than American

As Sherman began to raise his children, who were separated in age by only two years, he weighed several factors about child rearing. Among these were his own upbringing, his wife's thoughts on the matter, and the social environment in which his small family was living. Thinking back on his own childhood, Sherman said,

My parents would have preferred that I be more Chinese than American. Even though we lived in the purely Chinese community that was Chinatown, it was still a part of the United States. In spite of there being so many aspects of Chinese life and culture there, American ideas and culture were also very strongly present. I think the biggest change was when I started school. Commodore Stockton is right in the heart of Chinatown but it was still a part of the San Francisco Unified School District. We were taught all the same things that any grade school kid in California or Colorado or Texas or Indiana or New York had to learn. It wasn't long before I started to forget how to say things in Chinese. The same thing happened to every one of my friends and classmates. So even though my parents desperately wanted me to retain the old traditions and not become the end of the line for the family in the Chinese sense of things, it couldn't be helped. The first and most powerful force that really changed things was the language barrier.

All during my childhood my parents never took time to explain the details of what we were doing to celebrate a traditional event. Nor did they ever explain why things were done as they were. As children we were just expected to go along, do what we were told, and come

to understand everything by rote over time. I could have asked questions, but I never felt a strong enough need to do so. I fully accepted my role as a child: stay out of the way, help when asked, and just do whatever it was that I was told to. By the time I was old and experienced enough to have questions, the opportunity to ask them had long since passed on by. Despite my prior fluency and my years of Chinese school, I had forgotten so much of our Chinese language dialect that I could not put enough vocabulary together to form a coherent question. That's how I lost touch with how to be really Chinese. I didn't learn enough about the old customs when I was really young and later, when I was losing my ability to speak Chinese, it was too hard to talk to my parents about them.

I think that as my parents watched me grow older, they understood that I was becoming more and more American. I did not openly fight or challenge my parents, but just gradually and not really consciously I changed over time. First, I was forgetting the language and speaking English all the time. Then I became less obedient and more questioning. They always allowed me to go out with my friends, but as I got older, I wanted to stay out later at night. It was no fun coming home at ten o'clock. They were being protective and they thought I might get in trouble or do something bad. Anyway, whenever they said to get home early, I would complain or argue that I didn't want to. Even if they didn't like it, I would stay out well beyond 10:00 PM. I was showing a form of independence that they would never have thought to try with their own parents when they were young.

So, when my two kids were growing up, I didn't put any expectations on them about being Chinese. I just let them be about it. I wasn't about to put them through the torture of Chinese school. I really never even thought about doing it. Besides, my wife spoke Chinese at home all the time. Even though she was from Hong Kong, my wife and I were in very close agreement about not forcing the Chinese heritage or culture on our two sons.

We observed some of the old customs, though. For example, my wife and I are very good and regular about bai-sun, *or honoring our ancestors. We go out to the cemetery twice a year, once in April and then later in October to pay respects to my parents in the traditional way. I know that there are maybe certain ways to do things that have specific meanings, but since I don't know the exact details, we do it mostly by the way I remember seeing the older people in the family do it when I was young.*

When I was younger, the main thing was for us to go as a family to the cemetery where our relatives, or our ancestors, were buried in order to honor them. [45.] *Sometimes the family brought food that we set up on a small table. If we didn't have a table, we would spread everything out on the ground on a blanket, almost like a picnic. We also put a few small cups of wine by the grave for our ancestors to enjoy. We usually used water instead of real alcohol. It was all the symbolic nature of it that really mattered. Then we burned some incense so that the food's spirit could go to our ancestors and keep them nourished and happy. We used to set off firecrackers, too. This was supposed to chase away evil spirits and also to keep the air clean and pure. Fireworks are illegal in California but the authorities in the Bay Area more or less let the Chinese set them off for things like* bai-sun. *We burned paper that represented money that the ancestors would need in the afterlife. Somebody said that the money could be used for bribes in case of trouble with bad spirits and things like that. Finally, we would light incense and, one by one, stand near the grave to bow three times as a sign of respect.*

The dates for bai-sun *are based on the lunar calendar, but my wife and I don't keep that kind of calendar at home and we depend on the cemetery to remind us. They send a postcard near the time and then my wife and I go. We used to take the boys to the cemetery, and we would burn the fake money, leave the cups of wine, and burn the incense. I always asked them to bow three times at each grave. My sons are grown now, and it's up to them what they want to do from now on. I will continue to do this, of course. I believe that I should honor my ancestors. I hope that my sons will remember about it, though.*

Then just like with bai-sun, *Chinese New Year was a large and important celebration for my parents and the rest of the adults in the family when I was a kid. I only remember parts of it, though. On the*

146

first night of the two-week long celebration, we always had a big dinner. It sort of reminded me of American holidays like Christmas or Thanksgiving, only in Chinese. I always had fun because I would get to see all my cousins and we would play together. And the kids always got lay-see from all of our aunts and uncles and other older relatives. We mostly got a quarter in each lay-see back then. Nowadays, I know parents who give as much as five or ten dollars. That's a lot. There was always a special dish called jai for the beginning of the New Year. You had to have it. It was vegetarian and a traditional dish of Buddhist monks. Then there was just about any kind of food possible: chicken, roast pork, all kinds of vegetable dishes, and more. People would also bring oranges or tangerines to each other for good luck.

When we were kids, we were always warned to be good during the New Year. We weren't supposed to say bad words or even to think bad thoughts. We had to be sure to behave so that our home would be blessed with good luck for the rest of the year. We would set off firecrackers to chase away bad luck and evil spirits. My mom made sure the house was clean and in good order, too. She decorated with flowers in a vase and burned incense. The flowers were a symbol of newness and the incense like at bai-sun, was for the ancestors.

We always celebrated Chinese New Year with our boys. Since I didn't understand that much about it anymore, my wife and I just did a basic version of it. Of course, my mother did a lot. It was fun for her, especially since my dad passed away very soon after my first son was born. He was already gone when my second son came along. I would tell the boys at New Year time, "We're going to Grandma's for dinner!" I kept it pretty casual in my mind.

5.
A Chinatown Photo Album
All photos by author unless otherwise credited

- A cable car at Powell and Washington Streets. Connecting it to North Beach, Fisherman's Wharf, Downtown, the Financial District and Nob Hill, cable cars have long been instrumental in bringing tourists to Chinatown.
- Post-war population growth led many Chinese families to find housing in neighboring Nob Hill.

- Practically every Chinatown kid got their first library card at the Chinatown branch library.
- One of Chinatown's three lookalike *Ping Yuen* housing projects erected in the 1950s. The primary concern of the Chinatown Community Development Center that currently manages the properties is to keep Chinatown housing affordable.

The Jackson Street *Medical Dental Building* opened in the early 1960s. Many Chinatown residents received treatment here. A former Chinatown kid said, "Any Chinatown Baby Boomer's pediatrician was probably Dr. Stanley Louie." Another added, "Anyone born at *Chinese Hospital* around 1945 – 1955 was likely delivered by Dr. Helen Chinn." The names of other Chinatown doctors of the time include A.B. Chinn, Grant Moy, Rolland Lowe, Serena Lowe, Margaret Chung, Rose Wong, Collin Dong and Lawrence Joe.

- The author, a former neighbor and playmate of Judy Wing Lee, stands by his childhood home at 50 Bannam Place. The alley is behind the 1400 block of Grant Ave.
- Recent migrants attend evening English class at *John Hancock* School.

- Jack's 1963 report card from *Francisco*.   *Last two photos by Jack Woo*

149

- Teenager Jack Woo sports the latest mid-60s American teen clothing and grooming styles. According to Jack, his two younger sisters, June and Joan "continued to honor the old traditions of China."
- Jack receives his grade school graduation certificate from his principal. Jack noted that she was one of the city's first school administrators of Chinese descent.

Both photos above by Jack Woo

- Stockton Street has replaced Grant Avenue as Chinatown's main shopping thoroughfare. Shoppers pick for the "best and freshest." Packed #30 buses lumber by.
- Chinatown's limited space has always made for small and crowded shops.

- No longer stacked in open crates on the sidewalks or displayed in built-in tanks whose thick glass formed seafood shops' outer walls, live fish are now kept in and sold from aquarium style tanks. Pans are still used for crustaceans and amphibians.
- *Kaye's* at Grant and Pacific is where most of Chinatown's Baby Boomers got their first pair of shoes.

Jeff Chinn recalls the *Grandview* theater and its upstairs apartments, "I occasionally give Bruce Lee related tours of Chinatown. Before moving to Seattle in 1959, Bruce lived on Jackson Street next to the *Grandview*. He roomed with a friend named George Long and they both practiced gung-fu as well as the cha-cha. George, in fact, was the California cha-cha champion. Bruce liked to get up early in the morning to go downstairs to practice gung-fu. After practice, Bruce would go over to a set of Chinese drums stored in a corner. He would bang away and wake up most of the building's tenants. After repeated complaints, George asked Bruce to please, stop drumming. Bruce simply could not resist and continued to drum after each of his practices. George was forced to evict Bruce!"

Jeff Chin

- *Ga-mo So*: The parental disciplinary implement (weapon) of choice

- *Du-buon gai.* Once called DuPont Street, Grant Avenue has never lost the Toishanese rendition of its original name.
- The *Sun Sing* theater offered Chinese films as well as live classical Chinese opera, or *dai hay*, performances.

The old *Grandview* theater as a fruit and vegetable market in 2018. Marilyn M. Chin remembers, "We used to live in the apartment building above the theater. Our parents' bedroom windows are on the right and our living room windows are on the left of what used to be the theater sign. When we went to the movies there, we had to go out to nearby shops for snacks. Except for a small and old popcorn machine the theater did not sell snacks."

Paul's Jewelry closed and shuttered. Michael Tam helped his father throughout his years growing up. Michael speaks about what he and many others experienced in family shops as the 50s and 60s yielded to the 70s and 80s. "I have lots of good Chinatown memories, but boy, things have changed so much that I don't even go back any more. I don't think Dad does either. The guy gave all he could, but at more than seventy years old, less than perfect health, and constantly rising rents, he just couldn't do it anymore. After a while he wasn't even making any money. We basically had to pull him out of that place. His last couple of years was just a donation to the community because he was losing money every month. It's sad that someone like him, one of the OG jewelry guys that knew everything about the business dating all the way back to his Hong Kong days would end up going out like that. And yeah, he and my mom knew everyone back then. They really gave everything they had to that business … and to us."

Drag'On *A' Go-Go* flyer from the 1960s. The club was located in Wentworth Alley. The alley was well known as "fish alley" for the pungent odors wafting forth from its many dried seafood shops. Mimi Chin Lee's husband, Lewis Chin, established the club. He featured bands that played Soul, Rock, and Rhythm and Blues for teens and young adults alike. A former patron recalls, "That old alley rocked on weekends!" As of 2019 Steven Lee is hoping to revive the club to an updated version of its once lively self.

Mimi Chin Lee

- The far end of St. Louis Alley where former Chinatown night club performer Pat Chin lived as a young girl. The end of the now enclosed alley once turned left and opened onto Grant Avenue. During the late 1800s and early 1900s the alley was where young women and girls were auctioned off either as prostitutes or domestic servants.
- A small shrine on a ground floor window ledge in St. Louis Alley. Offerings of incense, *lay-see* and a cup of tea have been left for ancestors.

- *Old Chinatown Lane.* A "charming," "must-see" tourist spots. Residents live daily life in its cramped single occupancy rooms and hang wet laundry on fire escapes.
- A traditional Chinatown funeral procession slowly makes its way along Grant Avenue.

Nam Kue Chinese School. Instruction was given in mainstream Cantonese that proved dificult for a lot of Chintown's primarily Toishan speakers to follow. Frustration and poor grades led many to drop out. One former student says that he even, "Wrote a proposal by hand to my parents on how much money they would save if they didn't force me to go to Chinese school where I would just cheat to get by, anyway. They warned me that I would regret leaving Chinese school. I did."

One rare student who enjoyed her time in Chinese school said, "I guess I'm the oddball. I really liked the two Chinese schools I attended. I went to *Nam Kue* for grades 1 thru 6 where I learned writing with ink brushes and Tang Dynasty poetry. Then I went to *Hip Wo* for 7th through 9th grade where I learned about the history, geography, literature and music of China, the latter in which I still indulge myself. As a language major in college, I furthered my education in Chinese. I can now read the ancient literature of China. Decades later, I'm still fluent in reading and writing Chinese and in spoken Cantonese and Mandarin."

Chinatown's *YMCA*. The *Y*, the *Chinese Recreation Center* and *Cameron House* are three institutions that offer safe and organized activities for Chinatown kids. Volleyball and basketball were always popular at the *Y*, but many Chinatown Baby Boomers remember it best for its large indoor swimming pool.

- Jack Woo and his two sisters at the *Chinese Recreation Center* during the early 1960s. The Center was renamed for Chinatown native Betty Ann Ong who grew up near the North Beach side of Broadway and Columbus Avenue. On 9/11 Betty was a flight attendant aboard American Airlines Flight 11. Betty stayed on the phone to keep ground controllers apprised of events on board her aircraft until the very end.

- Jack's mother Hing Woo and aunt Lan Ying Quon near the Woo family home in the late 1950s. *Both above photos by Jack Woo*

- Pat Chin (far right) with the *Chinese Vanities*, 1954.
- Pat Chin with "her pal" Frank Sinatra and Andy Wong, owner of the *Chinese Sky Room*. The club was used as a set for the filming of *"Pal Joey"* in 1957. Unfortunately, all those scenes and Pat's dancing were ultimately cut from the final version of the movie.

Both above photos by Pat Chin

- The *Grant Avenue Follies* with one of the group's original founders, Ivy Tam in the center
- Pat Nishimoto and Dennis Tom with the *Grant Avenue Follies*.

Both above photos by Frank Jang

- The statue of Sun Yat Sen, founding father of the Chinese Republic, in *Saint Mary's Square* where Raymond Lee often played baseball. The statue served as home plate. As a troubled youth, Bill Lee would go to the park in order to assault and rob the *hom-sup low,* or dirty old men, who sometimes hung out there.
- The aged and weathered plaque in *Saint Mary's Square* that commemorates Chinese and Chinese-American servicemen who lost their lives defending the United States in either World War One or World War Two.

- Waiting for the Number 55 bus at the corner of Stockton and Sacramento, 2018.

Chinatown was small and crowded. Everybody knew everybody else because we lived so close to each other. We worked, studied and played at all the same places. Our friends were like brothers and sisters and all our parents were parents to all of us. We often forgot that we were poor and that things could be hard. We were a community that stuck together. We helped each other make do.

Quote from Harold Lee

6.
Changes and Innocence Lost
Things Were Not Perfect Even Before the Chinese Playground and the Golden Dragon

In the mid-1970s a number of events, one being a brazen gang shooting at a popular family-style Chinatown restaurant, placed the neighborhood in the national spotlight. Named after the restaurant where it took place, the bloody incident was dubbed the "Golden Dragon Massacre." A nearby space that had long been a haven for innocent childhood fun and games, the Chinese Playground, had fallen into the hands of rival gangs who fought turf wars for its control. Chinatown, a popular tourist destination, if not a national treasure, had long been viewed by visitors and native San Franciscans alike as an exotic, interesting and fun place for shopping, dining and people watching. The neighborhood's residents were widely viewed as friendly, cheerful and model citizens. Crime, violence and guns in Chinatown were the furthest things from anyone's mind. Still, even prior to the 1970s such things were not wholly unprecedented.

Liz Wong [46.]
We Were Amazed to See Bullet Holes -- Lots of Them -- in The Walls

Burning trash cans and demands for protection payments as in the case of Judy Wing Lee's family *gai-chong* were not necessarily the worst of Chinatown's early baby-boomer era vices. Liz Wong described a 1961 Chinatown shooting at the Long Kong Tin Yee Four Families Association at 924 Grant Avenue. Liz's family had a small apartment in the building and she recalled that,

My family originally lived in San Francisco, but my father was transferred by his civilian job with the Navy from Hunter's Point Naval Shipyard to Mare Island Naval Shipyard in the late 1950s. It was too far to commute, so we all moved to Vallejo. The family included my parents and a brother and a sister. I have an older brother who was already an adult and working in the City as an architect when we moved. My father rented a small apartment in the 924 Grant Avenue building that also served as the headquarters for our family association, the Lews. We only used Wong as a convenience because our paternal grandfather was a paper son. My older brother lived in the apartment alone, but we would use it whenever we came down to San Francisco to visit family on weekends.

Our neighbor across the hall, Lew Fook You, was a bachelor that we were required out of politeness and respect to call "Uncle." One night in 1961 there was quite a racket. The noise came from upstairs and it was about 6:00 or 7:00 at night. The sounds were muffled, but we could still recognize shouting voices, thumping and banging as if heavy objects were being thrown around or knocked over, and a familiar noise that made us think of firecrackers going off. Between being scared by all the noise and being told by my parents to stay inside, we did not go out to see what was going on.

The next day, however, the three of us, my two siblings and I, who

were close in age and still in grade school worked our way upstairs to satisfy our curiosity. We quietly sneaked into the ballroom that served as the family association meeting place. It was nicely furnished with heavy Chinese rugs and sturdy teakwood furniture. The chandeliers gave off plenty of light so we could see. We were amazed to see bullet holes, lots of them, in the walls.

Being so young, neither Liz nor her brother or sister knew the circumstances of the prior evening's events. Many years later she came across an old clipping from the San Francisco *Chronicle* dated August 1961 which described what took place.

The blood of two "brothers" stained the escutcheon yesterday of Chinatown's revered Lung Kong Tin Yee – the Four Families Association – on which the words "Honor, Virtue, Stability, and Peace" have ridden rampant for 16 centuries. One of the association's brothers, George Kwan, 56, lay dead. Another, Peter Kwan, 52, Four Families Association president ... was in Chinese Hospital with critical wounds. And a third, Lew Fook You, 55, had vanished after turning a .38 caliber revolver on elders of the largest Chinese combined family association in the Western Hemisphere. Shortly after 1 A.M. this morning, Lew returned to his apartment at 1115 Stockton Street, where he was taken into custody. Officers said Lew whipped out a pistol when they approached him with guns drawn. They had to wrestle the firearm away from him, they said. The shooting, first in the local history of the Four Families Association in nearly sixty years, took place at the Association's opulent headquarters at 924 Grant Avenue. ... (P)olice received "excellent cooperation from the Four Families." Normally the association would have given Lew Fook You sanctuary, but because one member was killed and another wounded, the association wanted him captured.[47.]

Accessed by a street level entryway, there used to be a five-and-dime in the building's basement. Liz is not absolutely sure, but says that according to her older brother, the shooter was somehow involved in an argument with the victims about the store's rent. Liz's father only knew the shooter casually as a neighbor but, adhering to centuries old Chinese customs of kinship and loyalty, he would take his wife and children on regular visits to Lew Fook You in prison.

Our father told us that even though the shooter had done something wrong, it would be right and our duty to still call him "uncle" out of respect. He was, according to my father, a member of the Lew family just like us and families needed to stay together. My father did not really know the man that well, not in China or in the United States, but he was very clear and firm about this. He did not like it that the family association had turned its back on a "brother."

Dad even went so far as to drive us to San Quentin where Uncle was serving a 15-year sentence. We went to visit him because Uncle did not speak English and we were his only connection to his old world. My sister Laura was six and I was eight when we went to San Quentin for the first time. I remember sitting on one side of a large "U" shaped table with Laura, Mom and Dad. Uncle and other prisoners walked out and sat on the other side of their visitors. I don't remember seeing handcuffs or chains. Guards stood a few feet off in the background. My father did most of the talking. Laura and I would just answer any of Uncle's questions the best we knew how. We must have visited about two or three times a year over a period of several – maybe five, I think – years. I remember that Uncle once drew a colorful picture of some birds which he gave to my sister and me. The experience was a real lesson in life for me from my father. There can be no greater thing than the strength of family support.

Don Ng [48.]
We Ran Wild and Did Bad Stuff

Don Ng was born in 1954 at Saint Francis Hospital, in San Francisco. Saint Francis was the next closest hospital to Chinatown after Chinese Hospital. It remains located on Hyde Street between Pine and Bush in Nob Hill. By the mid-50s the population of Chinatown had grown to such a point that families began moving into the neighborhoods bordering it: North Beach to the north and Nob Hill to the west. Don was raised in Chinatown right at the edge of North Beach on Broadway and Powell Streets. The family home was on the street level of the entrance to the Broadway Tunnel. Living just across the street, Don attended Jean Parker grade school.

He then attended Francisco Junior High School and Lowell High School.

Don's family spoke Thlay Yip and came originally from Toishan. Don's father was born in the United States and his first wife was also an ABC. They had one child, Don's half-brother, who was born in 1928. Don described his father as a man who, in his youth, enjoyed a bit of the fast life by hanging out in Chinatown drinking establishments and nightclubs. Following his divorce from his ABC wife, Don's father-to-be travelled back to China where he married a younger woman who would ultimately become Don's mother. Due to the Chinese Exclusion Act then in effect, Don's future mother was forced to remain in Hong Kong. After the Exclusion Act was lifted in 1943, Don's mother was finally free to enter the United States. She arrived in San Francisco in 1950. Don adds that his father was a strict and ill-tempered man who forbade any language but Chinese to be spoken at home. He was quick to hit Don at the slightest perception of a misdeed. The father was chronically under-employed. According to Don he was too proud to sign up for any form of government assistance.

As Don was unhappy at home, his older brother helped him find a job as a way to get out of the house. The brother knew John Choy, the owner of the Union 76 Station on Columbus Avenue. It was located across the street from the landmark Bimbo's 365 Club. Just 14 years old at the time, Don was interested in cars and, wanting to learn about them, was willing to work for free. He wound up pumping gas, sweeping floors, and cleaning bathrooms. John paid Don a modest salary, however, and Don ultimately spent 9 years working as a mechanic at the station.

Don worked at the gas station during the mid-1960s and early 1970s. Its proximity to Chinatown led many of the day's ABC hot-rodders and motorcyclists – four to five years Don's senior – to hang out there. Don was impressed by their cars, apparent freedom and what he called their "coolness." The older guys liked Don and would give him rides and allow him to tag along with them which he immensely enjoyed. According to Don, they were mostly ABC hoodlums such as the Leeway Boys and the Junior Raiders. These groups, despite their generally tough appearance and demeanor and their propensity for troublemaking, were far less of a menace than their later non-ABC counterparts. These later gangs, mostly comprised of overseas Chinese who began arriving in San Francisco in the mid-60s, would include significant numbers of teens and young adults who had been toughened up on the streets of Hong Kong. Some even had connections to adult gangs and criminal associations there. One of the more notorious San Francisco Chinatown gangs with roots in Hong Kong was the extremely violent Wah-Ching that would become one of the Golden Dragon Massacre's participants.

According to Don,

I thought the older guys with their cars and their Harley choppers were cool. I was poor and didn't have much in the way of a family, so I liked to hang out with them. We ran wild and did bad stuff, like breaking into cars and stealing things, fencing stolen items, and doing drugs, but we weren't as violent as the foreign- born gangs that really got going in the seventies. The guys in my day who came around the station and sold dope sometimes offered me to get high on some of the 'heavy stuff.' I was hesitant about trying any of the hard-core drugs, and one of the station owner's sons finally said to me, '...ah, that's OK. You're probably better off not doing stuff like this, anyway .... better to make something of yourself when you grow up'

By the mid-1960s U.S. Government legislation had removed the long-standing restrictions against non-European immigration. Relatively large numbers of newly arrived Chinese settled into Chinatown. Unlike the majority of young Chinatown residents who had been born in the 1940s and 1950s, the newcomers were not connected to Toishan, but to Hong Kong and the areas of Canton Province adjacent to that city. Instead of the Thlay Yip or the Sam Yup from Toishan, they spoke Cantonese. Unfamiliar with American culture, they stood out in dress, mannerisms, and language. The teenaged students from among them, most of who attended Galileo High School, tended to stick together and speak Chinese. They appeared "uncool" to the American-born Chinese who began to call them "FOBs" for fresh off the boat and "China Bugs," or just "Bugs" for short.

Out of expedience, the newcomers, many street-wise and hardscrabble survivors of the tough Hong Kong environment, began to band together for their own protection. The newcomers proved to be more willing to resort to violence than the ABCs. By the time Don reached high school age, the foreign-born youth gangs had morphed into something much more violent and even deadly. Members of the ever hardening Wah-Ching settled into the three high schools most attended by ABCs: Galileo near Chinatown, Washington near the Richmond District to which a large number of former Chinatown families had moved, and Lincoln, in the Sunset on the south side of Golden Park where many former Chinatown residents had also moved. Don recalls,

When I was finishing up junior high at Francisco, some friends and I got together to talk about things. Our natural high school assignment would be to Galileo because it was the closest one to Chinatown where we lived. Well, by that time the Wah Ching were all over Galileo and we ABC did not want to go there, knowing that we would get our asses kicked. We applied for admission to Lowell. *We were lucky and we got in.*

Lowell is located in the far western end of the city, not far from Lake Merced, Ocean Beach and the Pacific Ocean. It is about as far as a student could get from Galileo which sits almost at the opposite end of the City, near Aquatic Park and San Francisco Bay. In the 60s, Lowell was looked upon as one of San Francisco's top academic public high schools. More than a few Chinatown parents and grandparents of the time were aware of Lowell's high academic standards and would encourage their children and grandchildren to attend that school. Don says,

I don't recall my knowing about Lowell being such an academic school. For me it was just an alternative to Galileo. We just wanted to get away from potential confrontations with the foreign-born gangs. Those guys didn't hesitate to use guns, and we weren't really into that. The ABC guys would "rumble," of course, but we didn't use guns to settle our differences. At Lowell the students were about 40% Chinese, mostly ABC, but some foreign-born, too. The rest was mostly Whites with a few Blacks and some Latinos, too. Sometimes we Chinese would almost get into a riot with the Whites. I mean, we didn't necessarily go looking for trouble, but if we – or they – felt that there was some kind of challenge, we would go at it.

Like so many of his contemporaries, Don began his college studies at San Francisco's City College. As he grew older, Don understood that roaming the streets looking for trouble would be a dead-end path. After high school he attended San Francisco State where he undertook a pre-med major before ultimately gaining admission to the University of California Berkeley where he earned a degree in engineering. Later, Don would enroll in and graduate from the UC Davis medical school.

Saki Lee
American-Born Versus Foreign-Born

By the mid-1960s life came with more questions and complexity for Chinatown's youth. The increased immigration into Chinatown raised feelings of disdain in Saki Lee and many of her friends and family towards the newcomers.

It was so strange that even though we still lived in Chinatown ourselves, we would refer to the immigrant children from Hong Kong who began to arrive in the mid-60s as Bugs and FOBs. This derogatory attitude was shared by some of our own relatives who, in their efforts to Americanize as much as possible, disdainfully thought of foreign-born Chinese as peasants who were simple minded, loud, and crude. Did I think that myself? Well, I never socialized with China or Hong Kong born kids. Even though some of my ABC friends had parents who never integrated into American life or spoke a word of English, we kids fell into the age-old trap of cultural discrimination. For us, the global conflict that was the Cold War had turned into a neighborhood conflict of the FOBs and the ABCs.

I remember the reciprocal animosity and disdain from the China-

166

born towards us ABCs. We were ridiculed for not speaking Chinese or knowing much about our culture, and they'd make fun of us by calling us nasty names in Chinese. By the time I was in high school, I no longer spoke any Chinese. My siblings and I were not sent to Chinese school and, despite living in Chinatown we had little contact, often by our own choice, with Chinese culture itself.

Unfamiliar with American culture, the newcomers stood out in dress, mannerisms, and language. The students from among them who attended Galileo High School tended to stick together and to speak Chinese. Those who spoke English did so with heavy accents.

Many of the new-arrival boys dressed in tight, or "pegged," black slacks and white shirts. They wore their hair slicked back. I don't remember how the girls among them dressed, but they presented what looked to me to be a deliberately less well-kempt look than other girls at school. The ABCs did not dress in any distinctive manner.

Saki Lee's Cousin [49.]
The Cafeteria Drop Kick

I remember a story that one of my cousins told me after we had graduated from high school. He was a few years older, but we were at Galileo at the same time for at least a year or two. I do not remember ever hearing about what had happened until he told me about it years later. I think that I am able to remember the story as well as I do because while in high school, I saw, felt and understood almost all of the things tied to the animosity between ABCs and FOBs that went into his narrative.

My cousin started by saying that there was a rumor, perhaps based on fact or perhaps a pure fabrication, that some of the Hong Kong girls made spending money by visiting the old bachelors in their tenement rooms on Kearny Street before school. Among other things, Kearny Street had long carried the reputation of being a hotbed of prostitution. The ABCs began to taunt those Hong Kong girls with the words, "Umm-mun-jee" which, meaning five-dollar bill, was quite a rebuke. It did not help their cause that the targeted girls never defended themselves with anything more than a smug glare. Our groups, ABC and FOB, were thoroughly polarized. Little was expressed verbally between members of the two groups, but even a slight glance by one towards the other raised tensions.

My cousin was in his senior year when a group of close friends that he delivered newspapers with were in their first year at Gal as we called the school. He was at lunch in the cafeteria with several of them. One of them, whom I actually knew, was named John. John was a short and stocky boy who wore horn rimmed glasses. According to my cousin, John got up from the table to get something. A flurry of motion and the sound of raised voices caught my cousin's attention. A group of about six FOB boys and two or three of their female companions were grouped around John. They were talking loudly and seemed to be on the verge of making physical contact with John. My cousin and his other friends could see that John, a quiet, almost "geeky" sort of boy, was in distress. My cousin hurried over, pushed John aside, and told his tormentors to back off. This request was met with derision and menace. They traded a brief and intense series of words. Suddenly one of my cousin's adversaries who appeared to be in a leadership role aimed a kick at his groin. My cousin dodged the kick. Then one of the girls threw a punch that connected. My cousin, for all the activity, decided that he could not hit a girl, so he slugged another of the boys who was rushing at him. My cousin then saw the boy who had kicked at him. He did something that I remember from watching wrestling on TV. He gave the guy a running drop kick to his chest which toppled him against a trash can. The fight ended at that point when adult supervision stepped forth, and the little gang of FOBs ran out a door.

My cousin was sent to the office, but the dean of boys believed and sympathized with his story. He just told my cousin to go on to class and not get into any more fights.

The fight turned out to be a pretty minor thing. Nothing happened after that and my cousin said that he does not remember ever running into any of the people he was fighting with ever again. I think that if this had happened just a few years later, like in the late 1960s or early 1970s things could have gotten bad. The newer immigrants had real gangs by then and they were into some pretty heavy stuff.

In a subsequent discussion of the cafeteria fight, Saki's cousin added the following,

I went back to class and sat at my assigned seat at a table for four. The other three students were an Italian-American girl, a Chinese girl from Hong Kong and a boy named Martin. I don't remember the girls' names and Martin was a recent immigrant. Martin and I got along well in class and, because he struggled with English, I helped him with classwork a lot. I even used to let him copy off of me for tests. I admired him because he lived with his widowed mother who was either handicapped or sickly. He couldn't participate in extracurriculars or weekend activities because he was always helping his mom.

Everyone in the class knew about the cafeteria scuffle. The teacher even made a joking comment about it. As soon as he had a chance, Martin whispered to me to tell him what had happened. I told him, but I cut out a lot of details. I didn't want to say who I had gotten into the fight with because I thought he might get upset. I liked Martin and I didn't want to jeopardize our friendship.

The Italian girl liked to tell me how cute she thought the Chinese girl at our table was. I never really thought much about it and would always just brush her comments off. The Italian girl would say things like, "You should get sweet on her," or "Just talk to her; wouldn't you like to go out with her?" Well, even though I didn't have a girlfriend or anything then, I just wasn't that interested. I mean, she seemed like a nice enough girl, but she was an FOB. [50.]

I Knew I Wanted Out of Chinatown: Bonnie Lim [51.]

As Don Ng, Saki Lee and others have said, the Chinatown of their youth evolved as the 60s ended and the 70s began. Teenaged scuffles in the school cafeteria gave way to more serious things that reached into the streets. Sometimes backed by criminally-minded adults operating from as far away as Asia, some Chinese youths became fully immersed into gangs and gang-related violence. Vendettas, honor-killings and murder encroached upon Chinatown in ruthless and bloody fashion. The weapon of choice was the gun. The neighborhood where everyone once knew everyone else and where doors were not often locked began to make news headlines that announced increasing crime and violence.

Bonnie Lim, who grew up with her brothers in one of the Ping Yuen developments, was walking through Chinatown one day in the early 1970s when she witnessed something that emphatically demonstrated Don Ng's previous comment that, "… those guys didn't hesitate to use guns."

Once when I was on Stockton Street across the street from Victory Hall, I heard what I thought were car tires popping. Curious, I walked over to see why a bunch of boys was running from the scene. It utterly shocked me to see my first murder victim, a 16-year old boy lying in a pool of blood. My knees buckled and I almost fainted. Weeks following, another boy was shot and killed at the Ping Yuen Housing Project where we lived. Witnessing these acts of violence, I knew I wanted out of Chinatown.

The shootings were likely related to rival gangs contesting control of firecracker sales activities. Long gone were the days when grade school boys roamed Grant Avenue in order to sell small packs of "Black Cats" and "Rockets" for a quarter each out of brown paper sacks to tourists. A few years after seeing the killing, Bonnie married her high school sweetheart, Tommy Lim, who was enrolled in optometry school in Chicago. She moved to be with him. She and Tommy later returned to California where they established and continue to have an optometry practice in San Jose.

Raymond Lee [52.]
The 1977 Golden Dragon Massacre and Beyond

In the early morning hours of 4 September 1977, members of the Wah Ching gang were dining at the Golden Dragon restaurant located in the heart of Chinatown. Members of a splinter gang, the Joe Fong Boys, walked in with a rifle, a revolver and a pair of shotguns. The two gangs had been at violent and, at times, fatal odds since the late sixties. This time the Joe Fong Boys were seeking to settle a score from two months earlier. Back in July a shootout over firecracker sales had left a Joe Boy dead and two wounded.

The Joe Boys opened fire. Four innocent diners and a waiter were killed. Eleven others were wounded but not a single gang member was shot. The San Francisco Chronicle called it "San Francisco's Worst Mass Slaying."

Raymond Lee lived with his younger brother and parents in an apartment above one of the family's two shops, *Kuen Luen* Company at 530 Grant Ave. Raymond and his brother, 10 years apart in age, were first-generation ABCs who had been born at Saint Francis Hospital. Raymond's parents had arrived separately in San Francisco as students from Taiwan in 1959. They eventually met, married, remained in San Francisco and became naturalized American citizens. The family, unlike the majority of Chinatown's Toishan descendants, spoke Mandarin at home. Raymond spent several years studying at the afternoon Chinese school at St. Mary's on Stockton Street near Clay where he learned Cantonese. St. Mary's was also Raymond's elementary school. After grade school Raymond attended Francisco Junior High and went on to Sacred Heart for high school. Chinatown was Raymond's world and he, like Allen Leong and Judy Wing Lee, recalls it fondly as the ideal place in which to grow up.

The entrance to our upstairs living area was next to the 540 Grant Avenue shop. My parents and brother occupied the third floor which had two bedrooms facing St. Mary's Square just across from the alley at the back of our building. The third floor also included an eat-in kitchen, walk-in closet, water closet (toilet only) and separate shower room. I was on the second floor where my bedroom, at the building's front, faced Grant Avenue. Our laundry room with washer and dryer was also on my floor as were a wash room, water closet and two spare rooms that we used to store stock for the shops. The wash room had a window which faced Saint Mary's Square.

We didn't have a back yard, of course, but we had Saint Mary's Square where my brother, friends and neighborhood kids would spend hours and hours playing. We played baseball with the steps of the tall Sun-Yat Sen statue as home plate. We also would go a few blocks to the Chinese Playground where there were sand boxes and playground equipment. It also had an adjacent basketball court where we engaged in pick-up basketball games for hours on end. Whenever we finished playing, we would dash off to any of a great number of places to get our favorite things to eat. My personal favorites included the house special chow mein and the deep-fried battered chicken drumsticks from Joe Jung's at the corner of Clay and Stockton, Coffee Crunch Cake from Eastern Bakery and steamed pork buns, or cha-siu bow, from Yong Kee on Jackson Street. Life was simple, fun and hassle free!

It was during his sophomore year at Sacred Heart when Raymond, watching the evening news on television, learned of what has since been called the "Golden Dragon Massacre."

Raymond remembered,

I was a high school sophomore who had just been given the responsibility of running my parents' Kuen Luen gift shop after school hours and on weekends. They also owned K.L. Art Co. at 540 Grant Avenue. I was shocked by the news and could not understand how anything like that could possibly happen so close to home. I also felt a deep sadness for the people who had gotten killed or injured. They just had to be at the wrong place at the wrong time. I remember feeling how awful it would be on their families.

My parents used the incident as an example for my brother Oscar and me of what happens when a teenager got mixed up with gangs. They reminded us that there could never be any good that would come from such pursuits. We did not feel that they were overly protective or that they were always watching us; they just wanted us to stay on the straight and narrow. One of the reasons my brother and I went to Catholic schools was that my parents wanted to make sure that we would not have contact with gangs or any other undesirable elements. Like so many Chinatown parents, mine were typically conservative with their children. As for myself, by the time I had started high school I figured that the best path to a good life and career was to focus on my schoolwork. With or without our parents' concerns neither my brother or I had any interest in gangs at all.

I never really even knew of anyone who was a gang member. There were a couple of classmates or neighborhood kids who my friends and I sort of suspected were gang members, but we had little to do with any of them. These particular people seemed to mainly want to be "tough guys." They would talk down to their classmates, vandalize their school lockers or pick fights. They dressed in black, wore bomber jackets and favored brand-name sneakers. Most did not openly challenge authority figures and, to my knowledge, did not carry weapons to class. This fact made the killings at the Golden Dragon all the more shocking to me. Firearms and their use were very foreign to me. Before the massacre the illicit activities perpetrated by the Wah Ching, Joe Boys or others occasionally made headlines, but otherwise had minimal or no impact on Chinatown residents or businesses. What happened at the Golden Dragon changed everything.

By the end of September, the Chinese Chamber of Commerce estimated that business throughout Chinatown had fallen by over half. The Chamber urged the police to quickly make arrests and to do what it could to ensure order. Ironically, it was the same Chamber and more than a few Chinatown business owners who five years earlier requested a soft approach to any similar Chinatown problems. Prior police sweeps of the neighborhood to forestall fights and prevent violence had been deemed as "bad for business" and, thus, were scaled back.

Immediately after the Golden Dragon shootings rewards of up to $100,000 were promised for any information that would lead to arrests of any persons responsible. A new 20-man Gang Task Force was implemented by the SFPD. Eventually all key perpetrators were caught, tried and imprisoned.

Raymond continued to express his personal reactions and thoughts about the Golden Dragon Massacre and its effects on the Chinatown community and on his family.

The impact of the massacre was keenly felt almost immediately. Both the local and national media covered the aftermath of the mass shootings almost daily. The torrent of gangland activities preceding and following the massacre was seen as a blight on the community, so much so that the SFPD established an Asian Gang Task Force to curb organized crime. Despite this, Chinatown was now regarded as too dangerous for tourists and locals to frequent. In the weeks and months to follow, Grant Avenue was a proverbial ghost town devoid of even casual browsers during the height of tourist season. My parents became ever more frustrated as they struggled to make ends meet due to the downturn in business for the rest of 1977 and all of 1978.

Over the next few years some of the merchants remained guardedly optimistic that their commercial ventures would return to the same levels as before the massacre. They never did. Even as the police and city politicians took credit for the eradication of local gang activities, the damage had been done. As fewer tourists came, the shops and restaurants cut back their operating hours. For example, the Golden Dragon used to stay open until 3:00 AM, but after the massacre it would close at 10. Outsiders no longer considered Chinatown as a clean, safe, if also a somewhat intriguing place to hang out. Instead many were reminded of a seedier past of dingy and smoky gambling joints or opium dens; the Tong wars of the late 19th and early 20th centuries and the scandalous sexual exploitation and trafficking of women and girls from China.

Renovations and upgrades to properties in the financial district and downtown resulted in an influx of new and lucrative businesses to those parts of the city. This exacerbated the ongoing loss of income related to gang activities by pushing up real estate values in Chinatown. By the mid-1980s a lot of Chinatown business operators quit because of rising rents. Those who, like my parents, hung on were forced to reinvent their shops. My parents could no longer survive on the inexpensive t-shirts, Japanese-made porcelain figurines, gilded lacquer boxes, silk kimonos miniature cable cars and post cards that had been staples of the neighborhood's tourist-oriented business for so many years. To meet ever-increasing overhead costs my parents turned to stocking a more "high-end" type of merchandise that tended to be heavily weighted towards jewelry fashioned from cultured pearls and semi-precious stones. Although profit margins were higher with the new merchandise, turnover was lower. Our stores tried to adapt by carrying goods that catered more to locals such as the nearby office workers who daily passed through Chinatown to and from work or on their lunch breaks. We began to stock things for home decorating like wall hangings, and silk embroidery. We also capitalized on the fashion preferences of the so-called hippie movement and turned to selling Native American silver and turquoise rings and bangles, brightly colored plastic bead necklaces and a wide variety of rings and bracelets.

My parents' shops as well as those of our neighbors had also become targets for extortion. In-person verbal threats of personal harm to shopkeepers or of damage to their property were made by teenaged Asian toughs. Our neighboring shop owners would drop by from time to time to talk about such confrontations. They also stopped by to commiserate whenever a fellow business owner had been shaken down or robbed. They collectively appealed for better and increased police support against extortion and overnight smash and grabs. Police foot patrols were made more frequently. Practically all businesses throughout Chinatown installed burglar alarms and roll-away metal gates. No such security measures had ever before been needed or used anywhere in the neighborhood.
I was personally confronted in Kuen Luen on two separate occasions. One afternoon a 16 or 17-year old Asian male entered the store and faced off against me. He appeared to be operating alone. He acted very nervous and whispered to me that he had a gun. He sounded more like an ABC than a foreign-born Chinese. He demanded that I open the cash register and hand him all the money. I did as he said. After he left, I called 911 and filed a police report. I felt victimized and helpless. Despite providing as detailed a description as I was able to, the perpetrator was not caught.

About three weeks later he returned. I had been mentally preparing myself for such a thing, and when I saw him, I steeled myself. He made similar threats and demands as he had earlier, but I stared him down. I addressed him directly and purposefully. As I called loudly for help, he got scared and quickly left. I did not bother with a police report and he never came back. In retrospect I am pleased that I was able to remain level-headed and calm. After thinking about the would-be stick-up guy for a while, I concluded that he was pretty much an amateur and small time. Judging by his nervous demeanor I surmised that he might have been pulling the robberies under orders of a senior gang member. He may have also been undergoing some sort of gang initiation rite.

Even discounting the impact of gang activities in Chinatown, time would not stand still and other changes occurred that affected me, my family and our Grant Avenue shops. Rents rose at a rate that outpaced normal inflation and our ability to make enough in sales to keep up. When we first opened in the mid-1960s, our rent was about $500 - $550 per month. It doubled in the 70s and by the 80s it had doubled again.

In those days of $2,000 monthly rents many of our friends and neighbors sold off and left. The old-timers moved into what we called "the Avenues," or the Sunset and Richmond districts on either side of Golden Gate Park. My parents operated in the red during the early 80s and sold out from Kuen Luen in 1983. By then I was in college at San Francisco State. I spent less time helping out to dedicate my time to study. My parents, now helped by my brother, hung on at K.L. Art Company and operated in the red over its last several years. They sold it in 1991.

The vacuum left by the long-time resident Toishanese merchants and their families began to fill up with new arrivals from Hong Kong, Taiwan and Mainland China. Toishanese, once the "native language" of Chinatown, gave way to Cantonese and Mandarin. The business people among the new arrivals came with a lot of retail experience and a lot of money to invest as well. They moved into the old-timers' places, renovated them and stocked them with high-end and pricey inventory. Some of the new jewelry shops had display

176

windows that featured gaudy and blinding displays of gold and jade such as Chinatown had never before seen. The hardy or stubborn holdovers from my parents' time could not compete with them.

I remained at State from 1980 until 1985. I finished with a bachelor's degree in Psychology and spent another three years to earn a Master's degree. Since my brother was helping my parents in Chinatown, I spent my senior and graduate student years working at State. I spent time employed in the campus bookstore, the university library and as a graduate teaching assistant. I then left San Francisco to go to Detroit where I would spend the next six years to earn my PhD and as a post-doctoral fellow at Wayne State University.

Whenever returning to Chinatown, though, I ponder the fate of the establishments and people – friends and neighbors – of the old days. Grant Avenue has been dramatically transformed from what it was in the days of Kuen Luen and K.L. Art Company. There are more non-Asian businesses and there seem to be homeless persons on each block from one end to the other of the street. Two decades ago, Chinatown's language was largely Toishanese with some Cantonese. Now it is Mandarin with smatterings of numerous other minority Chinese dialects which I mostly do not recognize. The neighborhood's cuisine has gone from flavors such as those of roast pork (cha-siu and faw-yuk), soy sauce chicken (see-yew gai), chow mein and other Cantonese fare to include signature dishes from Szehuan, Hunan, Shanghai and Xi'an. On each visit I encounter ever less of the old familiar things I have always loved so much.

Each time my grade school friends and I gather together our conversation revolves around how much our old neighborhood has changed and how we so terribly miss the Chinatown in which we grew up. I think that I took much of my life in Chinatown for granted. The levels of urban decay and crime in Detroit easily eclipsed anything that I had seen at home. Finished at Wayne State, I moved to Winnipeg, Canada in 1991 and, like Detroit, it offered yet another stark contrast to my old neighborhood. Winnipeg's staid and placid lifestyle was so distinct from the colorful hustle-bustle of old Chinatown. I was fully aware of the changes that had come to my

177

old home neighborhood, but I still missed it. Settling into my second home in Saint-Denis, an historic, ethnically and culturally diverse town about five miles north of Central Paris, France, I finally found an ambience that was much closer in sights, sounds and flavors to the Chinatown of my memory. Saint-Denis' central district is alive with energy, crowded day and night, chock-full of mom-and-pop shops, produce and meat markets and all manner of bistros, cafes and restaurants. All of this is a mere five-minute walk from the apartment my wife and I share.

Bill Lee's Memoir [53.]
Chinese Playground is Still Contested Turf

Bill Lee, a native son of Chinatown, published his memoirs in 1999. The book, *Chinese Playground: A Memoir,* was initially released in March 1999, and Bill gave a book talk that same year through the San Francisco Public Library. In a little over an hour Bill, spoke about his younger days and his gang affiliations, read excerpts from his book and responded to audience questions. Lee was steadfast and consistent in stating that his hope for the book was to have it educate readers and steer them away from the type of activities and life that he once so intimately knew. In efforts to reach as many youths as possible, Bill has also visited many San Francisco schools to talk about his life and his book. He additionally has provided counseling to serious juvenile offenders in San Francisco and Marin County.

During his library presentation, Bill stated that Chinatown's gangs operated largely through tactics of fear and secrecy. He added that because he had once been an insider, publishing the book had put him in violation of the gravest of all taboos. He had revealed the inner workings of, among others, the Joe Boys, his former gang and the perpetrators of the 1977 Golden Dragon Massacre. He had ignored the sacred terms of loyalty and secrecy to which he had once been sworn. Now both Bill and his son were receiving threats and Bill's public appearances, the library talk included, were being monitored by the police. Nonetheless, as he spoke, Bill made an open call to gang members, actual or potential, to "break the pattern and to share what was going on" and to turn their backs on the processes of "recruitment and of victimization."

When he was a child Bill's mother was often away from home to labor long hours in a *gai-chong*. His father; whom Bill stated was a gambler, alcoholic and womanizer, worked as an herbalist and practitioner of traditional Chinese medicine. The father, born in China, had been sold as a very young child to a barren couple. He was eventually brought to San Francisco as a paper son. Having been married twice before, Bill's father was back in China when he took an 18-year old bride in an arranged marriage. The couple arrived in San Francisco in 1949, and Bill was born out of the union in 1954.

Not wanting children, Bill's father had concocted a formula for his wife to drink in order to terminate her pregnancy with the child who was to become Bill. When it did not work there was talk of selling the child as the father had been sold years earlier back in China. Bill speculated that his father possibly harbored some regret and did not see the plan through. Once born, Bill grew up with an often-drunken father who took his frustrations out on Bill in the form of routine beatings. Bill's older brother also administered beatings to both Bill and their sister. The family lived in a small and cramped apartment in a building on the corner of Washington and Stockton streets. Bill said that from a very early age he clearly "sensed not being wanted."

At the age of five, Bill was shining shoes on the streets of Chinatown. He tended to hang out at St. Mary's Square Park, across California Street from Old Saint Mary's church and behind Raymond Lee's family shops. The standard charge was a dime, but generous or satisfied customers often rewarded Bill with a quarter. The downside of the little park, according to Bill, is that it was there that he learned to be street tough: to fight and to steal. There was also danger from lurking *hom-sup low,* or dirty old men who favored young boys. In collusion with older boys, Bill learned to bait these men and then jump them and rob them. Not even old enough for school, Bill had already begun to master the art of "hiding emotions and masking vulnerabilities" in the rough and tumble confines of St. Mary's Square and the Chinese Playground. By the time he was in the second grade, Bill and two friends from Hong Kong frequently talked about running away.

The Wah Ching, rivals of the Joe Boys to which Bill would become a member, dominated the Chinese Playground of Bill's childhood. Whenever Wah Ching members entered the playground, everyone else would quickly yield space to them. Basketball games would end as players vacated the courts for the convenience of the Wah Ching. The gang also had clubhouses further down on Clay Street across from another popular recreation spot, Portsmouth Square. Bill wanted to get close to the gang, but quickly became disconcerted by what he called their ubiquitous tendency towards hidden agendas. No favor, however small, tendered by the Wah Ching could be expected to go unpaid. There was always the unspoken expectation that, sooner or later, one had to make good on everything.

Bill recalled a time when he was at the Sun Sing movie theater on Grant Avenue. He had become a hard-core aficionado of the kung-fu films that played there. The Sun Sing had become Wah Ching turf, and during a film, about 15 of them called on a lone individual to meet with them outside. Bill watched the individual get up to follow the gang members but, before exiting, they jumped him. They methodically beat him and took turns cutting him with broken bottles. The film continued to run, patrons got up and hurriedly left, but neither management nor police came to intervene. The victim managed to limp away. Twelve-year old Bill, who said that the scene remained with him for a long time, stayed to watch the movie. Bill spoke about his disappointment at his own weakness. He later listened in at the Chinese Playground as gang members would brag about robberies, beatings that they administered and how they could get free meals at restaurants for just walking in and taking a seat.

Bill remarked that for many youngsters in Chinatown the presumed benefits of having hardworking parents were offset by their continual absence and the resultant lack of supervision. Left to their own devices many would fall under the influence of gangs and the allure of seemingly easy money, flashy cars, access to plentiful supplies of material goods and sex. Low self-esteem and resentment at his home life gradually led Bill to cast his lot with the Joe Boys whose urges for power were served by the gun. Firearms were even given as prizes to promising young gang affiliates. Bill reckoned that shootings were relatively easy in Chinatown. The streets were always busy and crowded. A gang member could walk up to a guy, shoot him and then run into the ever-present crowd. There would be nobody bold enough to try to stop him or to later identify him to the authorities.

Bill's gang days ended with the Golden Dragon shootings. Although a member of the Joe Boys, Bill was not present that early morning. He was supposed to have been there, but his sister had called and insisted that he perform an errand for the family. Nonetheless, Bill was the first person called in by the police for questioning. This led some of his associates to believe that he had turned informant. There were informants, but Bill says that he was not among them. The gang splintered and became weaker than it had been prior to the shootings. Bill looked at it as the time to get out of the gang lifestyle.

For the twenty years prior to the publication of his book, Bill remained deliberately out of contact with his former gang mates. Soon after the book's release, Bill began to do promotional signings. It was at one of these events that he received death threats. The upshot of the threats was that they alerted Bill and City authorities that the gangs were still an active threat. A shooting at the Chinese Playground a year earlier, in 1998, prompted Bill to believe that the public facility was still a piece of contested gang turf. The persistence of such activity only further motivates Bill to continue to counsel troubled youth and to keep speaking at middle and high schools to try to sway students away from gang influences and the gang lifestyle. He stated that the families that had two working parents who had little or no time to adapt to American society and culture and who also, for financial expedience, neglected their children were the most frequent and easy source of new gang recruits. The ability of the gangs to act as surrogate caretakers and providers of money, cars, weapons and sex to youth made vulnerable by weak family ties further fuels Bill's desire to do everything within his power to reach out and hopefully stem the tide or break the cycle of violence and criminal activity that, however quiet or unnoticed, continues to plague Chinatown.

The *Golden Dragon* has been replaced at its original location at 816 Washington Street by the *Imperial Palace*. The restaurant's address places it on a moderately inclined hill between Grant and Stockton and just across the street from Waverly Place. The jade green exterior wall of the Imperial Palace looks very much the same today as it did when it was a part of the *Golden Dragon*.

7.

The Grant Avenue Follies
Preserving the Legacy of The Golden Age of Night Life in
Chinatown

Since its foundation in 2003, the *Grant Avenue Follies* has refined its repertoire and put on numerous lively and cheerful shows that never fail to delight audiences. The group is a not-for-profit organization. All of the *Follies'* performances are for benefits, charities or simply as pro-bono entertainment. The group has danced for organizations that include *On-Lok*, *Laguna Honda* and *Habitat for Humanity*. *On-Lok,* meaning "peaceful and happy abode" in Cantonese, provides quality care for Chinatown's elderly residents. The *Follies* danced for a five-person 100th birthday celebration there in 2017. The eldest of the celebrants was 108 and another was *Follies* co-founder Cynthia Yee's mother, Mildred Fong. *Laguna Honda* is a long-time San Francisco skilled nursing facility and rehabilitation center where the *Follies* schedules annual performances during Chinese New Year and the Moon Festival.

The *Follies* has additionally performed for the benefit of San Francisco historical and art preservation organizations such as the *San Francisco Natives Tours* and the *San Francisco Art Deco Society*. The energy and enthusiasm that Cynthia applies to her activities with the *Follies* as well as through her association with other community groups has earned her the National Jefferson Award. The award recognizes contributions to public service through volunteerism at the community level. The *Follies* has gone as far as Hong Kong at their own expense to dance at a close friend's 80-year birthday party. They plan to head back there soon for a repeat performance for their friend's 85th. The group even wanted to revive Dorothy Toy's traditional visits to San Quentin, but new prison policy prohibits such visits. The *Follies* went to Cuba on a tour and cultural exchange in the fall of 2018.

Pat Chin
We Have Been Kept Pretty Busy!

Former *Sky Room* chorus girl and one of the *Follies'* original members, Pat Chin spoke about how the group formed and some of its activities.

I was happily married for 45 years before my husband passed away in 2002. After a while I felt that I needed to keep busy, so I started to go back to my roots and look for dance classes. I was able to reconnect with other former professional dancers among whom were Cynthia Yee, Ivy Tam and Isabel Louie. The four of us had a lot of fun dancing together, and we really enjoyed one another's company. When an opportunity arose, we put our heads and talents together and came up with our dance group, the Grant Avenue Follies. In addition to the social and fun parts of dancing as a group, we all wanted to give something back to our old Chinatown neighborhood and the people who were still living in it. We organized the Grant Avenue Follies as a not-for-profit group and started to participate in fund raisers and entertaining in assisted living facilities and Veteran's Administration Hospitals. I think that people seem to be interested in what we do because it goes back to the glamorous days when people dressed up to go out to supper clubs to be entertained.

Trina Robbins, one of our classmates in tap class, who is also a prolific illustrator and author, was so intrigued by us, that she decided to investigate our background for a book. She eventually completed "Forbidden City: The Golden Age of Chinese Night Clubs." When Trina's book was published in 2009, we helped her promote it by performing at her book signings at the Old San Francisco Mint, the San Francisco Public Library and the Asian Art Museum.

Local film-maker and writer Arthur Dong produced a documentary called "Forbidden City, USA" about the Chinatown night clubs and performers from their beginnings through to their final days in the late 1960s. He also wrote a book based on the film. He used the same title as he did for the documentary and included the Follies and our pictures in his book. We had also performed at a few of his book signing events. All these events seemed to increase our popularity, so we have been kept pretty busy!

Trina Robbins' and Arthur Dong's works serve to remind the public of the pioneering nature of all the former Chinatown nightclub performers. The books and film address the courage that it took for young Chinese American women to escape the centuries old traditions, values and expectations of their parents. Perhaps the most important contribution that the club performers are shown to have made was the breaking of racially based stereotypes that had for so long constrained Chinatown's citizens from full inclusion into the American melting pot. Each of the girls and young women as well as their male counterparts showed the world that the Chinese were fully capable of being so much more than houseboys, laundrymen, maids and servants. Pat continued,

We have performed in almost too many venues for me to remember. Some include the Art Deco Society of California, and we have been honored annually since 2011 by the Burlesque Hall of Fame as Living Legends in Las Vegas, Nevada. We have also been making regular annual appearances with the San Francisco Women's Breakfast Club at the Fairmont Hotel. We were all very excited about making our cultural exchange trip to Havana, Cuba in 2018.

Among its current members are dancers from Chinatown who have neither worked in any of the old Chinatown clubs nor even danced other than casually and for fun. One such *Grant Avenue Follies* "novice" was retired and widely-known dentist Bernice Pun. Bernice, raised in Chinatown, had attended St. Mary's school on Stockton Street, graduated from UC Berkeley and gone to dental school at the University of Pacific. She kept a practice in Chinatown for many years and very few post-war Chinatown Kids do not know of her. For a great number of them Bernice had been their first dentist. Two other members who only began dancing as retirees are Mimi Lee and Pat Nishimoto.

Mimi Lee [54.]
A Lifetime of Fun and Activity

Although she has never been a professional dancer, many of the activities that Mimi Lee enjoyed over her lifetime have been a great help in preparing her for her role as the *Follies'* featured ribbon and fan dancer. As a student in Chinese school she was a baton twirler and majorette. As a teenager she spent time performing as a Southern China-style lion dancer. After high school Mimi became a hair dresser. She continues to practice Tai-chi through which she performed from 2015 through 2018 in the August Moon Festival in Chinatown.

Mimi is a native San Franciscan. Like many of her contemporaries, she is a first-generation ABC with a humble and immigrant family background. Her father arrived in San Francisco as a young man who was able to learn English quickly in classes offered by a Chinatown church. He served in the American military during World War II. With American citizenship earned through his time in uniform and with the Chinese Exclusion laws permanently stricken in 1943, Mimi's future father was able to send for his wife from China. Once reunited the couple started a family that included Mimi, another daughter and three sons. The family qualified for housing in one of the *Ping Yuen* housing complexes where Mimi and her siblings grew up.

Mimi attended regular school at Chinatown's Commodore Stockton and continued with afternoon Chinese school at *Jing Kwok* on Stockton Street. Unlike many of her baby boomer contemporaries, Mimi truly enjoyed Chinese school. She was enthralled by every aspect of it and happily absorbed all that she was taught. Mimi says that Chinese school helped make her who she is today. She has been forever grateful to her mother for enrolling her at *Jing Kwok*. It was there that Mimi "began my lifelong interest in Chinese cultural celebrations, dance and song." She adds that, "Chinese school was more than just about the language. The history and the way of life in China and so much more were not just interesting to me; they were vitally important."

Mimi and her older brother were a part of the *Jing Kwok* drum corps in which Mimi was one of the baton twirlers. Those old Chinatown parade viewers who can still picture the corps on the march will remember that its typically petite girls were noted for the height and length of time that they could keep their batons spinning in the air. They were agile and acrobatic enough to rarely, if ever, miss a baton as it returned towards earth. Mimi became a majorette and describes herself as, "twirling that baton like a champ." The competition was most certainly stiff, so Mimi is more than justified to do a bit of bragging. She enjoyed a moment of youthful fame when she and the rest of the corps were privileged to march for then-presidential candidate Richard Nixon in 1960. After Nixon lost to John Kennedy, another noted Chinatown Chinese school group, The Saint Mary's Drum and Bell Corps, would be honored with an invitation to march in Kennedy's inauguration parade in Washington D.C.

Later, during her high school years at Galileo, Mimi's brother who was then in the Cathay Post Drum and Bugle Corps drum line recruited her to be a flag girl. The post's corps was well-respected by its peers. Mimi was a participant with the 1964 corps that placed second in California's statewide competition. She remains deeply proud of that achievement. "All the other corps that were there were really good. You can hardly imagine what it was like; the uniforms, the marching and the music were all top-notch." After high school and her time with the corps, Mimi "enjoyed the honor of being invited back to be featured on the Cathay Post float in the annual

Chinese New Year parade." She added, "I did that two years in a row. It was such fun to stand on the float and wave to the crowd as we passed by."

Mimi's preparation for her current role with the *Grant Avenue Follies* continued when, once again, her older brother recruited her for an activity. This time it was to be a lion dancer with the Golden Lions, a Southern China-style troupe. Lion dance groups are most typically associated with kung-fu clubs, but the Golden Lions was not. Nonetheless, its routines were just as rigorous in their demand for agility, strength and stamina. Each lion is made up of two performers: one holds and operates the head while the other follows the head and works the elaborately decorated tail. Extra duress during performances was (and continues to be) created by the long strings of exploding firecrackers that are so often part and parcel of lion dancing. Kids and more than a few adults would contribute additional torment for the dancers by deliberately tossing firecrackers, sometimes entire packs of them, at the lion. The only protection afforded to the performers was, at most, cotton ear plugs and an extra pair of thick socks. The person performing as the "tail" of the lion could sometimes help by kicking or using the lion's fabric end to sweep away or smother the explosives. Mimi performed in the 10-10 (October 10th Chinese Independence Day holiday) and Chinese New Year parades as the tail and she laughed as she said, "I was all over the place with those firecrackers. I hopped, dodged, kicked and swept at those darned firecrackers like I was crazy. It was loud, scary and really tiring, but I had so much fun doing it."

A much more relaxed activity that Mimi used to develop her current set of performance skills was found at the dance parties held by Chinatown's teens and young adults around the neighborhood, around town and even across the Bay in Berkeley, Oakland and even beyond. There were numerous bands made up of local kids who performed pop music, much of it based on the Soul and Motown sounds popular at the time. Mimi clearly remembers the names of some of the groups: *The Agents*, *Bold Rebels*, *Intrigue*, *Enchanters*, *Wanderers* and *Jest Jammin'*. All but *Jest Jammin'* have given way to adulthood, family-life and careers. *Jest Jammin'*, perhaps like the *Rolling Stones*, refuses to age. Mimi says, "I participated in many of these soirees and I knew all the members of some of the groups, too." She has unquestionably retained her youthful loose limbs and supple back. She denies any innate talent, but does admit that she seems to always been possessed of, "a sense of rhythm and a bit of soul." For the past twelve years, Mimi has been working diligently to stay in shape and remain very active as a practitioner of Tai-chi Yuen. Mimi said, "Through Tai-chi Yuen I have learned patience, self-control and meditation. I participate with my Tai-chi Yuen group in competitions and events that include the Chinese New Year parade and the August Moon Festival. I was very proud to participate in the recent (2018) August Moon Festival."

In addition to all her past and current physical activities, Mimi says that she has been able to perform with the *Follies* as a result of friendships with and guidance from people with deep knowledge and understanding of the performing arts.

One of her friends, Mai Tai Sing, was a one-time performer at the *Forbidden City*. She was a part of the husband-wife team, the *Tai-Sings*. that also toured the country. She also eventually became a partner and hostess of the *Rickshaw Club* in Chinatown. The *Rickshaw*, which remained in operation until 1970, hosted a number of major celebrities that included Frank Sinatra, Sammy Davis, Jr., Judy Garland and the Beatles. Mai Tai was also a fashion model, and later in life she opened and operated the well-known San Francisco *Mai Tai House of Beauty*.[55] Mimi says that her friend, "… impressed upon me the importance of 'carriage' and I try to carry myself in the same majestic style of Mai Tai." Mimi has also worked with San Francisco native Preston Mui who is a choreographer and Movement Coach. Preston lives in Los Angeles where he has also guided an impressive list of names that includes Reese Witherspoon, Nicole Kidman, Janet Jackson and Britney Spears. It would seem that Mimi has been in excellent hands.

Mimi also says that her late husband Lewis Chin, was at least an indirect but immense help to her as a Follies dancer,

He was the owner of Dragon-a-Go-Go on Wentworth Street in the late 60s just when Forbidden City and the Sky Room were closing

out. He also owned the Hippodrome which later became the Stone. He owned the building but leased it out when it changed from the Hippodrome to the Stone. Jerry Garcia and the group Metallica are a few of the performers that I remember from the Stone. My husband was also the founder of Basin Street West on Broadway and a lot of big names went through the club. There was another club that has become today's Penthouse which is an up-scale gentleman's club. I learned my sultry performance style by stopping by the club back before it became the Penthouse to watch the alluring showgirls' stage acts on their dance poles.

The Penthouse continues to operate on Broadway between Montgomery and Kearny. It features a steakhouse for dining, dancers called the "Key Girls," and for several days in November 2018 hosted President Donald Trump's nemesis, Stormy Daniels, as a guest performer. Mimi adds,

Dancing with the Follies never ceases to bring me joy. With the Grant Avenue Follies, I have traveled to Las Vegas, Honolulu, and Seattle. I continue to look forward to new places and new experiences with them.

Pat Nishimoto [56.]
Bringing Joy to Our Audiences

Pat Nishimoto is another member of the *Grant Avenue Follies* who is not a former nightclub performer. Pat whose former husband came from a Japanese background, is a first-generation San Franciscan and ABC. Her paternal grandfather, or *yeh-yeh*, had been brought to San Jose in the early 1900s to work as a houseboy for a Mrs. Boyd. Although it was at a time when the Chinese Exclusion Act was still in full effect, Pat's grandfather somehow managed to get his then 12-year old son and Pat's future father to California. It is possible that Mrs. Boyd vouched for the boy to immigration officials. Pat's father was young enough to quickly adapt his to American life. He was also able to learn English without difficulty through school. Pat believes that as an adult her father's fluency in both Chinese and English allowed him to secure work with the Merchant Marine as an interpreter on shipping routes to and from China. On one of his trips to China, he married and fathered a daughter, Pat's older sister. The girl was born in Fau Shek, Hoisan. Pat's father later served in the Army during World War II. After the war he travelled back to China in order to bring his wife and daughter to California. Including Pat there were four children in the family. The three girls and their brother grew up in the Nob Hill outskirts of Chinatown on the corner of Jones and Jackson Streets. The children went to school at nearby Spring Valley Elementary School. They were also sent to Chinese School at *Jung-Wah* on Stockton Street in the middle of Chinatown. According to Pat, the additional hours of schooling after a full day at Spring Valley,

... were definitely not fun as the teachers were very strict. Chinese school lasted only two years for me. I think my parents thought it was too long of a day and decided to let us discontinue Chinese school.

In lieu of learning Cantonese at *Jung Wah,* Pat and her siblings retained and practiced their family's native Hoisan dialect of "thlay yip" at home.

Mom spoke little English which may have been better as we had to speak thlay yip to converse with her. English was really my second language. My siblings and I went on to Marina Middle School. I would later attend Lowell for high school after which I went on to San Francisco State College.

The family moved from their Jones Street home in 1960 when, as Pat says,

Dad made a wise investment and bought a home in the Cow Hollow neighborhood. This is the "trendy" part of Union Street with its numerous boutiques and cafes. The neighborhood sits between the well-heeled Pacific Heights and Marina District neighborhoods. Back then, just as the Civil Rights movement was making headway in the southern states, Chinese were not allowed to purchase homes in either of those very upscale areas.

My parents worked hard. Dad co-owned Darnell Liquors on

Fillmore Street between Geary Boulevard and Sutter Street when I was very young. He later sold out and went into retail as a salesperson. The store was later torn down and an overpass was built above Geary. Dad usually worked swing shifts so it seemed like we did not see him too often. Mom worked as a seamstress in a gai chong. It was on Stone Street, the alley just off the side of where the old Chinese Hospital building was. Mom often brought her work home at night to work on after dinner. In spite of her take-home sewing, she would always have a wonderful dinner ready for us every evening. The usual fare always included fresh meats, fish and veggies all purchased from Chinatown each day. Mom also made the best Chinese soups. We never owned a car so Mom trekked up those hills each day with groceries! Both of our parents emphasized studying hard, doing our homework and being "good." That was our "job."

I didn't realize it while growing up but, in comparison to other kids, we were "poor." Unlike them, we did not have bikes, lots of toys, or store-bought clothes. We never owned a car and did not get to go on vacations. Overall, I would say that my parents were also very frugal. Looking back, I guess we really didn't need a lot. Mom used her sewing skills to make some of our clothes. We didn't have a lot of toys. Hula hoops, jacks, four square balls, and roller skates were about it. We spent a lot of time playing at the local Helen Willis Playground which is still on Broadway near Van Ness with its swings and slides, basketball hoops and tennis courts. We were mostly good kids. We liked reading as much as playing, so we would also check out books at the library. If we wanted to go a little further from home, my sister Kate and I had a spool of cotton fishing line with a hook at the end. We would bring some bacon from home and walk down about two miles to Fisherman's Wharf and have so much fun catching bottom feeders and throwing them back in. Kate and I walked all the way to the North Beach area to go "swimming," as we called it. It was really just a lot of splashing around in the public pool at North Beach Playground. Mom would give us 25-cents in case we needed a snack or drink. If I didn't use the money, I'd put it in my piggy bank. I always felt I had money. We kept ourselves busy in our neighborhood. In recollection it was fun and safe to hang out on the sidewalks to play with our neighborhood friends.

Except for one wonderful vacation when I was 13, our family only took the simplest of trips. We went by airplane to Disneyland where we stayed in a hotel. Our usual trips were ones like riding the Muni to the long ago torn down amusement park out across from Ocean Beach: Playland. The rides, eating sno-cones, cotton candy, popcorn and caramel apples have left me with many happy memories of childhood. I also need to mention how delightful I found the park's "official greeter," an animated mannequin of a buck-toothed and guffawing old woman named "Laughing Sal." The sight of her will stay with me always.

Not ever owning a car, we all once took the Greyhound from the old bus station at Seventh and Market to visit Mrs. Boyd in San Jose. By then yeh-yeh no longer worked for her. In fact, he had returned to China. Mrs. Boyd owned a lot of Chinese art objects, and I remember that she told my father to take whatever he would like. We did select a few things which we carried back on the bus later that evening. I think that Dad made several further trips to visit Mrs. Boyd. I have since inherited several of those beautiful antique art pieces.

My dad was an avid baseball and football fan. He liked to have both the TV and radio on at the same time so he could follow multiple games at once. I think that because he was an Army veteran, Dad would have us stand up at home when the National Anthem was played on the radio or TV. Dad took us to Giants baseball games since a family member who knew Horace Stoneham, the Giants' owner, would sometimes give us tickets. Being from the owner these were VIP seats right above the Giants' dugout. I was in the fifth and sixth grade at that time so that really gave me something to brag about at school. We still packed our own food to bring to the games as we thought that the snacks sold at Candlestick Park were way too expensive. I will always cherish fond memories of going to Giants games with Dad and my brother and sisters.

I Would Have Loved to Take Dance Lessons

From a very early age, Pat remembers always being fascinated by music and dancing. Growing up, her experience in them was limited to passive enjoyment. Pat's fascination with stage, movie and television performers grew as she herself did. She wistfully dreamt of dance lessons and would act out her song-and-dance fantasies at home.

When I was young, I watched Shirley Temple tap and sing. I watched Annette Funicello and the Mickey Mouse Club Mouseketeers on TV also. They made me feel that I could dance and sing too! I would pretend to be a ballerina and prance around on my toes in my Chinese slippers. One day when I was a first-grader I saw my very first live play: "Puss 'n Boots." I was so taken by that performance! I loved the costumes and the makeup. I imagined that I was on the stage acting, singing and dancing right along with the players. I was mesmerized. Woweee, I thought. If only I could be like that, too!

Although my mother didn't have much time for anything besides work and taking care of us kids, she did manage to take us to live performances of Chinese Opera a few times. I think that the theater we would go to was the Dai Ming Sing, or Great Star on Jackson Street. I was amazed at the white powder and makeup on the faces of the actors and actresses. I couldn't take my eyes off of the colorful, bright and dazzling costumes! I didn't understand what the singing was about. It was so completely different from Shirley Temple and Annette! It sounded like a bunch of cats meowing and screeching! I would turn to my mother and ask, "What are they singing about?" All she would say was that these were famous actors and actresses. She never explained any of it. I don't think it mattered. I was so impressed with the costumes and the musical instruments. I didn't need words or a storyline. It was extra fun getting to eat Chinese snacks like watermelon seeds and dried salted plums at the show. I loved it all so very much.

Mr. Joe Tanzi was the performing arts teacher when I attended Marina Junior High School. During the Spring of 1963, Mr. Tanzi directed the musical "Flower Drum Song." A few of my girlfriends and I were asked to learn the song and dance number "Grant Avenue, San Francisco" for the show. We all got to wear a turquoise blue happy coat, black tights and a Chinese straw hat! It is still unforgettable to this day. It was my very first taste of being on stage and I loved it.

I would have loved taking dance lessons, but that would not have ever crossed the minds of my old-fashioned parents. Dad, who was strict and stern passed away when I was in high school. Mom, who had the warmest smile and kindest heart, never wavered from her dedication to the four of us. Still, it was never part of her way of life back in China to be taking dance or music lessons. My mom and her family worked as farmers in the rice paddies. Things like "enrichment activities" and "school extra-curriculars" were completely unknown to her. She, as well as my dad, only wanted me and my siblings to have good lives, so for them the only thing that made sense was for us to study, check out books from the library and do well in the classroom. Even without our father around to help her, our mother rarely asked us to do chores. She continued to work long hours at her piecework sewing, and when she got off each day, she hurried home to cook, clean, and handle the household alone. She wanted to give us all the time we needed to study hard and excel academically in school.

Even with the complete difference between her old-country childhood and ours in America, Mom was not unreasonable. She understood that life for us should not be only about hard work and toil. She knew that we were studious and pretty good kids. Mom, and Dad before he died, trusted us to make good decisions, so she made sure that we could have time for friends. She wanted us to go out and have fun with them.

During my teen years, I joined and belonged to two very special places, the YMCA and Cameron House. They both had very well organized and supervised girls' clubs that were the best places to hang out on Friday nights and weekends. We had wonderful club leaders that steered us and kept us on track. All of us ABCs knew each other and it did not matter that we went to different schools throughout the city and never bonded as schoolmates. We just mixed together at the Y or at Cameron House and had fun. There were always lots of activities and a couple of my favorites were the girlie chats and meeting boys. We'd even_go over to the Chinese

Playground just to watch the boys play basketball after our club meetings. Another after club meeting thing was, we would all go out for siu-yeh, or snacks, at those good old places like Jackson Cafe, Sun Hung Heung and Sam Wo. Last, but not least were dances. I loved being out there on the floor. I didn't need lessons to have a good time rockin' like my teen idols to that wonderful 60s music.

I Knew I Had Some Rhythm but Tap Was a Whole New Ball Game

Surrounded by her loving mother and siblings, Pat thrived and grew as a teenager. She went to Lowell High School, kept her grades up and never deviated from being an all-around "good kid." She attended San Francisco State for college and earned her BA in Sociology. Pat enjoyed a long and satisfying career in the San Francisco public school system.

I worked with the San Francisco Unified School District for over 35 years. I worked as a Paraprofessional for half of those years in the Elementary schools and the other half as the school secretary at different elementary, middle and high schools. I really enjoyed working with students and being surrounded by their high energy. For recreation my then-husband and I started playing tennis when I was 25. We really got into it and pushed one another to study and practice the sport. We emerged from the process as self-taught tennis players. We must have done things properly, because I wound up being pretty competitive on the court and ended up playing in United States Tennis Association matches over the next 42 years. Meanwhile, my development as a tennis player did not go unnoticed or unappreciated at the high school where I worked. I was talked into assuming the role of girls' head tennis coach in the fall and boys' coach in the spring. I did this over a period of five years.

After retirement in 2013, an acquaintance asked me if I was interested in taking beginning tap classes with the San Francisco Park and Recreation department once a week. I didn't hesitate at all. I had never lost my desire to do some sort of dancing. Shirley Temple time! I was excited and went out and bought tap shoes to be prepared for the first class. Well, the first class was not a beginner's class as

I expected. It was an intermediate class lasting an hour and a half that was followed by an advanced class. I did not know it at the time, but Cynthia Yee, the former club and road professional dancer and one of the co-founders of the Grant Avenue Follies, and several of her long-time dance associates and friends were in that advanced class. I was completely and utterly stunned at what they could do as dancers. At the same time, some of the other class participants were there just like me to learn the basics.

I know I have some rhythm but tapping was a whole new ball game. The instructor was a talented woman named Jean who also happened to be the choreographer for all of the Follies' dances. I felt very intimidated, but I was also determined. If I wasn't going to learn how to dance now, when would I ever do it? Jean was very strict too, and not very encouraging with newbies. Each 90-minute class involved doing warm up tap steps, reviewing old dance numbers, then moving on to learn new choreography. I was impressed and overwhelmed. I thought to myself, "If only I could learn one of their numbers, I would be so happy and proud!"

I felt like I was always behind every week with these intermediate and advanced dancers. The friend who got me into tap class quit after two months. After three months I was ready to quit, too. One of the dancers whom I knew from Lowell High School encouraged me to hang in there. My thoughts were, "How will I ever learn? Could it be done by osmosis?" There was another dancer named Sheena who, while not a Follies member, was a tapper with decades of experience. She would pull me aside during each class to break down the steps and choreography with me. I was fully resolved and committed to learn, catch up and stay current. Just like when I worked to learn tennis on my own, I pushed on with my dancing every night at home. I referred to YouTube to fill in the gaps in my understanding. I watched the videos at length and in detail to try to get where I needed to be. I was on-line a lot during that time. I also taped Jean in order to be able to review what she taught us in class. I was fully bent on learning at least one dance number!

Cynthia suggested that, in addition to our Wednesday class, I also attend the Tuesday session that was geared towards advanced beginners. I took her advice and went to tap class twice a week. Sheena was also there on Tuesdays and continued to freely and gladly give me extra attention.

Several months of hard work passed. Cynthia must have noticed my dedication and improvement. One afternoon after class she approached me to ask if I was interested in dancing with their group. The Grant Avenue Follies! I was going to class because I had always wanted to learn to tap dance, but something like the Grant Avenue Follies was the last thing I would have thought. I was excited and honored to be asked. I had seen the Follies perform on stage once before I took tap classes and was very impressed. They looked so sharp in their costumes that evening: black top hat, black tuxedo with scarlet gloves and black fish nets. Cynthia wanted me to learn one number, the longtime favorite of San Francisco's Chinese community: "Chinatown, My Chinatown."

"I'll give you three months and you can perform the number with us at Laguna Honda Hospital during the holidays," she said.

I took up her challenge, learned the choreography and when the time came, I went on and performed with the Follies at Laguna Honda. That was in December 2013 just a half-year after that terrifying first tap class with Parks and Recreation. I did it and I felt so proud of the accomplishment. My new career with the Follies had begun.

I Made My Solo Debut at Herbst Theater

I very much respect and admire Cynthia who is an experienced performer and dancer. I was honored and flattered when she asked me to perform a fan duet with her in 2017. It turned out to be so exciting and fun! Then later in the year she thought it would be a good idea for me to perform a fan number by myself. I was accompanied only by a singer. I chose the song "Can't Help Falling in Love with You" which also happened to be the singer's favorite. Prepared through lessons, pointers and tips from experienced fan dancers I made my solo debut at Herbst Theater in January 2018. The theater is a part of the War Memorial Performing Arts Center in the City's Civic Center. We were there as a part of San Francisco's annual show honoring our veterans and seniors.

My big sister Sue was sitting in the audience and I surprised her with my solo fan dance. She was teary eyed and so proud of me! And there it all was; the dream I had held onto since I was six years old: dancing on stage.

Over time the thrill of performing with the ladies of the Follies remains as strong as it was on that first December evening. Each one of the group's members is a talented legend in her own right. It is so heartwarming to perform and see the smiles on the faces of our audience members. Whether we are at a fund raiser, or a community event or at a venue for the elderly we often receive standing ovations. I never dreamed that retirement would be so fulfilling!

8.
Home Again
Reflections on Chinatown, Friends, Family and Heritage

Whenever they are back for a stroll along Grant Avenue or Stockton Street, Chinatown's baby-boomers frequently catch themselves feeling as if they had never grown up or moved away. After making it up the incline of Jackson or Sacramento Streets they now, as never before as kids, take pause to catch their breath. As they rest, familiar sounds and scents reach them from the upper floors of tenement buildings and from open air food stalls and upon the breezes that flow from the neighborhood's labyrinth of alleyways. While they are not always as they might once have been, many former homes and favorite places are still quickly recognized. Time can seem to slip into reverse as childhood memories awaken to stir in special corners of the hearts of those who have come back for a visit.

Amy Chung [57.] is a Chinatown native. A graduate of Hastings Law School, Amy has a strong relationship with the Chinatown

Community Development Center. Amy is a staunch advocate for Chinatown as well as for those who live and work there. She offered the following thoughts on what Chinatown means to her.

I thought it was a pretty nice place to grow up (and I) feel the connection to this community. It's that connection ... culturally and historically ... the context within which you are living ... little bits and pieces of history and culture ... that make you who you are.

Saki Lee
Rediscovery of My Chinese Identity

Having lost touch with her Chinese heritage as a teenager, Saki left Chinatown and the Bay Area almost as soon as she graduated from high school. She wanted to better understand the world around her even as she simultaneously sought the means by which to make a positive mark upon it. Looking back at her past and her roots in Chinatown, Saki offered the following thoughts.

My childhood and adolescent impressions of Chinatown must have stayed in my subconscious because right after graduation from high school I applied to VISTA. VISTA stood for Volunteers in Service to America and was the domestic version of the Peace Corps. Its main goal was to fight poverty and to offer support for the underprivileged in America. I was accepted probably because I came from an impoverished inner-city neighborhood myself. After training in Denver, I was placed in the inner city of Kansas City, Missouri where I worked at a community center as an assistant to the director of social services. I was able to meet members of the Black Panthers, the militant Chicano group of Corky Gonzales, and the non-violent United Farm Workers leader Cesar Chavez and some of his loyalists. I had grown up among quiet and non-assertive Chinese people so this was a culture shock. But I wanted to learn something about racism and poverty in America. Staying in Chinatown would have sheltered me from any such possibility.

After my time with VISTA I stayed on in the Kansas City black community as an intake interviewer for single mothers needing social welfare and support. While studying world literature at the

University of Missouri in the evenings, an unanticipated window opened for me. The course exposed me to Taoist and Buddhist teachings that led me to something new and exquisitely Chinese that I had not known while growing up in Chinatown. An inner hunger to find meaning and something I could identify with had arisen within me. I felt more motivated than ever before to seek out something substantive and inspiring from within the Chinese culture which, of course, was also my own culture.

As a young adult one of my favorite relatives in San Francisco was an uncle who was married to one of my mother's sisters. Uncle Mon embodied a deeply refined and artistic temperament. He was passionate about Chinese art and culture. Whenever I returned to visit Chinatown, I would drop by his Grant Avenue curio shop for a chat. His quiet and peaceful demeanor had a calming effect on me. Uncle Mon talked to me about Tai Chi which he practiced. He demonstrated some of the movements. He also showed me antique scrolls hanging in his shop or in art books that he kept behind the counter. He lovingly pointed out how the calligraphy and the paintings were formed from smooth, flowing, and graceful motions by long-tenured masters. He mimicked some of those moves for me. I marveled at how his wrist, arm, and shoulder literally danced over an imaginary scroll in the making. My uncle had taken me into what was for me a secret and astoundingly beautiful corner of the Chinese world. I realized that I had been longing to know beauty, and I wanted to somehow capture it to treasure deep within my heart.

Saki explained that the personal discoveries she had made as a world literature student meshed with the things that she learned from her uncle. These, in turn blended with her memories and her experiences from the day as a lost five-year old who had been sheltered in a Chinatown *gai-chong* to her time spent on the harsh streets of Kansas City and the lettuce fields of California's Central Valley. Saki began to understand and embrace the concept of synergy in which multiple things can be combined in order to produce an even more positive result than if they had been applied separately towards a similar goal.

In the mid-1970s Saki moved to Holland. She fell in love with the country, married a Dutch national and has remained in Europe ever since. She was delighted by the opening of Holland's first ever school of Traditional Chinese medicine into which she eagerly enrolled in 1980. She completed the four-year curriculum and, not unlike Melody Chan Doss-Wambeke's grandfather a generation before her, established herself as a practitioner of the healing arts.

Today I am happy and content for I have finally recovered so many of the essential elements of my life that had gone missing during all those years of alienation from my Chinese identity. I have enjoyed and shared the positive effects that can emerge from weaving sometimes disparate healing strategies together into my practice. I remain in a continual state of learning and discovery. I have gotten deeply satisfying results from blending Taoist teachings with dance, yoga, music, acupuncture, meditation, breathing exercises, herbal medicine, and more. I don't actually use everything at once, of course, but I pick and choose what to blend on a case by case basis. There is Tuina, for example, which combines manipulative therapy with tai chi, acupuncture, fire cupping, herbal treatments, meditation, and breathing exercises. I don't see the world or human activity as unidimensional. Things and people are meant to mix and blend together so that the whole can be so much more than just the one.

The short and simple version for me is that I feel that I have overcome the uncertainty that plagued me as an adolescent and young adult. I don't see things as ABC against FOB, Chinese or non-Chinese, or black or white anymore. I fully accept my Chinese background as it interacts with my thoughts and feelings as an American. Simultaneously, those two parts of me blend with the Dutch and the broader European parts of me. From the gai-chong *of my childhood through my early days of school and the turbulence and confusion of being a teenager to my early adult life I have learned that I am many things and that each of them comes together to make me what I now am. I am very much at peace with this.*

Jack Woo
Imagine Having Friends From 60 Years Back – and Still Counting!

Jack moved away from Chinatown for work and to raise his family, but he never left San Francisco.

I still visit Chinatown because my mother still lives in the house that I grew up in. It is on Mason Street, not far from the Cable Car barn. After I visit with my mother, I usually go on down to Chinatown where I go to the old places. Many of my long-time favorites like the Nam Yuen restaurant and Jackson Café are now gone and I miss them. I went to those a lot when I was still in school. I can still enjoy the "Pork Chop House," though. It is on the corner of Beckett Alley where it intersects with Jackson. On the other corner of the alley is the old bar, Red's Place. The real name of the restaurant is something else, but I think people just started to call it the "Pork Chop House" and so that's what it is now.

Well, I'm retired now, but I keep pretty busy. I even took up ballroom dancing which reminds me of a little story. There used to be some night clubs with exotic floor shows in Chinatown. They all closed down in the late 50s or early 60s and one was called The Forbidden City. After his days as a performer in the Forbidden City Revue, Tony Wing, took a job at the YWCA on Clay Street teaching ballet to the local kids. I remember going down there once a week to pick up my two sisters who took lessons from him. At that time, I didn't know anything about him except that he was a ballet teacher. Then around 1988 my wife and I decided to take up ballroom dancing and we found this little studio in the Richmond District near 20th Avenue. Lo and behold, it was Tony Wing who was teaching it! I reminded him that I used to pick my little sisters up at the Y. My wife and I took lessons from Tony for over ten years!

I still have a lot of my old buddies, and we hang out together a lot. Some still live in San Francisco and some are in other places in the Bay Area. We aren't too far from each other. We take fishing trips together and I always enjoy their company and we remember the good old days. Some of us golf, too, like at Lincoln Park's municipal course and other places. It gives us an easy and relaxing time to talk and everything. When I'm with my old buddies, it's just like we're back in junior high school again.

It's unfortunate that there are no other generations except for us Baby Boomers that have such loving and memorable ties to the Chinatown community. It was wonderful for me while growing up and even beyond. The only example of a tie to old Chinatown for the generations after ours is Cameron House. It is still very active in the community. A few of my friends try to recreate that old closeness to Chinatown by sending their kids there, but I don't think the younger generation can ever achieve or recreate the same closeness the kids of my generation were fortunate to have. We lived in Chinatown and walked to Cameron House in a matter of minutes. Today my friends drive their kids to and from Cameron House. They live way out in the Avenues or even down the Peninsula or across the Bay. How could it be the same for those kids? They might be friends while at Cameron House, but they split up right away when their parents arrive to pick them up. When I was at Cameron House, my friends and I stayed together when our time there was over. We walked through Chinatown. We stopped for snacks, or siu-yeh. We played in the park or in the alleys and we took our time getting home.

Growing up in San Francisco Chinatown was a wonderful and unique experience in my life. It provided me with a lifetime of memories. It was the place where I came of age and what I experienced and learned as a youth helped guide me into my adult life. If I have to make a choice regarding the best time of my entire life, I would have to say that it was the period of the 50s and 60s and growing up in Chinatown because most of the childhood friends that I made remain as my closest friends to this day. Imagine having friends that are still a big part of your life from 60 years back ... and still counting!

The closest I ever got to duplicating my type of childhood for my kids was having them learn to cook some Chinese dishes. I once managed to get them to make "duong" which they referred to as "Chinese burritos!"

Judy Wing Lee
I Wish My Kids Could Have Grown Up in the Chinatown of My Childhood

While Judy still keeps a home in San Francisco that she frequently visits, she has retired and is now living in Hawaii. Judy observes that,

I realize now that we lived during a golden age that made it easy to grow up in Chinatown. It's defined a lot of who we are now. Our parents worked hard and instilled that into us. We didn't have much supervision, but we learned how to make good choices. We were not coddled, so we became self-sufficient and independent. Because we had siblings and friends who lived so near to us that they might just as well have been siblings, we learned to be responsible for each other. Above all else, we had parents who loved and sacrificed for us. I just wish my kids could have grown up in my Chinatown era. It truly was a 'golden age' for me and my contemporaries.

Now my overly protected grandkids are growing up in the suburbs where they will need to drive a car just to leave the house. Their parents use tons of wipes to keep them spotless. They have piano, dance, gymnastics, soccer, basketball, Kung fu, swimming lessons, and vacations in Disneyland and Hawaii. I wonder what they will reflect as their 'golden age'?

Deb Lem
Thoughts About Growing Up Chinese in Chinatown

Deb remained in Chinatown through college and her early working years. Although college was a bit too far for commuting, she returned home frequently during those four years. She worked close enough to Grant Avenue, however, to return nightly after work.

I went to college at Humboldt State University in Arcata, CA. I went there to study oceanography. I soon changed my major to geography because I thought that I might pursue an advanced degree in Urban Planning. I never got around to doing that once I started working. I was first at City Hall in the business tax department. Later, I got a job at Ampex Corporation in Redwood City. After working there for a few years, I decided to attend Palmer College of Chiropractics in Davenport, Iowa. It was my truly first time away from my Chinatown home. I met my husband in Iowa and graduated in 1981 with a Chiropractic doctorate. Shortly after graduating, my husband and I went even further from Chinatown when he took a job in Italy working in their socialized medicine system as a chiropractor. I, however, did not work there. Italian healthcare did not hire women because the patient load exceeded 100 persons per day. The system felt that a heavy load like that was simply too grueling for women. After returning from Italy in 1985, my husband and I opened a joint practice just outside of Philadelphia where my husband is from.

We tried, but I had no success in getting pregnant. In 1998 we went to China to adopt our first daughter, Maia. We went again the next year to adopt our number two, Lily. We decided to go to China for adopting not necessarily because I am Chinese, but at the time, the China program was just starting to ramp up. It was relatively easy to do your mountain of paperwork and pay your money and have a lovely child at the end of it all.

My husband and I have tried to expose our children to many different cultures. It has been our consistent desire to raise them to be "global" citizens. We have been with them to Europe numerous times and to South America. It's a bit far to travel to Asia from the East Coast but, the girls grew up as knowledgeable as I am about our Chinese heritage. They know about the Chinese Exclusion Acts, inequity throughout the world, racism and segregation. They also understand how important inclusion is to a society. They are firm believers that people are all more alike than we are different. They also appreciate it that they have been given opportunities as children in our American society that they would not have had as orphans in China. They are presently 20 and 22. Maia just graduated from college with a degree in digital forensics and Lily is a rising senior majoring in data analytics and math.

I worry about Chinatown and San Francisco each time I see them. They both seem to be changing so drastically and so rapidly. I can't help but feel that Chinatown has really become gentrified. I cannot say whether gentrification in Chinatown is good or bad. I don't think it is as simple as that. I know that San Francisco is not a very large city and gentrification has long since adversely affected the Hispanic Mission District. Rents there have gone up so much that members of both the long-time Hispanic residential and small business communities find it hard to stay there. Still, I also think that some amount of "improvement", shall we say, is necessary. But what does that mean? Chinatown cannot remain the same as it has always been. That said, where do the recent immigrants go? Where do the people from China, Cambodia and points east go? Not everyone wants to go to San Jose or the East Bay, and they're not any less expensive.

On a personally happier note, I am glad and proud to have grown up in Chinatown in the 50s and 60s. It really was like a small town where people knew you. I belonged to a community where people looked like me. Everyone was supportive of each other. You felt safe walking everywhere: to school, dance lessons at the old YWCA with Tony Wing, piano lessons, Cameron House, or anywhere else. I really appreciate Cameron House for helping me to meet new friends, providing me with guidance in all manner of life's experiences, and even teaching me about the history of Chinatown that my parents didn't even know.

I feel that I had the best of two worlds - especially the Chinese one. I was living in America, but I had easy access to my Chinese roots. Even today, I live in an East Coast suburb, but thank goodness, there is a Chinatown nearby where I go to get a fix of my old Chinatown comfort foods. My best friend in Pennsylvania is Chinese. We talk about Chinese food a lot. Oddly enough, some of my Chinese actually comes back when I listen to her whenever she happens to speak it. I know that I look different from the people in my neighborhood or in pretty much all the places I go. That's a good thing, though. We are all different, and we need to embrace and cherish that fact.

I will always love that I grew up in Chinatown. I keep my home address as it was when I was a child close to my heart: 1046 Grant

Avenue, San Francisco, 11, California. Similarly, my family telephone number will forever be in my heart as Yukon 2- 0775.

Irene Dea Collier
Through My Mother's Experiences I Was Gradually Able to Understand

In 2007 Irene and her mother went back for a visit to their native village. Irene said,

I was able to see my mother's vegetable garden. It was beautifully well preserved because my father had continued to send money back to the village for the care and upkeep of our family's property. All of our relatives in the village had been rice farmers, but while they tended to the paddies every day, they still needed someone to grow food and cook for them. Before she left, this had been my mother's job. She was a wonderful and prolific gardener. She cultivated all kinds of greens as well as taro and sweet potatoes. She was not just a good cook, but a creative one as well. She had to do whatever she could to make the two to three meals a day that she had to cook for seven or eight other people as tasty and variable as possible. Except for pulling an occasional fish out of the village pond or the nearby river, everyone's diet was a vegetarian one.

I am very happy that my mother got to go back to see her garden as it had been when she was still tending it. This is especially true as she has since passed away. My second daughter, Lora, visited our former village five years later. She reported that much had changed there. There is now a paved road leading to the village, but our old house has been neglected and abandoned. It still stands next to a new one, but it is only used as a storage site. I suppose that change is inevitable. I was deeply saddened when my daughter told me that Mom's garden had no longer been cared for and was completely weeded over.

Through my mother's experiences, I was gradually able to understand why she was as reserved or quiet and as conservative and frugal as she was. When she was growing up there was very little order in China, and once the Japanese invaded in the mid-

1930s, conditions became harsh and frightening for ordinary people. She saw firsthand how Chinese soldiers could not protect their people. This left her unable to have any faith or trust in authority or government. She could not even trust nature. The area where she lived was frequently subject to flooding. This in turn ruined crops and led to food shortages and even famine. She maintained a quiet demeanor, or low profile, because she was fearful of discovery and deportation. This caused her to never want to spend any more money than absolutely necessary. She did not hoard; we never had enough for that, but she saved for the "rainy day." Her general suspicions and paranoia were not helped by the pessimistic and tragic themes of so many of the Chinese movies that we so often went to see.

I think that two of my strongest personality traits, frugality and a quiet nature, were directly absorbed from my mother. I am so tight with money that my kids get frustrated with me. They constantly tell me, "Oh, for goodness sake, Mom! It's not that big a deal to buy something! Just do it!" And, in the end, despite the badgering of the kids and my own battles with my conscience, I still can't.

I also think that, even though all three of them are grown and married with families of their own, I sometimes intimidate my kids. I know that I'm quiet and reserved, but I can be really sharp and opinionated and critical when I talk to my children. It's the Chinese mother in me. My mom was like that to me. It wasn't being mean or anything, it was just the way she was. Take the vegetables, for instance. I tried and tried for years and years to cook them like my mother. I asked her to show me how, and I think I did everything the way I was supposed to. But no. I just couldn't satisfy her. Not even remotely. She would shake her head and speak in tones of exasperation to tell me that they were never tender enough. She conveyed her sense that I was hopeless as she would gripe that they were never succulent. It was always something: I cooked them on too high a flame or I used too much oil. I just couldn't learn how to do it right. One thing I did learn, though, was how to be a tough and demanding Chinese mother. I try to be careful, but every now and again, oh boy!

Now that I've mentioned cooking, I need to say that I love to cook. After all, I learned from the best - my mother. I spent years and years as her "sous chef." She took great pride in preparing food from ingredients and in the manner of the old village. I strive to continue with that tradition of doing things like they were done back in the village. Even down to how to properly kill a chicken. I don't actually do it, but I clearly remember how my mother taught me. You start by folding its wings back just so while holding the feet in a certain position. Then you're supposed to lift the neck just before making a quick and clean slash across with your knife. You keep a hold of the bird and let all the blood drain out from the neck.

After I had been cooking for a while, my son took an interest and wanted me to teach him. Of course, I did and I think that he's really pretty good at it now. My daughters also turned out to be quite good at it. A group of friends and I sometimes get together for "Chinese Soul Food" dinners. We each cook a dish and do a potluck. Recently I have made chicken cooked in whisky, pig's feet in balsamic vinegar sauce, and jee-yuk-beng; steamed diced pork. Good jee-yuk-beng is usually flavored with hom yue; dried salt fish.

I'm also trying to emulate my mother and raise a garden. Just the thought of raising my own vegetables to use in my cooking is so exciting. Between the sandy soil and the raccoons of San Francisco's outer Richmond district, though, I'm really having a hard time with it.

Don Ng
I Felt Like I Should Give Something Back to the Community

Over time, Don Ng who as a teen "ran wild and did bad stuff," overcame his tendency towards delinquency. His transformation towards greater maturity may have begun at Cameron House. The establishment, located on Sacramento Street, was founded in the 1870s as a haven for Chinese women, many of whom had been smuggled into San Francisco for the purposes of domestic servitude or prostitution. These women were not only protected and sheltered by the Presbyterian institution, but they were taught life skills and Christian Faith as well. Social conditions in Chinatown had

211

improved drastically by the mid-twentieth century. Many of Chinatown's youth of the 1950s and 1960s and well beyond spent time enjoying the sports, arts, and fun coeducational social activities that Cameron House had by then adopted. A great many of Chinatown's baby boomers harbor happy memories of it. More than a few have returned as volunteer workers or to provide financial support to the place that they feel had been so good for them when they were children. Don recently said,

I started going to Cameron House (as a teenager) *only because I had heard that there were pretty girls there. I was also more interested in the fun activities and the sports there than I was about learning anything serious. I tolerated the preaching they did and put up with it because I had to in order to participate. I made some good friends there ... guys from Galileo, Lowell, and Washington High Schools. We became close and formed a bond during that time that has lasted up until the present day. When not doing stuff through Cameron House, my buddies and I would stay up all night just hanging around together. We would go to Chinatown restaurants like* Sam Wo *or* Kuo Wah *that used to stay open really late for "siu yeh," or late-night snacks. We also went to those dumpy movie theaters like Sun Sing on Grant Avenue to watch Kung Fu movies.*

While Don may not have been the type of model youth that the institution's namesake Donaldina Cameron would have most envisioned, he nonetheless absorbed enough through Cameron House's declared missions to return there as an adult leader.

After I got my degree in Engineering at UC Berkeley and was working, I felt like I should give something back to the community. I went back to Cameron House and, with some of my friends, we got together to form a Leadership Group. We wanted to mentor some foreign-born teenagers who had been hanging around outside of the building. We took some of the kids on ski-trips and we also took some them camping ... things like that. A lot of them were troubled or going in the wrong direction and we just wanted to help them out. We couldn't 'save' every one of them, but I recently ran into one of the kids ... well, he's grown now, with a son of his own who goes to Lowell High School, and it was nice to see that he was doing well.

Don is currently the Medical Director of the General Medicine Clinic at the Osher Building of UCSF's Mount Zion Campus. Even through a busy and demanding schedule, he continues to reach out to younger people. In a recently made video aimed at encouraging new college students Don spoke about his own background and his current beliefs. On the video, "UCSF Leaders and Scholars Reflect on First Generation College Experiences," Don says,

Around 1969 there was a lot of gang activity in San Francisco and in Chinatown. I was a bit delinquent around that time myself ... and I decided to apply to Lowell, and then after I was there a while along with some friends who were close to me and in sort of a similar situation, we started to think about what we wanted to do in our lives ... and having known people who were either in gangs or got murdered or ended up being murderers and ended up being in jail, we just said, you know ... that's not the kind of future we want.

What is your potential ... what are your skills ... and how can you use those skills to one; further yourself, and, number two; give back to your community and society?

Harold Lee
. Helping people like myself gave me a sense of purpose, and my identity as a Chinese American grew stronger for it.

Vietnam and Marine Corps veteran Harold Lee, like Don and many others of his old neighborhood acquaintances, found himself drawn back to Chinatown. More than for nostalgia or for some of his favorite foods, Harold felt that he wanted to return and somehow give something back to the place that had so long ago given so much to him.

It was after I left the Marines in 1970 that life for me started to change. I attended City College of San Francisco and then transferred to San Francisco State University where I took up studies in sociology. I also took courses in Chinese American history. One very strong influence on my thinking at that time was a Chinatown historian named Philip Choy. I remember that he was

ABC and a World War II veteran. Since I was veteran, the fact that he, too, had served meant a lot to me. He used to give talks and lectures about Chinese-American history in Chinatown and other places around the Bay Area. He wound up teaching the first class ever on Asian-American history at State in the late 1960s. I could feel that he was upset, or even mad, at the way history courses had been ignoring Asian contributions to the making of the United States. I remember how fired-up he was one time when he was talking about how it was the Chinese, and only the Chinese, who built the whole Central Pacific Rail Road by hand. I never thought about it until then and it kind of got me riled up, too. Especially the part about how hard and dangerous it was to dig the tunnels and lay the track over the Sierra Nevada Mountains. It was like nobody cared how dangerous it was and if Chinese died or suffered, it was like, "Oh, Well" or "Whatever." He also helped get the Angel Island immigration center built up so it is open to visitors as a history exhibit. He was a real inspiration to me. Everything I heard about from Mr. Choy combined with my Chinese American history classes caused me to begin to look seriously at my own Chinese identity.

I got very involved as a volunteer at the Chinatown YMCA. Working with young Chinese Americans gave me the time to look at myself. The young people and the atmosphere at the Y were generally positive. I gradually began to think about my own sense of self. I liked doing things that could be helpful to the Chinatown community. I remembered how much I got out of the Y and Cameron House as a kid, so I felt like I was really doing some good for a lot of Chinatown people as a volunteer at the Y. I don't think that I thought about it purposefully, but I sort of combined the bad experiences I had in the military with the positive things I was seeing at the Y. I really started to feel and understand how important tolerance and acceptance could be in a community of people. The more time I spent as a volunteer at the Y, the stronger these ideas became to me. The community had lots of needs in areas like health care, housing, and transportation. I felt that since I was Chinese, I should try to be helpful and give back to a community that was facing things that most people outside of Chinatown didn't have to deal with. Helping people like myself gave me a sense of purpose.

214

My identity as a Chinese American grew stronger for it.

Steven Lee
Bringing Back and Giving Back

Steven Lee is not a native of Chinatown. Although his mother was from San Francisco and his grandparents lived just about a half mile from Chinatown on Leavenworth at Filbert Street, Steven was born and raised in Vacaville. Vacaville lies on Highway 80 between Vallejo and Sacramento, and Steven did not leave it until 1976 when he enrolled at San Francisco State and moved into the dorms. His first introduction to Chinatown, other than as a child, was through ABC friends from college who would bring him there for the good, plentiful and inexpensive dinners for which it was so famous. Steven fondly remembers many a late night or early morning sojourn to Chinatown standby restaurants such as *Sai-Yon*, *Nam-Yuen* and *Sam Wo* for "good old Chinatown comfort food."

While he was a serious student, Steven also enjoyed the college social and party scenes. He had so much fun at the frequent student gatherings for music, dancing and liquid refreshments that he very quickly took it upon himself to plan and host similar events on his own. He recalls that his first such efforts were based at the SF State Student Union. These affairs gradually outgrew campus venues and moved to larger sites off campus all around the Bay Area. Combining the know-how gained through his studies as a broadcast major along with his natural penchant for having fun, Steven's parties featured some of the most accomplished dee-jays of the day. His soirees rapidly became huge favorites of weekend party-goers. The cover charges levied at the door were reinvested into ever bigger and better parties.

Steven's "career" as an accomplished, if amateur, empresario took a step forward when another popular Chinatown-based party organizer, Benji Wong, took leave from hosting parties at the well-appointed, bright and booming *Rickshaw Club*. The *Rickshaw*, located on the 400-block of Grant Avenue, was just half a block downhill from the former site of Andy Wong's famed *Chinese Sky Room* at the corner of Pine Street. The other end of the 400-block is at Bush Street and the Chinatown Gate which form the border between Chinatown and the City's Downtown and Financial District. Enthusiastic partiers from these neighborhoods easily found their way to the *Rickshaw* where they mingled with their Chinatown contemporaries to pack the perpetually swinging club. As the mid-70s were a time of gang activity that severely impacted Chinatown's economy and reputation, Steven states that he was always gratified to be able to bring a little life, joy and money to the area. Steven says that he personally knew a number of Chinatown's most prominent gang members, the nationally notorious "Shrimp Boy" Chow among them. He used to make it a point to ask them to please "behave" whenever they stopped by to party at the *Rickshaw*. Steven was relieved that they always did.

Steven recalled that a group of friends had invited him to dinner just a half block down from the *Golden Dragon* restaurant on the very night of the infamous 1979 "Massacre." Steven does not remember precisely why, but he declined the invitation and drove home instead. He was happy to miss the event. He is sure that he would have run into some of those involved. The mark left on Chinatown by that incident was to be a deeply devasting and long-lasting one. Like Raymond Lee of the family run *Kuen Luen* and *K.L. Art Company* on Grant Avenue, Steven says that his greatest sorrow came through having to helplessly watch Chinatown's lights darken as shops and restaurants closed ever earlier, and ever fewer tourists came to visit.

Even as the gangs were gradually swept underground by law enforcement, new challenges arose to threaten the family-oriented, homey and nurturing nature of Chinatown that so many who grew up there in the 50s and 60s remembered. In the mid-90s a wave of immigrants abandoned Hong Kong in the face of Britain's promise to fully return the territory to China by 1997. Significant numbers of these newcomers transferred considerable wealth to Chinatown. The underlying results belied the general belief that such infusions of capital would benefit the area. Some of the new arrivals bought or leased properties with little concern for the cost. Such free spending eventually caused many long-established mom and pop businesses such as flower shops, beauty salons, hardware stores, bakeries,

216

stationary stores, and groceries to lose their own hitherto affordable leases. Rising real estate values also forced low-income apartment dwellers to either scramble after greater income sources or to relocate. As the 2000s have progressed, the technology boom that created Silicon Valley, and the increasing pressures of gentrification threaten to overwhelm Chinatown and its remaining residents altogether.

By 2011, a majority of the Chinatown restaurants that Steven had so enjoyed in the 1970s and 1980s had shuttered for good. *Sam Wo*, a community staple since the early post-earthquake days, had been shut down for health and safety reasons. *Sam Wo* had for many years been home to the wise-cracking, oft-times verbally abusive and internationally famed "rudest waiter on earth," Edsel Fong. Over the years San Francisco's favorite hometown columnist, Herb Caen of the *Chronicle*, had penned a number of flattering, if not endearing, pieces about both the establishment and Edsel. Fong was simultaneously reviled and beloved by *Sam Wo* patrons. He and Caen brought the restaurant into the public eye, and from the late 1960s onwards, *Sam Wo* bore a cult-like reputation among non-Chinese San Franciscans and out of town visitors alike. San Francisco tour books made it a point to tout it as a "must-see" location. Nonetheless, the owners were disinclined to spend the money needed to fix things as time took its toll on the restaurant. By 2010, it appeared to Steven that another part of old Chinatown was on the verge of being lost forever.

Deb Lem shared a few of her memories and thoughts about *Sam Wo*.

Who can forget Sam Wo! It was just the best, always-can-count-on-them-being-open restaurant. It was so narrow. I think it was probably the narrowest restaurant in Chinatown. Maybe in all of San Francisco! I will always remember the dumbwaiter. The place was so narrow and the stairs were so steep that the only way to get the food from the ground-floor kitchen to the upstairs dining spaces was by the dumbwaiter. My favorite dish there was the jook. *It was the best! I've been to the new place on Clay Street, and I think it is great that the old and tiny marble-topped tables made it there. And those banged up stools.*

By the second decade of the 2000s, Steven had firmly established himself as a successful businessman. He had also become a nightclub owner and operator, a board member of the California Music and Culture Association, and Commissioner of Entertainment for the City and County of San Francisco. He proudly states that he is the first Chinese-American to have ever been appointed to the latter post. He also maintains an ongoing involvement as a volunteer with, among others, internship programs for Asian-American students interested in Government and Public Affairs and the Chinese Railroad Workers Memorial Project.

In 2015, along with a group of hopeful, and even sentimental, investors, Steven took it upon himself to reopen *Sam Wo* at a new but nearby location on Clay Street. He states that while it is a business venture, he is deeply motivated to keep the restaurant open and successful primarily because it is such a vital part of Chinatown's history and legacy. He has enthusiastically stated, "I want to save it!"

To that end, Steven has made all attempts to ensure that much of *Sam Wo's* menu retains the restaurant's old dishes. He is also adamant that they be prepared in the same manner as always. Among these dishes are *won-ton*, tomato beef chow mein and that universal Chinatown staple and favorite - *jook*. Steven has brought the restaurant's operations into the 21st Century with on-line ordering and an app through which deliveries by truck can be arranged. Steven, a long-time car enthusiast, purchased and refurbished a 1957 Dodge panel truck to which he attaches magnetic "*Sam Wo*" signs. Partly because he loves driving his truck so much, Steven himself often serves as the "delivery boy." The restaurant also sells t-shirts, participates in street fairs city-wide, and recently hosted a performance and photo session with the *Grant Avenue Follies*. Steven derives his greatest satisfaction from *Sam Wo* through the knowledge that it has brought back a bit of the old-time vitality and character with which Chinatown has always been associated. Steven says that he does not envision turning the restaurant into a "chain," but is contemplating opening a second location at the San Francisco airport.

Over the years, Steven's youthful energy has not abated. As of 2019, he is also deeply involved in a Chinatown night club renovation and revitalization project. He hopes to create an upscale club in the old Wentworth Alley space where Mimi Lee's husband, Lewis Chin had his *Drag'on A-Go-Go* that once "*packed 'em in*" in during the mid-1960s. He says that he would like to feature bands in the style of those popular in the old *Forbidden City* or *Chinese Sky Room* alongside with groups familiar with classic pop sounds such as by Madonna, Earth, Wind & Fire, or Michael Jackson. He also wants to include more contemporary sounds such as those of Bruno Mars or Beyoncé.

Again, a large part of Steven's motivation stems from his desire to keep Chinatown alive and well. He is disturbed and saddened at the sight of so many of the neighborhood's buildings being run down to the point of condemnation. He also frets for the safety and welfare of Chinatown's residents. He, as does Chinatown Community Development Center executive director Norman Fong, wants to keep housing affordable and community services and personal comfort readily available for newly arrived Chinese or other Asian immigrants for whom the neighborhood is the gateway to the United States. Steven believes that ventures such as his *Sam Wo* and as yet named nightclub will stand alongside those like Brandon Jew's Michelin-Starred *Mister Jiu's* and the *China Live* complex on Broadway Street to bring new activity and spending to Chinatown. He further expects to see an economic trickle down into the rest of the neighborhood. Like so many other San Francisco ABCs of his generation, Steven understands that his roots are in Chinatown. Saving it may be beyond his means, but he insists that he must do whatever he can to give something back to the place where his grandparents came to live and work. It was, after all, their dedication and their sacrifice that provided him with the opportunities to enjoy a type of life about which they could only dream.

Tommy Lim
Growing up in North Beach-Chinatown changed my life

After moving back to the Bay Area in 1977 (from Chicago and optometry school), *I took a job in San Jose. We purchased a home and from there on I knew we would not be moving back to San Francisco, but we still attended the Presbyterian Church in Chinatown whenever we could. On August 25, 1979, our daughter Kelly was born. As if it wasn't already difficult enough to attend church in San Francisco, it seemed an impossible task with a newborn. In 1981, Bonnie and I opened* Berryessa Optometry, *putting even more demands on our time. On July 26, 1983 our son Aaron was born.*

With the birth of our second child we decided that perhaps we needed to find a church in San Jose. That search lasted for a few years. I took Kelly, then five years old, to visit prospective churches while Bonnie stayed home with Aaron. The churches we attended were very welcoming but they were missing something, and I just couldn't figure out what it was. I shared my concerns with my closest friend, Reverend Norman Fong. I had thought that the problem was my own inability to adjust. Together we figured out that the missing piece was the Asian- American factor.

This eventually led Bonnie and me to become involved in the South Bay Asian-American Presbyterian New Church Development in San Jose that we helped start. It was an exciting period of time for the small group of core families involved. After about ten years, a decision was made to close the church. However, all those years of hard work with the South Bay Church resulted in some very special life-long friendships; and these friendships eventually led us to the First Chinese Baptist Church in Chinatown.

Who would have guessed that my spiritual life would run full circle and I would end up attending a church in San Francisco Chinatown again, just down the street from the Presbyterian Church that had nurtured me during my growing up years? Life at FCBC has been good, but I am still in the process of finding my place in the life of the church. I joined the Church Choir and the Men's Chorus (something I never expected to do), and found sharing God's love through music to be my most fulfilling experience at church so far. I am looking forward with anticipation for what the future will yet bring.

We are very proud of our children. Kelly is a graduate of the University of California in San Diego, and she now works in the human resources and recruiting department of a San Francisco tech company. Aaron graduated from UC Davis and works as a senior business analyst in another tech company in the City. He lives in an apartment right by Cameron House. I am pretty pleased that even though my optometry practice keeps me in San Jose, Kelly and Aaron, at least, are still physically close to our roots. I wouldn't have it any other way.

Growing up in North Beach-Chinatown changed my life and how I felt about myself. I was finally comfortable being a Chinese-American and not wishing I were white. Chinatown gave me a sense of belonging to a community where I finally fit in. I found a home. And of course, I met the love of my life, Bonnie, in Chinatown.

Laura Wong [58.]
Family, love, history, culture - they are all a very connected set of things that Chinatown instilled in me

Laura Wong is Liz Wong's sister. Their grandfather was a paper son, but Laura, Liz, their brother Dennis and their father were all born and raised in San Francisco. While she was very young, Laura's family moved to Vallejo.

Although we didn't live there, I always felt connected to San Francisco's Chinatown. I have many warm memories of experiences shared with my numerous San Francisco cousins. My parents, two brothers, sister, and I spent many a Christmas, New Year and Easter vacation (before it came to be called "Spring Break") playing with cousins and going to fun places around the city. Chinese New Year luncheons meant battered and deep-fried chicken drumsticks, chow mein and Fanta orange soda. Whenever we went to San Francisco, our aunts and uncles made certain to shower us with love, food,

221

presents and lay-see for which a dime was typical and a quarter was a fortune.

Chinatown always felt comfortable and familiar to me. As soon as we drove across the Bay Bridge, I would anticipate the food, the stores, going to see Chinese movies and the specific sounds and smells of the neighborhood. We would often have a family meal at Sun Wah Kue where my father always ordered the full roast beef platter that included clear soup, dinner rolls and the choice of ice cream or orange, apple, or custard pie for dessert.

We spent time at different family associations for special occasions. My father liked going to the Lung Kong Association as well as to those of the Lew (our family), Quan, Jeung, and Chew. Those are the four family surnames derived from the classic novel, "Romance of the Three Kingdoms." We kids must have switched effortlessly from English to Chinese because I don't ever recall being at a loss for words when talking to all the "uncles" and "aunties" at the associations. Family, love, history, culture; they are all a very connected set of things that Chinatown instilled in me.

Allen Low [59.]
I hope that Chinatown is a place that remains a community

Allan Low spent most of his growing up years hanging out at the Chinatown YMCA. During this formative period of his life Allan was able to explore and closely know Chinatown. While he no longer lives there, he expressed his hopes for the neighborhood to continue to serve as a place that nourishes its residents, young and old, as it once did him.

I hope that Chinatown is a place that remains a community. It is a community of opportunity for newcomers when they first come to the United States. It's an opportunity for small businesses, for workers, also for community-based organizations to help (it) continue to be a place for seniors, families to raise children, and for those of us who move out of Chinatown but come back to support and help each other ... I want to continue to have those opportunities available for future generations.

Margret Gee [60.]
Chinatown is particularly important to me

While Margaret Gee harbors fond and deep memories of the Chinatown of her youth, she, like Allen Low, also expressed her hopes for its future.

Chinatown is a place that is culturally relevant for generations to come ... Chinatown is particularly important to me. Not only did my father bring me to Portsmouth Square when I was a child, but also when my grandmother migrated from China, she chose to live in Chinatown. Rather than live with one of her children (outside of the neighborhood) *she chose to live in Chinatown because it was a place where she could live independently, where she could go grocery shopping on her own, she could talk to her friends, go out and be self-sufficient and not be isolated in other parts of the Bay Area. I hope that Chinatown remains (to be) that place where people can connect to their roots and (to) serve the new generation to come.* [4.]

Sherman Wong
I'm glad that I grew up in Chinatown

Sherman Wong the frequent radio contest winner who "grew up in a sewing factory" reflected on what Chinatown has been to him.

In 1979 I went with my brother to visit my father's village in China. The family house was still in good condition. It looked pretty much like it was back at the time when my parents moved to San Francisco. It was three stories high. Some of the family photos from San Francisco that my parents had sent back to relatives were on display by the hearth. Nobody actually lived in the house at the time, but there was a caretaker who helped keep an eye on it and keep it in good shape. I'm pretty sure my father sent him money from time to time so that he would do his job. I used to have to help him write the address in English on the envelopes. He wrote the Chinese part and I wrote what needed to be done in English. He probably sent money back to some of his relatives also.

Even though our family house was nice, the village was sort of underdeveloped. They still had to draw water from the well with a bucket. My brother did most of the talking and he knew some of the people. They all seemed pleased or at least amused that we were there. I couldn't really say much because my Chinese wasn't that good anymore, but I could understand a good deal of what people would say. I mostly just answered with a yes or a no and a few simple phrases and very basic sentences.

We lived in South San Francisco when my sons were very little. Since my wife and I worked in the city, we would drop them off at my mom's before work and pick them up on the way home. It was pretty convenient. We used my mom's address when we had to sign the boys up for school so they went to school in San Francisco, and my wife and I could continue the routine of driving them to and from Grandma's. It was just like my parents' old trick of using the sewing factory address to make after school care for me easier when I was little. All the Chinese that our sons know came mostly from my mother and my wife. Like me, they began to go all English and all American once school started.

When they were in the fifth and sixth grade, we moved further down the peninsula to San Carlos. They went to an all-white school that had maybe a handful of other Chinese kids. They had no problems with racial issues. If you were Asian in an all-white community like San Carlos, you were OK. I don't think it would have been that way for African Americans or even for Hispanics. The boys got along fine, and they got a good education in San Carlos. They grew up white. We were in the suburbs, and they grew up doing all the typical all-American things: little league, soccer, and all that. One of them is now a dentist in San Mateo. The other is a chef in New York City. My dentist son went to NYU for dental school, and his brother studied at a culinary school located in New York also. I think they just wanted to go someplace outside of California to see something different.

I think young kids today have it pretty easy. It isn't for them like it was for us back in Chinatown. We were really disadvantaged in a lot of ways. It could sound odd, but I sort of miss some of the aspects of being disadvantaged or living in a ghetto. Even though it was hard, people made do. In a lot of ways, I didn't know that my family and those of most of my friends were disadvantaged. I wasn't unhappy. I pretty much had fun as a kid. I never thought about Chinatown being a ghetto. I think it was because people were close to each other and there was a very strong sense of community. Kids had to help their parents to make it financially. Lots of us worked for our parents in their little businesses, or we did things in the house and for the family when our parents were away working. I didn't mind it. I still always found time and ways to enjoy myself.

There was a sense of belonging in the old neighborhood of Chinatown that I really miss.
Growing up in San Francisco's Chinatown gave me the opportunity to appreciate my cultural heritage. Chinatown was such a small and crowded place that we practically lived and worked on top of one another. The physical closeness opened the way to special deep emotional ties that I was able to forge with my parents, family and friends that persist today. Living in Chinatown also enriched all those little things that help make life enjoyable: food, school, friends and so much more.

Chinatown has filled me with countless wonderful and fond memories. All things must change, though. I grew older and I moved away. Chinatown, by the natural forces of evolution has changed from what it was for me in the 50s and the 60s. That's the way it is in life. San Francisco Chinatown as my generation knew it will never be the same. Our memories and recollections will be our only testament and legacy.

I'm proud to be Chinese American. I enjoy knowing that I came from a background that has a great history and a great culture. I know that I have lost some of it and I hate it that I have. Knowing about what China and the Chinese people have been, however, is comforting. I am Chinese no matter what.

NOTES

1. Allen Leong. Facebook post used with permission. November 2016.
2. Melody Chan Doss-Wambeke. All anecdotes provided to author by Melody Chan Doss-Wambeke through e-mail exchange. September – December, 2016. Melody has provided additional anecdotes, stories and information from 2016 – 2019.
3. Chinese Hospital was founded in 1925. It replaced the Tung Wah Dispensary that had been established in 1899 to offer medical care to the Chinese in San Francisco.
4. Judy Wing Lee. All anecdotes provided to author by Judy Wing Lee via e-mail. August – December 2016. Judy has provided follow-up e-mails, Facebook messages and photos from 2016 – 2019.
5. The 1906 earthquake and fire destroyed practically all birth, death, marriage and immigration records held in San Francisco. Numerous people would eventually take advantage of the loss of such records. Claims that a person was a legal immigrant or natural citizen could no longer be disproven.
6. Judy's grandmother remained in China during her husband's travels to and residence in the United States.
7. Pat Chin. All stories provided to author by Pat Chin via e-mail exchanges. July – August 2018 and May 2019.
8. Irene Dea Collier. All anecdotes from Irene Dea Collier were told to the author in-person, by phone or by e-mail exchanges. October - November 2016, March 2017, March 2018 and July 2019.
9. Sherman Wong. All anecdotes were told to the author by Sherman Wong in phone conversations. October - November 2016.
10. Tommy Lim. All anecdotes from Tommy Lim were shared to the author by telephone. October -November 2016. Reviewed and revised by Tommy in June 2019.
11. Chan, Sheryl. "Looking Back with Gratitude," in Chuck, James, editor, Chinatown, More Stories of Life and Faith. First Chinese Baptist Church. San Francisco. 2008. p.14.
12. Saki Lee. All anecdotes shared by Saki Lee were provided to the author by means of e-mail. November, 2016.
13. The *Ping Yuen* housing project in Chinatown included three complexes built in the 1950s and a fourth completed in the early 1960s. They were built in response to overcrowded conditions in Chinatown and, since their inauguration, have been available specifically to low income renters.

14. *Hip Wo* which means "Unity and Harmony" was founded in 1924. Non-church affiliated members of the Chinatown community combined with members of the Chinese Congregational, Methodist, and Presbyterian churches to establish the school.

15. October 10th (10-10); the National Day of the Republic of China. The date marked the start of the Wuching uprising in 1911. The final result was the ouster of dynastic rule in China and the establishment of a republic.

16. Jack Woo. All anecdotes from Jack Woo were provided to the author by means of e-mail. August – November 2016. Jack continued to provide follow-ups, additional stories and family photos from 2016 – 2019.

17. *Frenesi* was a Big Band hit from the World War II era. It was made famous by Artie Shaw and was a huge favorite among American servicemen both during and after the war.

18. *Americans We,* by Henry Fillmore 1929. Fillmore was from Cincinnati and he enjoyed conducting the song so much during concerts at the city's zoo that it was often called *"The Cincinnati Zoo March."* The song also became a tradition at halftime of the Orange Bowl for many years.

19. Cynthia Yee. All anecdotes from Cynthia Yee were provided by telephone conversations and e-mails with the author. July 2018.

20. Lyrics for the song "Grant Avenue" were transcribed from the "Flower Drum Song" soundtrack by the author.

21. Dong, Arthur. Forbidden City, USA: Chinese American Nightclubs, 1936 – 1970. Deep Focus Productions, Los Angeles, California. 2015. p. 202.

22. Dong, p. 48.

23. Dong, p.48

24. Dong, p. 144.

25. Dong, pp. 71.

26. Lyrics for "Chinatown, My Chinatown" by Chris Connor. https://www.lyricsmode.com/lyrics/c/chris_connor/chinatown_my_chinatown.html#!

27. Pat Chin. E-mails, in addition to those of 2018, and photos were shared by Pat with the author in April and May, 2019.

28. SF Gate. 23 January, 2005. https://www.sfgate.com/news/article/WONG-Andrew-C-2703662.php

29. SF Gate. 22 July, 1995. https://www.sfgate.com/news/article/OBITUARY-Walton-Biggerstaff-3028604.php

30. Dong. p. 168.

31. Jeffries was noted for his roles in Western films as a "singing cowboy." Although he was less than ¼ black he considered himself to be African-American. He later changed his status to white in order to marry the famous exotic dancer Tempest Storm free of any racist criticism.
32. Norman Fong. Anecdotes provided by Norman Fong to author by telephone conversation. April 2017.
33. Nakao, Annie. "Remembering When Chinatown Rocked and Rolled." SF Gate, October 24, 2004. Web. Accessed 29 December 2016.
34. Nakao.
35. Nakao.
36. Nakao.
37. Nakao.
38. Chin, Flo, "Thank God for His Loving Grace," in Chuck, James (editor), Chinatown: More Stories of Life and Faith. First Chinese Baptist Church, San Francisco. 2008. p. 26.
39. Owyang, Virginia (Ginny) "God Will Direct Your Paths," in Chuck, James (editor), Chinatown: More Stories of Life and Faith. First Chinese Baptist Church, San Francisco. 2008. p. 101.
40. Harold Lee. "Harold Lee" is a pseudonym selected by an interviewee who prefers that his true name not be revealed. The name is not associated with any other person called Harold Lee, living or dead. All anecdotes by "Harold Lee" were provided to the author by telephone and personal conversations. October 2016 and March 2017.
41. Hom, Franklin, "Much to be Thankful For," in Chuck, James (editor), Chinatown: More Stories of Life and Faith. First Chinese Baptist Church, San Francisco, 2008. pp. 67 – 68.
42. Chapin, Dwight. "Willie 'Woo-Woo' Wong." USF's Little Big Man. San Francisco Chronicle. April 23, 2005.
43. Mark Zannini. All anecdotes provided by Mark Zannini to author by telephone conversations. October – December 2016.
44. The Cheung-sam is a long (expressed by the word 'cheung') one-piece dress that is tight fitting. It is usually sleeveless or short sleeved and has a high collar that is buttoned at the neck. The skirt has a sensually revealing slit that reaches to mid-thigh. The color red symbolizes happiness.
45. One key purpose for honoring the ancestors lies in the belief that they are the ones who keep watch over the fortunes of those left behind.
46. Liz Wong. All anecdotes provided to author by Liz Wong by means of personal conversations. February 2017 and March 2018.
47. San Francisco Chronicle, 03 October 1961. The article has been kept by Liz Wong and was shown to the author in March 2018.
48. Don Ng. All anecdotes from Don Ng were provided by e-mail and telephone conversations with author. October, 2016.

49. Saki Lee's cousin requested that his name be kept anonymous. These anecdotes were taken from the e-mail correspondence between Saki Lee and the author in 2016.

50. Anecdote from Saki Lee's cousin provided to author by personal conversation. February 2017. Martin is the real name of the cousin's classmate. Saki's cousin and Martin remained friends for many years.

51. Lim, Bonnie, "It's All Linked," in Chuck, James (editor), <u>Chinatown: More Stories of Life and Faith.</u> First Chinese Baptist Church, San Francisco. 2008. pp 87 – 88. August 2018.

52. Raymond Lee. All anecdotes from Raymond Lee were sent to the author by e-mail correspondence with author. June, 2018.

53. Bill Lee. <u>Chinese Playground,</u> a Book Talk at San Francisco Public Library. September, 2015.

54. Mimi Lee. All anecdotes from Mimi Lee provided to author by e-mail and telephone conversations. August 2018 and follow-up phone conversations in April 2019.

55. LA Times. 15 July, 2018. <u>http://www.latimes.com/local/obituaries/la-me-obit-mai-tai-sing-2018-htmlstory.html</u>

56. Pat Nishimoto provided all quoted material in written form to the author. But for minor editing, it is as she originally wrote it. June 2018 and February 2019.

57. Chung, Amy in "The Legacy of San Francisco's Chinatown." BBC World News America. 19 July 2010.

58. Laura Wong. All anecdotes from Laura Wong provided to author by e-mail. March 2017.

59. Low, Allen; in "Building Community, Chinatown Style," video, Chinatown Community Development Center, November 2015.

60. Gee, Margaret; in "Building Community, Chinatown Style."

ADDITIONAL NOTES

- The quote at the end of the introduction by Debbie Gong Chin is from <u>New York City Chinatown Chinese, Vol. II</u> by Jean Lau Chin, 2017. The book is available through:

www.ceoservices.wix.com/nycchinatownoralhist

- All anecdotes from Deb Lim were provided by her through a series of e-mails to the author during May and June 2019.

- All anecdotes from Steven Lee were provided by him through several phone conversations and follow-up e-mails in May 2019.

The Author

Edmund (Ed) Wong was born at *Chinese Hospital* in San Francisco. He lived with his family above its shop, *Kim's Fine Art* at 417 Grant Avenue until he joined the Navy in 1967. He returned to graduate from SF State in pre-med in 1973. Ed married and spent two years in the Peace Corps in the South Pacific. He and his wife, Elizabeth, moved to Louisville, Kentucky in 1979. Ed retired as the head of Jefferson Community College's foreign language department in 2013. He now pursues his lifelong interest in writing. His first two books are *Growing Up in San Francisco's Chinatown* and *The Sea Takes No Prisoners*. When not writing, Ed enjoys riding horses, model railroading, photography, military history, and travel.

The Illustrator

Leland Wong, born in 1952, is a San Francisco Chinatown native. Growing up in a family curio shop in Chinatown, he worked alongside his parents at *Fueng Wah Company*. Surrounded by the store's inventory of Asian art, Leland developed an early interest in drawing and art. Leland earned his BFA from San Francisco State in 1975. He has since been mostly self-employed as an artist, screen printer and photographer. Traditional Asian styles and themes influenced by growing up in the family store can be readily identified in much of Leland's artwork. Leland's art has been widely exhibited in venues that include the Corcoran Gallery in Washington, D.C., Golden Gate Park's de Young Museum, the National Japanese American Historical Society, and the Chinese Culture Center. He still lives mere blocks from the heart of Chinatown where he continues to practice his art

On the Cover

Clockwise from Top-left

Pat Nishimoto (at left) by father and sister, Kate. Pat's mother holds Pat's brother, Ray. Family friend at table.

Jack Woo with sisters June (on Jack's right) and Joan.

Washington Irving Third Grade. Gary Wong holds the flag.

Mimi Lee at left. Uncle Jack, Mom and brother Douglas in back. Brother Walter between grandparents and sister Mabel at end.

Sherry Lee, Ed, and Ed's mother, Ada Wong.

Also by Edmund S. Wong

- *Growing Up in San Francisco's Chinatown: Boomer Memories from Apple Pie to Noodle Rolls* (Arcadia). 2018.
- *The Sea Takes No Prisoners: Stories from the Men and Ships of the Royal Navy in the Second World War* (Unicorn, UK). 2018.

Visit Ed at:

https://growingupichinatown.wordpress.com/

https://www.facebook.com/growingupinchinatownsf/

and

https://www.amazon.com/Edmund-S.-Wong/e/B077J3QNML